AMC
MAINE
MOUNTAIN
GUIDE

Seventh edition

APPALACHIAN MOUNTAIN CLUB BOOKS
BOSTON, MASSACHUSETTS

Awaiting copyright data from Library of Congress

Distributed by The Talman Company

Library of Congress Cataloging-in-Publication Data

The paper used in this publication meets the minimum requirements of the American National Standard for Information Sciences—Permanence of Paper for Printed Library Materials, ANSI Z39.48–1984.∞

**Due to changes in conditions,
use of the information in this book
is at the sole risk of the user.**

Printed on recycled paper.

Printed in the United States of America.

10 9 8 7 6 5 4 3 2 1   93 94 95 96 97

Contents

Key to Maps

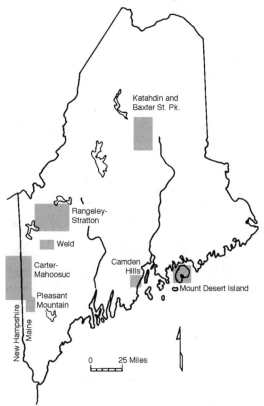

Katahdin and
Baxter St. Pk.

Rangeley-
Stratton

Weld

Carter-
Mahoosuc

Camden
Hills

Mount Desert Island

Pleasant
Mountain

New Hampshire

Maine

0   25 Miles

MAPS FOLDED IN BACK POCKET
Carter-Mahoosuc/Rangeley-Stratton
Katahdin/Camden Hills/Pleasant Mountain
Mount Desert/Weld

To the Owner of This Book

With the object of keeping pace with the constant changes in mountain trails, the Appalachian Mountain Club publishes a revised edition of this guide at intervals of about five years.

Hiking and climbing in the Maine mountains should provide a combination of outdoor pleasure and healthful exercise. Plan your trip schedule with safety in mind. Determine the overall distance, the altitude to be reached, and the steepness of the footway. If you are returning to the starting point the same day, allow ample time, as your morning quota of energy will have lost some of its get-up-and-go. Read the caution notes where they appear in this book. They are put there for your guidance and protection.

We request your help in preparing future editions. When you go over a trail, please check the description in the book. If you find errors or can suggest improvements, send a note to the committee. Even if the description is satisfactory, "Description of such-and-such trail is o.k." will be appreciated. Do not be deterred by a lack of experience. The viewpoint of one unfamiliar with the trail is especially valuable.

Address: Maine Mountain Guidebook Committee, Appalachian Mountain Club, 5 Joy St., Boston MA 02108.

Introduction

This, the seventh edition of the Appalachian Mountain Club's guide to the mountains and trails of Maine, describes nearly two hundred summits in all sections of Maine—from Mount Agamenticus in the southwestern corner of the state to Deboullie Mountain in northern Aroostook County, and from Mount Aziscohos close to the New Hampshire line in northwestern Maine to Pocomoonshine Mountain, near the St. Croix River, which forms the New Brunswick border. Some examples are the trail-rich Mount Desert Island summits, the compact and scenic Camden Hills, the low but frequently climbed hills in southwestern Maine, and the isolated and interesting mountains close to the Quebec and New Brunswick boundaries.

This guide is intended for use as a pathfinder; therefore it does not include extended historical references or descriptions of views. In general, it describes trails for the ascent. Any difficulties going down a trail that would not be encountered going up are mentioned at the end of the description. Where a trail follows a range, this guide describes it for the direction usually traveled. Signs mark many paths, but hikers cannot rely on them because they often fall down or disappear. Also, trails are constantly changing. Logging may destroy them, heavy storms may obscure them, and new trails are occasionally added.

This guide strives to remain current by adding or deleting trails or mountains depending on present conditions.

MAINE FOREST SERVICE FIRETOWERS

For years, the Maine Forest Service maintained firetowers on many mountains. The trails built to the summit towers made excellent hiking paths. During the last two decades most of these towers have been abandoned as the state forest service switched to aircraft for forest fire patrol. Several of the towers have been removed or converted to other uses such as microwave or cable television relay.

Some of the firewardens' cabins have been sold to private owners; others are in disrepair or have been vandalized or torn down. Do not expect to use them for camping or emergency shelter.

In many cases, continued use by hikers or adoption by volunteers has kept trails to firetowers open; in other, more remote regions, the trails are becoming overgrown. No group has offered to maintain them. Before heading for the more isolated areas with summit towers, hikers should check trail conditions with the local Maine Forest Service office.

DISTANCES AND TIMES

The distances and times that appear in the tables at the end of trail descriptions are cumulative from the starting point at the head of each table. Estimated distances are preceded by *est.*

Times are based on a speed of 2 mph, plus an additional half hour for every 1000 feet gained in elevation. Times are included only to provide a consistent measure for comparison among trails and routes. When no time is given, the route described may be considered a leisurely walk or stroll. With experience, hikers will learn how to correct these standard times for their own normal pace. Bear in mind, however, that if your average pace is faster than the standard time, it will not necessarily be so on trails with steep grades, in wet weather, if you are carrying a heavy pack, or if you are hiking with a group. And in winter, you should estimate roughly twice the time it would normally take for you to complete a hike.

The final entry in the distance-time summaries at the end of trail descriptions gives the metric equivalent of the total distance. The metric equivalent for the elevation of each summit is also listed.

GUIDELINES FOR WILDERNESS HIKERS AND CAMPERS

Below are some fundamentals of living in the outdoors without destroying it. Following these simple rules will help preserve the backcountry for all to enjoy.

Camp in Designated Areas

The backcountry can no longer withstand indiscriminate camping and hiking. Please cooperate.

Bring Your Own Tent or Shelter

Shelter buildings are often full, so each group should carry all needed equipment for shelter, including whatever poles, stakes, ground insulation, and cord are required. Do not cut boughs or branches for bedding.

Use a Portable Stove

In some camping areas, a "human browse line" is quite evident, because people have gathered firewood over the years: Limbs are gone from trees, the ground is devoid of dead wood, and vegetation has been trampled by people scouring the area. A carefully operated stove puts the least pressure on the forest.

Help Preserve Nature's Ground Cover

If a shelter is full, or if you camp away from shelters, find a clear, level site on which to pitch your tent, away from trails and streams. Site clearing and ditching around tents are too damaging to soil and vegetation.

Hammock Camping

Some campers use hammocks rather than tents. Hanging between trees eliminates even that crushing of ground cover caused by tents. (Hammocks, however, have certain limitations during bug season!) We can all practice low-impact camping by making conscious efforts to preserve the natural forest.

Water for Drinking and Washing

Wash your dishes and yourself well away from streams, ponds, and springs. It's handy to carry a small screen or cloth to filter the dishwater, so you don't leave food remnants strewn about the woods.

Most hikers drink from the streams without ill effect, and indeed, the pleasure of quaffing a cup of water fresh from a (presumably) pure mountain spring is one of the traditional attractions of the mountains. Unfortunately, in many mountain regions the cysts of the intestinal parasite *giardia* are present in some of the water. A conservative practice is to boil water for 20 minutes or to use an *iodine*-based disinfectant. *Chlorine*-based products, such as Halazone, are ineffective in water that contains organic impurities, and they deteriorate quickly in the pack. Remember to allow extra contact time (and use twice as many tablets) if the water is cold.

Think About Human Waste

Keep it at least 200 feet away from water sources. If there are no toilets nearby, dig a trench 6 to 8 inches deep for a latrine and cover it completely when you break camp. The bacteria in the organic layer of the soil will then decompose the waste naturally. (Don't dig the trench too deep, or you will be below the organic layer.)

Carry In–Carry Out

Trash receptacles are not available in trail areas (except at some trailheads), and visitors are asked to bring trash bags and carry out everything—food, paper, glass, cans—they carry in. Cooperation with the "carry in–carry out" program so far has been outstanding, and the concept has grown to "carry out more than you carried in." We hope you will join in the effort.

Use Special Care Above Timberline

Extreme weather and a short growing season make these areas especially fragile. Footsteps alone can destroy the toughest natural cover, so please try to stay on the trail or walk on rocks. And, of course, don't camp above timberline.

Limit the Size of Your Group

The larger the group, the greater the impact on the environment and on others. Please limit the size of your group to a dozen or fewer.

CAUTION

Hikers should always carry a map and compass, knife or small ax, waterproof matches, water, adequate food, a windbreaker, rain gear, a spare sweater or shirt, gloves or mittens, a hat, and extra socks. In addition, at least one member of the group should carry a lightweight survival kit that includes first-aid supplies (bandaids, gauze pads, and adhesive tape; moleskin or a similar blister preventive; an antiseptic; and an analgesic), high-energy emergency food, a flashlight with extra batteries, a large plastic trash bag, some foil, a needle and thread, safety pins, cord, paper and a pencil, and perhaps a space blanket.

Before entering the woods, tell someone where you are going and when you plan to return, and get to know the area. Study a good map, and know how to use your compass. Pick out reference points along the trail after you start your hike, and check your compass from time to time. Dress for the terrain and weather. Don't depend on cotton clothing for warmth; once it is dampened by perspiration or precipitation it will pull warmth from your body. Wool and some synthetics such as polypropylene provide better insulation even when wet. Dress in layers: Remember, you can always take off what you have on, but you can't put on what you don't have with you.

Compass directions given in this text are based on true north instead of magnetic north. This is important information, because in Maine the compass needle points up to 20 degrees west of true north.

Note: With reference to streams, the terms *right bank* and *left bank* mean right and left when facing downstream. Other abbreviations used frequently in the text are listed below.

HYPOTHERMIA

Hypothermia, the most serious danger to hikers, is the inability to stay warm because of injury, exhaustion, lack of sufficient food, or inadequate or wet clothing. Most cases occur in temperatures above freezing; the most dangerous conditions involve rain with wind. The symptoms are stumbling, poor coordination, garbled speech, amnesia, disorientation, and agitated behavior. Progressive lethargy, uncontrollable shivering, and coma will follow if no treatment is given. The result is death, unless the victim (who usually does not understand the situation) is treated, and it is not unusual for the victim to resist treatment and even combat the rescuers.

If you suspect a person is hypothermic, find him or her shelter from the wind and rain, and remove any wet clothing. Place the victim in a sleeping bag without clothes or with dry garments. Be sure to cover the head and neck, and provide insulation from the ground. If the victim is fully conscious, supply quick-energy food and warm (not hot), nonalcoholic drinks. Keep the victim inactive until signs of improvement appear. Allow adequate rest before moving on; do not hesitate to send for help if there is any doubt that the victim should proceed.

Uncontrollable shivering is evidence of advanced hypothermia. This shivering will eventually cease on its own, but that is an indication that the hypothermia is becoming even more severe. In severe cases, only professional treatment offers hope for survival. Reduce exposure to wind and rain, prevent further heat loss, and send for help. Do not try to rewarm in the field.

The prevention of hypothermia is infinitely easier than its treatment and should be a prime concern of hikers during any season. Sources of detailed information on causes, prevention, and current treatment are available through the AMC's Boston or Pinkham Notch headquarters.

GETTING LOST

If you get lost in the Maine woods, it is not necessarily a serious matter. First *stop,* sit down, and think. If you are familiar with the territory, you may be able to find your way back to the trail or to a high spot to survey the area. If you are unsure which direction to take, *stay where you are!* If you have informed someone of your trip plan, then you will probably be found quickly. *Don't panic.* If you have the proper equipment, you can improvise a shelter (near water if possible) and wait for help. Build a fire for warmth and to draw attention. (Be careful to keep the fire under control, of course.) The main thing to remember is to *stay put* and *stay calm.*

SEARCH AND RESCUE

The Department of Inland Fisheries and Wildlife is empowered to conduct search-and-rescue operations in Maine. All Maine telephone books carry the 800 number of the nearest Warden District.

The text of the relevant sections of Maine law is given below; for more information write to the Commissioner, Department of Inland Fisheries and Wildlife, 221 State St., Augusta ME 04333.

Title 12, Sec. 7035, No. 4; Powers

Search and rescue. Whenever the commissioner receives notification that any person has gone into the woodlands or onto the inland waters of the State on a hunting, fishing or other trip and has become lost, stranded or drowned, the commissioner shall exercise the authority to take reasonable steps to ensure the safe and timely recovery of that person; except in cases involving downed or lost aircraft covered by Title 6, section 303.

A. The commissioner may summon any person in the State to assist in those search and rescue attempts. Each person summoned shall be paid at a rate set by the commissioner with the approval of the Governor and shall be provided with subsistence while engaged in these activities.

B. The expenses of the department in search and rescue efforts shall be paid from the General Fund. The Joint Standing Committee of the Legislature having jurisdiction over Inland Fisheries and Wildlife shall report out a bill during each regular session requesting General Fund monies for the full cost of the search and rescue.

C. The commissioner may enter into written agreements with other agencies or corporations, including commercial recreational areas, allowing partial search and rescue responsibility within specified areas.

D. The commissioner may terminate a search and rescue operation by members of his department when, in his opinion, all reasonable efforts have been exhausted.

Any person who has knowledge that another person is lost, stranded or drowned in the woodlands or inland waters of the State shall notify the Warden Service Division of the Department of Inland Fisheries and Wildlife.

Sec. 7036, No. 4; Prohibited Acts

Failure to notify. Except as otherwise provided through written agreement, a person is guilty of failure to report a lost, stranded or drowned person if he has knowledge that a person is lost, stranded or drowned in the woodlands or inland waters of the State and fails to give notice of the incident by quickest means to the Warden Service Division of the Department of Inland Fisheries and Wildlife.

FIRES AND FIRE CLOSURE

The following is a summary of regulations that govern building fires in various areas:

1. In Acadia National Park and in state parks, regulations permit fires at designated places only. In Acadia National Park, consult a park ranger before building any fire.
2. In the White Mountain National Forest, permits are no longer required, but hikers who build fires are still legally responsible for any damage they may cause.
3. In other areas:
   a. In *organized* territory (i.e., within the boundaries of a township with its own local civil government), fires may be kindled on private land only with written permission from the landowner. The landowner's permission must be presented to the town fire warden, who may then issue a permit.

    b. In *unorganized* territory (i.e., where the local government function is performed by state or county authorities a permit for outdoor cooking and warming fires may be obtained free of charge from any MFS ranger.

    c. Fires may be built without a permit at the following places:

        (1) MFS authorized campsites and lunch grounds

        (2) State Highway Commission roadside picnic areas

        (3) Appalachian Trail shelter sites

        (4) Baxter Park and Recreation campgrounds and campsites (but see park regulations and discuss with rangers)

        (5) Maine Bureau of Parks and Recreation campsites and picnic areas

        (6) Maine Bureau of Public Lands authorized campsites

    d. Specific and detailed information on fire permits may be obtained from any MFS ranger or the forest service's Augusta office.

During periods when the danger of fires is high, the governor, through proclamation, may prohibit all outdoor fires or may close the woods altogether. Check with the MFS before embarking on a trip for any restrictions that may be in effect. They will have the most up-to-date and accurate information regarding fires and permits required.

We cannot stress enough the importance of care in using fire in the woods. Hikers as a group have compiled a fine record, but a forest fire traced to the carelessness of a hiker could result in the closing of much land and many trails.

CAMP TRIP LEADERS' PERMITS

Those who lead summer camp trips in Maine should be aware of a law that regulates issuing permits for camp trip leaders. The text of the legislation is given below; for more information write to the Commissioner, Department of Inland Fisheries and Wildlife, 221 State St., Augusta ME 04333.

Title 12, Sec. 7322; Permits for Camp Trip Leaders

Boys' and girls' camps licensed by the Department of Human Services, or located in another state and licensed in a similar manner, if the laws of the other state so require, conducting trip camping shall: provide at least one staff member over 18 years of age for each 6 campers and ensure that the staff member in charge of the trip holds a valid trip leader permit. Any person wishing a permit shall submit an application on forms provided by the commissioner and shall pay the application fee. To qualify initially for a permit, an applicant must show successful completion of an approved trip leader safety course or complete an application provided by the commisioner outlining in detail the applicant's experience and training as a trip leader; and meet any other requirements adopted by rule of the commissioner. Waiver of the course requirement by the commissioner on the basis of the applicant's experience and payment of the application fee shall qualify the applicant for a trip leader permit.

With the advice of the board, the commissioner shall review and adopt a trip leader safety course curriculum which shall include, but not be limited to: training in first aid; training in water safety, including lifesaving techniques as appropriate; and trip leader qualifications and required experience for the special waiver procedure in subsection 4. The commissioner shall publish the curriculum adopted or approved by the board and a current list of courses, with the approved curriculum, by name and address.

Wardens of the department and the rangers of the Bureau of Forestry and rangers of the Bureau of Parks and Recreation may terminate any trip which is considered unsafe or in violation of this section.

The initial qualifying fee for a trip leader permit is $14. The permit may be renewed upon payment of $9 if requirements of the department are met.

POLICIES OF LANDOWNERS IN NORTHERN MAINE

Maine's economy depends very much upon its woodlands. These lands are owned by a large number of small-lot owners and by a small number of companies that own large areas. These private holdings include many of Maine's mountains; generally, owners allow recreational use of their land.

The opening of the Allagash Wilderness Waterway and improved highways and roads leading to northern and northwestern Maine have increased the flow of hikers, hunters, fishermen, canoeists, and others to the forest country. At the same time, continuing technological advances in logging have led to greater use of trucks to haul lumber and pulpwood. The timberland owners constantly extend their system of private roads, many of which are open to the public. These roads offer access to many areas that used to be difficult to reach. In 1971 the North Maine Woods, an association of landowners, was established to control recreational use of the area west of ME 11 and north of a line that starts several miles north of Baxter State Park and runs around Telos and Caucomgomoc lakes and then west to the Canadian border. The line extends north along the border to Estcourt, south to St. Francis, southwest to Fish River, south into T8 R6, and west toward Baxter State Park. The Katahdin Ironworks/Jo-Mary (Gulf Hagas) area is also under the association's management. The MFS has transferred control and management of most of its forest campsites in this area to North Maine Woods, which operates traffic-control centers on the major private roads into the area. Users must register at the control centers and pay fees, which vary somewhat from year to year and are at times higher for out-of-state residents. There are also fees for use of campsites within the controlled area.

The landowners have established some basic rules for their roads. Speed limits are posted. *Trucks always have the right of way* on these private roads. Do not leave unattended cars that block passage on any road; large logging trucks may need to pass or access could suddenly be needed to fight a forest fire. Pull well off the road when stopping, even for a few minutes.

Each land-owning company has particular rules, and prior permission is often needed to use a company's roads. For instance, some companies do not allow trailers or RVs on their roads, and others limit vehicle length and width. Anyone coming from a distance to enter an area should check ahead of time with the companies concerned.

For a map showing the locations of control centers and for the latest regulations and information, send a written request and $2.00 to North Maine Woods, P.O. Box 421, Ashland ME 04732 (207-435-6213). The Paper Industry Information Office, 15 Western Avenue, Augusta ME 04330 (207-622-3166), offers some maps of company-owned lands in northern Maine and in other areas of the state and information regarding public use of privately held lands.

MAINE'S MOUNTAINS IN WINTER

For those who are properly prepared, winter hiking and climbing in Maine offers challenge and satisfaction. The general comments in the *AMC White Mountain Guide*'s section on winter climbing apply equally well to winter climbing in Maine. An added factor in Maine winter climbing is that unplowed access roads frequently lengthen a trip. Many trips that take only a day in the summer may take two or more in the winter and require camping.

Snowshoes are a must. (The bear-paw type is best for climbing.) Climbers should also carry crampons if they are likely to travel on ice or "boiler plate" snow. Other required gear includes an ice ax or ski pole if you are climbing on open slopes. For brisk snowshoeing, a light shell over a wool shirt is usually sufficient, even in very cold weather. At rest or above timberline, you will usually need an insulated parka and wind pants, and perhaps a face mask and goggles also. Be sure to carry spare pairs of wool socks and warm mittens and an extra hat. Ordinary leather boots are inadequate. Waterproof insulated boots are recommended, and they should not be too tight.

Deep snow can make route finding difficult. In steep areas or when snow is not compacted, hiking time is much longer than in summer. Be prepared to make an early start and to return after dark using artificial light. Trips should be planned carefully.

The trail descriptions given in various sections of this guide usually apply in the winter, with the qualifications that unplowed roads may add distance and trail markers may be hidden. Winter hikers should avoid high peaks and steep rocky slopes unless they have a lot of experience.

Any hikers climbing the higher and longer routes in winter should be fully aware of the danger of low temperatures and high winds. This danger is infinitely greater in winter than in summer. The wind-chill chart in this guide gives some indication of how cold it can be. Hikers should plan their trips with such weather in mind.

WIND CHILL CHART

Estimated Wind Speed in MPH	Actual Thermometer Reading (°F)											
	50	40	30	20	10	0	-10	-20	-30	-40	-50	-60
	Equivalent Temperature (°F)											
calm	50	40	30	20	10	0	-10	-20	-30	-40	-50	-60
5	48	37	27	16	6	-5	-15	-26	-36	-47	-57	-68
10	40	28	16	4	-9	-21	-33	-46	-58	-70	-83	-95
15	36	22	9	-5	-18	-36	-45	-58	-72	-85	-99	-112
20	32	18	4	-10	-25	-39	-53	-67	-82	-96	-110	-124
25	30	16	0	-15	-29	-44	-59	-74	-88	-104	-118	-133
30	28	13	-2	-18	-33	-48	-63	-79	-94	-109	-125	-140
35	27	11	-4	-20	-35	-49	-67	-82	-98	-113	-127	-145
40	26	10	-6	-21	-37	-53	-69	-85	-100	-116	-132	-148

(wind speeds greater than 40 mph have little additional effect)

LITTLE DANGER (for properly clothed person)

INCREASING DANGER

GREAT DANGER

Danger from freezing of exposed flesh

SKIING

A number of Maine's downhill ski areas are mentioned briefly in the text. To locate them easily, refer to the index under *Skiing*.

In summer, ski trails offer routes that, because of their width and their usually zigzag course on the steeper slopes, are likely to have better views than do regular summer trails. On the other hand, ski trails are less shady, the footing may be poor and rough, and some of them cross swampy places.

BUSHWHACKING IN THE MAINE MOUNTAINS

This guide deals mainly with mountains in Maine that have trails, but it does include a few peaks where hikers must bushwhack for short distances. It leaves out countless other bushwhacking sites, ranging from rather low hills to mountains approaching 4000 ft. The AMC Maine Mountain Guide Committee feels that such areas should remain without trails so that interested hikers can gain experience in bushwhacking. Some of the mountains are close to existing roads and trails, but many others are accessible only by water or long approach walks. Various topographic maps will show many of these named and unnamed trailless peaks.

Only people who are fully experienced in route finding, using a compass, and map reading should try to bushwhack the higher and more distant mountains. Bushwhackers can encounter a variety of problems and should take extra care to carry sufficient food, clothing, shelter, compasses, first-aid equipment, and similar supplies. Bushwhacking is much more time consuming than ordinary hiking, and hikers should be prepared to spend the night out if necessary.

Since most trailless mountains are located on private property, hikers should obtain permission from an authorized person prior to starting out. They should also be extra careful to leave word with a responsible party of their routes and destinations.

Bushwhackers should *not* mark their routes. The usual markers, such as rags and tapes, deteriorate rapidly. Missing markers may mislead those who subsequently attempt to follow them. Markers destroy the concept of a mountain without trails. If you plan to take the same route out that you take in and you want to mark it to save time on the return, please remove your markers as you leave.

MAPS

Extra copies of the maps at the back of this guide may be purchased separately from the AMC, P.O. Box 298, Gorham NH 03581 (or call toll-free 800-262-4455). Elevations of mountaintops and other points can be found on the maps. Remember, though, that a map cannot indicate the condition of a trail. This is a function of the text. Never assume the existence of a usable route merely because there is a dotted line on the map. Consult both the text and the map.

Other Maps, Guides, and Literature

Among many maps and books covering the mountainous areas of Maine, the following may be particularly valuable.

USGS topographic quadrangles have been published for all of Maine. The 7.5-minute series is replacing the old 15-minute series. In this book, the text indicates the quadrangle available for a given mountain. An index map showing all USGS maps is available at many sporting-goods stores and bookstores throughout the state. The index map and individual maps are also available from the USGS National Center, 12201 Sunrise Valley Dr., Reston VA 22092; (703-648-6045) or (800-872-6277).

DeLorme Mapping, Main St., Box 298, Freeport ME 04032; (800-227-1656; in Maine 800-734-5780) publishes *The Maine Map and Guide,* an accurate and regularly updated map of Maine. *The Maine Atlas and Gazetteer,* by the same publisher, provides detailed sectional maps indicating roads, trails, and significant topographic features (no contour lines).

The 1992 edition of the *Guide to the Appalachian Trail in Maine* contains further information about the Appalachian Trail and maps (seven) for the entire AT in Maine. Copies are available at many retail outlets and from the Maine Appalachian Trail Club, PO Box 283, Augusta ME 04330-0283.

For further detail on Baxter State Park see *Katahdin* by Stephen Clark, published by North Country Press, Unity ME 04988.

Information about state parks, public lands, and fire permits may be obtained from the Maine Forest Service (207-287-2275); Bureau of Public Lands (207-287-3061); and Bureau of Parks and Recreation (207-287-3821).

The AMC's journal, *Appalachia,* periodically publishes material on the mountains of Maine, and the *AMC Maine Mountain Guide* contains references to some of these articles.

COOPERATION

The AMC earnestly requests that those who use the trails, shelters, and campsites in public lands know the rules and follow them, especially those pertaining to fires. The same consideration should be shown to private landowners.

The New England Trail Conference advises that trails should not be blazed or cut on private property without the consent of the owners and definite provision for maintenance. Trails should not be cut or marked on public lands without the approval of the park or forest officials.

The main purpose of this book is to furnish accurate details, both in the text and on the maps; we will gratefully accept corrections from any source. If you find inaccuracies, signs missing, obscure places on the trails, or a map that needs correcting, please send a report to Maine Mountain Guidebook Committee, Appalachian Mountain Club, 5 Joy St., Boston MA 02108.

ACKNOWLEDGMENTS

The Maine Mountain Guidebook Committee appreciates the help received during the preparation of this book from members of the AMC and many others. Publication of this book would not have been possible without their assistance.

MAINE MOUNTAIN GUIDEBOOK COMMITTEE

Editor
Elliott M. Bates

Seth Briggs
Dean Cilley
Susan Cilley
Mike Cooper
Dennis Crispo
Eugene S. Daniell III
Lester Kenway
Rick McVey
Roy R. Schweiker
Steve Spencer
Steve Tuckerman
Ed Walsh
Paul Wentworth

ABBREVIATIONS

The following abbreviations are used in the trail descriptions.

min.	minute(s)
hr.	hour(s)
mph	miles per hour
in.	inch(es)
ft.	foot, feet
yd.	yard(s)
mi.	mile(s)
m.	meter(s)
km.	kilometer(s)
est.	estimate
AMC	Appalachian Mountain Club
AT	Appalachian Trail
BSP	Baxter State Park
CTA	Chatham Trail Association
FR	Forest Route
MATC	Maine Appalachian Trail Club
ME	Maine
MFS	Maine Forest Service
NH	New Hampshire
NPS	National Park Service
US	United States
USFS	United States Forest Service
USGS	United States Geological Survey
WMNF	White Mountain National Forest

SECTION 1
Katahdin Area

Katahdin, the highest mountain in Maine at 5267 ft., is about 80 mi. north of Bangor, between the East and West branches of the Penobscot River. It is as wild and alluring as any mountain in the East. The name, in Indian dialect, means *greatest mountain.* It lies within Baxter State Park (BSP), created by a gift of former Governor Percival P. Baxter in 1931. By the time of his death in 1969, Governor Baxter had extended the grant to more than 200,000 acres. A condition of his gift—there are variant wordings and differing interpretations by Governor Baxter and others—is that the area "shall forever be left in its natural wild state, forever be kept as a sanctuary for wild beasts and birds and forever be used for public forest, public park and public recreational purposes." Since 1921, the mountain and most of the neighboring summits have been part of a state game preserve.

KATAHDIN

Katahdin, an irregularly shaped mountain mass, rises abruptly from comparatively flat country to a gently sloping plateau above the treeline. It culminates on its southeastern margin in an irregular series of low summits, of which the southern two are the highest. These peaks are 0.3 mi. apart, and Baxter Peak (5267 ft./1605 m.) to the northwest is the higher of the two. From the southeastern South Peak (5240 ft./1597 m.), a long, curved, serrated ridge of vertically fractured granite, known as the Knife Edge, hooks away to the east and

1

northeast. About 0.7 mi. from South Peak, this ridge ends in a rock pyramid called Chimney Peak. Immediately beyond Chimney Peak and separated from it by a sharp cleft, is a broader rock peak, Pamola (4902 ft./1494 m.). It is named for the Indian avenging spirit of the mountain. To the north, the broad rock mass of Hamlin Peak (4751 ft./1448 m.) dominates the plateau or tableland, which ends in the series of low North (Howe) Peaks (4734–4612 ft./1443–1406 m.). Refer to the Katahdin map in this guide.

Katahdin was first climbed in 1804 by a party of eleven, including Charles Turner, Jr., who wrote an account of the ascent. There may have been unrecorded ascents during the next 15 years, but we know the mountain was climbed again in 1819 and 1820. After this date, ascents became more regular.

The tableland, nearly 4 mi. long, falls away abruptly from 1000 to 2000 ft. on all sides. After that the slope becomes more gentle. Great arms stretch out to embrace glacial cirques, known locally as basins. The Great Basin, with its branch, the South Basin, is the best known. In the floor of the latter, at an altitude of 2910 ft., Chimney Pond lies flanked by impressive cliffs and bordered by dense spruce forest. It fills about eight acres and is a base for many varied mountain climbs. North of the Great Basin, but still on the eastern side of the mountain, is the North Basin (floor altitude 3100 ft.), whose high, smooth-ledged sides surround a barren, boulder-strewn floor. The nearby Little North Basin has few visitors. On the western side of the tableland, the little-known Northwest Basin lies at about 2800 ft., and farther south there is a broad valley known as the Klondike. Klondike Pond rests in a small glacial arm of this valley, just below the plateau. At 3435 ft., it is 0.3 mi. long, deep, narrow, and remarkably beautiful.

From the peaks at its northern and southern ends, the tableland slopes gradually toward the center, known as the Saddle. From the eastern escarpment of the Saddle, the land falls off gently toward the dense scrub that carpets the northwestern edge. Many avalanches have scored the walls of the tableland, but only two of these scorings are now climbing routes—the Saddle Slide at the western end of the Great Basin and the Abol Slide on the southwestern flank of the mountain.

Katahdin's isolated position makes for an exceptional view that takes in hundreds of lakes, including Moosehead; the many windings of the Penobscot; and to the south, the hills of Mount Desert and Camden. Mount Washington seems to lie in a direct line behind Mount Abraham and is not visible.

Katahdin is the northern terminus of the Appalachian Trail, which includes the Hunt Trail on Katahdin itself. The great mountain lies on the southeastern side of a scattered group of smaller mountains, many of which offer interesting climbs and good views, particularly of Katahdin. The text describes these mountains following the description of Katahdin and covers them in a clockwise direction—west, north, and then northeast.

West of Katahdin, the following mountains form an elbow-shaped range: the Owl, Barren Mountain, Mount O-J-I, Mount Coe, South Brother, North Brother, and Fort Mountain. Sentinel Mountain and the striking Doubletop Mountain offer fine views from the west side of Nesowadnehunk Stream. Mullen Mountain and Wassataquoik Mountain are in the remote area between Fort Mountain and Wassataquoik Lake. Sprawling Traveler Mountain is the principal mountain in the northern section of the park. The South Branch Ponds and campground sit at its western base. Turner Mountain is to the northeast of Katahdin and offers magnificent views of it.

In all, there are at least 46 mountain peaks in the park. Eighteen of them exceed 3500 ft.

Camping facilities that accommodate about seven hundred persons are available at ten different public campgrounds, from which most trails are accessible (see the Katahdin/Baxter map). The campgrounds are: Roaring Brook, Abol, Katahdin Stream, Nesowadnehunk (Sourdnahunk), Kidney Pond, Daicey Pond, South Branch Pond, Trout Brook Farm, Russell Pond, and Chimney Pond. Russell Pond and Chimney Pond are accessible only by trail; park roads serve the other eight. All the campgrounds have lean-tos (except Trout Brook and Kidney Pond) and tent sites (except Chimney Pond and Kidney Pond); some have bunkhouses. Daicey Pond and Kidney Pond have cabins. All these sites offer only the most basic facilities. There are no hot showers, grocery stores, or gasoline stations, and the water is untreated. Campers and visitors supply their own food and cooking utensils.

There are areas for groups of 12 or more at Avalanche Field, Foster Field, Nesowadnehunk Field, and Trout Brook Farm. Backcountry campsites for smaller hiking parties are at Davis Pond, Pogy Pond, Wassataquoik Stream, Wassataquoik Lake Island, Little Wassataquoik Lake, Little East, Webster Stream, Long Pond, Middle Fowler Pond, Lower Fowler Pond, Upper South Branch Pond, Billfish Pond, Round Pond, Littlefield Pond, Matagamon Lake, and Webster Lake. Park headquarters in Millinocket handles all reservations for park facilities. Visitors can rent canoes at South Branch Pond, Russell Pond, Kidney Pond area, and Daicey Pond.

In recent years, use of the facilities at BSP has increased considerably. At the same time, park authorities have begun limiting the number of campers in the park. During most of the summer, the campgrounds are completely full. *Reservations are strongly recommended and are the only way to guarantee space. Reservations must be confirmed and paid for in advance; the park accepts no phone reservations.* The address is Reservation Clerk, Baxter State Park, 64 Balsam Dr., Millinocket ME 04462 (207-723-5140). When allotted spaces have been filled, no more overnight campers are allowed in the park. To avoid unnecessary driving and disappointment, campers without reservations should call the reservation clerk before starting a long trip to the park.

If park facilities are filled, campers can try a number of private sporting camps and campgrounds in the area around the park. The MFS maintains several campsites in the general area.

The park is open to the public 12 months a year at usage fees that differ for Mainers and out-of-staters. Nearly all of the 180 mi. of trails are blue-blazed. The only exception is the white-blazed Appalachian Trail. Remember that at various points on the tableland of Katahdin, and particularly near its summit, local variation in declination makes the compass somewhat unreliable.

Roads to the park run through Millinocket, Patten, and Greenville. These routes are shown on the official Maine Highway Map (or any other general highway map). Roads in the BSP area are indicated on the Katahdin/Baxter map with this guidebook. To reach the southern and eastern entrances to the park from points to the south, follow I-95 north to the Medway exit, and then go west on ME 157 to Millinocket and the park area; or continue on I-95 to Sherman Mills, and then follow ME 11 to Patten and ME 159 west past Shin Pond to the northern portion of the park. The approach through Greenville to the southern entrance is rougher, longer, and more time consuming than the other, but it is very interesting and offers good views of the Katahdin area.

Currently, the park has four entrances. As they enter or leave the park, all visitors must stop at the entrance gate house to register and to pick up or leave passes. Visitors can also find out about the status of hiking trails on the mountains and get other information at the gatehouses.

The southernmost gate house is just north of Togue Pond, about 18 mi. from Millinocket. Immediately past the gate house, the road forks. The right fork leads 8.1 mi. to Roaring Brook Campground and trails to Chimney Pond and Russell Pond. The left fork leads to Abol Campground (5.7 mi.), to Katahdin Stream Campground (7.7 mi.), and to Nesowadnehunk Field and Campground (16.8 mi.).

The second control point is on Matagamon (First Grand) Lake on the approach road to the northeastern part of the park. It is 24 mi. from Patten and ME 11. Follow ME 159 west from Patten past Shin Pond. Trout Brook Farm Campground is 2.6 mi. to the west on the perimeter road. South Branch Pond Campground is 9.6 mi. Drive west at first on the perimeter road, and then south about 2.5 mi. on a well-marked turnoff.

There is a third control point on the park's western boundary at Nesowadnehunk Campground. It is 58 mi. from Greenville or 51 mi. from Millinocket to Nesowadnehunk Gate over rough, privately owned logging roads. A fourth entrance is at Telos Gate, 10 mi. north of Nesowadnehunk Campground. Inquire from BSP headquarters about route and road conditions before starting out.

You can reach most campgrounds and other facilities in the park from the perimeter road. To meet the terms of former Governor Baxter's deeds of trust, the roads are unpaved and relatively unimproved. The perimeter road extends 50.5 mi. from Togue Pond Gate House to Matagamon Gate House. It is a very narrow, winding, dirt or gravel road. Except in a few places, the dense foliage along the road restricts the view. A trip to the park is not really worthwhile unless you plan to hike or camp.

From the Togue Pond Gate House, the perimeter road first leads northwest and then generally north. It skirts the southern and western flanks of Katahdin. During the first 5 mi. of the drive, the mountain is briefly visible a few times. After passing Abol and Katahdin Stream Campgrounds, the road reaches Foster Field, where you can see Doubletop, O-J-I, and other mountains in the range west of Katahdin. After that the views are very restricted all the way to the Matagamon Gate House. Most of the perimeter road follows the routes of old logging roads. For clarity and consistency, the older, more colorful, road names have been dropped in favor of the term *perimeter road*.

People planning to camp, hike, and use the facilities in the park should know the rules and regulations, which are revised annually. They can be obtained by writing to Baxter State Park, 64 Balsam Dr., Millinocket ME 04462. The latest versions of the most important rules are summarized below.

Camping is allowed only at authorized campgrounds or campsites. A responsible adult at least 18 years old must accompany groups that include five or more persons under 16 years of age; there must be one adult for each five minors. Larger camping groups may be restricted to authorized group-camping areas. The rules *prohibit bringing pets* into the park and also limit the entry and use of larger recreational vehicles. They also prohibit airplanes, motorboats, motorcycles, trail bikes, and other all-terrain vehicles. Currently, snowmobiles may be operated only on the perimeter road of the park. They may not be used on the South Branch Pond Road or the Roaring Brook Road, except by authorized park personnel.

Warning. Increased use of BSP in recent years has resulted in more accidents; several people have died on the mountain. The upper summits are very high and are rugged and bare above the timberline, and the park is fairly far north. As a result, the weather and trail conditions can change very quickly, even in the middle of summer. The weather on Katahdin is similar to that on Mount Washington, but longer access routes can make conditions even more dangerous in many cases.

Hikers planning to go to higher elevations should take plenty of food, water, and warm clothing. No hired packers serve the park; hikers who do not want to carry their own packs should make needed arrangements before arriving. The trails on many of the routes are among the steepest and most difficult in New England. Hikers should be in good physical condition if they plan to climb the higher and more distant summits; those who are not in good shape should limit their activities accordingly. *Do not* leave the trails (unless bushwhacking is suggested in this guide), particularly on Katahdin or during severe weather or limited visibility.

Hikers entering the park via the AT must register at the first campground, Daicey Pond.

Hunt Trail

The white-blazed Hunt Trail, the route of the Appalachian Trail up Katahdin, climbs the mountain from the southwest. It was first cut in 1900 by Irving O. Hunt, who operated a sporting camp on Sourdnahunk Stream. The trail leaves from Katahdin Stream Campground. From the treeline to the tableland this trail is steep and rough. Heed the warnings in the previous paragraphs.

The trail follows the north side of Katahdin Stream. At 1.1 mi. from the campground it passes the trail to the Owl on the left, crosses Katahdin Stream, and shortly after that a trail leaves left to Katahdin Stream Falls. The trail steepens through the spruce and at 2.7 mi. reaches two large rocks that form a cave, which will

shelter four people. There is a *spring,* undependable in
dry periods, 50 yd. down the trail from the cave.

The trail passes through a growth of small spruce
and in 0.2 mi. emerges on the bare, steep crest of the
southwestern shoulder, called the Camel's Hump. There
cairns mark the trail, which goes on to wind among
gigantic boulders. The trail then traverses a broad shelf
and climbs steeply 0.5 mi. over broken rock to the open
tableland (at 3.7 mi.), where two slabs of rock mark the
"Gateway." The trail continues east, following a worn
path and paint blazes, until it reaches Thoreau Spring (at
4.2 mi.), where there is *water* except in dry seasons. (At
the spring, Baxter Peak Cutoff goes off to the left and
reaches the Saddle in 0.9 mi. This trail avoids the summit and is the best route in stormy weather for traveling
between Thoreau Spring and the Saddle. To the right,
the Abol Trail descends 2.8 mi. to Abol Campground.)
From the spring, the Hunt Trail climbs moderately
northeast for 1 mi. to Baxter Peak, with its commanding
panoramas and surprising view of the South Basin.

Hunt Trail

Distances from Katahdin Stream Campground
- *to* Owl Trail junction: 1.1 mi., 45 min.
- *to* cave: 2.7 mi., 2 hr. 55 min.
- *to* the Gateway: 3.7 mi., 4 hr. 25 min.
- *to* Thoreau Spring and junctions with Abol Trail and
  Baxter Peak Cutoff: 4.2 mi., 4 hr. 35 min.
- *to* the Saddle (via Baxter Peak Cutoff): 5.1 mi., 5 hr.
  30 min.
- *to* Baxter Peak: 5.2 mi., 5 hr. 20 min.
- *to* Chimney Pond Campground (via Baxter Peak
  Cutoff and Saddle Trail): 6.8 mi., 6 hr. 30 min.
- *to* Chimney Pond Campground (via Baxter Peak, the
  Knife Edge, and Dudley Trail): 7.6 mi.(12.2 km.),
  7 hr. 45 min.

Abol Trail

The Abol Trail is believed to be the oldest route up the mountain, and evidence exists that the first recorded ascent took place near this trail. It follows a great slide up the southwestern side of Katahdin.

Caution: This trail is *dangerous* because of its steepness and the great amount of loose rock and gravel in the slide. Climb and descend with great care.

The trail leaves the perimeter road at Abol Campground. It crosses through the campground and at 0.2 mi. enters an old tote road and reaches the south bank of a tributary of Abol Stream. It continues along the south bank of the stream for 0.6 mi. The trail then bears right (northeast) away from the brook and leads sharply right. It reaches a gravel wash of old Abol Slide (1.3 mi.) and climbs the slide, reaching a more recent slide at 1.9 mi. Beyond this point the slide is steeper and becomes entirely bare. Huge boulders and increasing steepness mark the latter part of this climb. On the tableland, paint blazes lead 0.1 mi. to Thoreau Spring and the Hunt Trail. Go right on the Hunt Trail and continue northeast up gentle slopes to the summit of Katahdin. Except in dry seasons, there is water at Thoreau Spring. It is possible to make a long but rewarding circuit using the Hunt and Abol trails. You can either leave cars at the Abol and Katahdin Stream campgrounds or walk the 2 mi. between them on the perimeter road. Going up by the Abol Trail is best.

Abol Trail

Distances from Abol Campground

> *to* foot of old Abol Slide: 1.3 mi., 1 hr. 20 min.
> *to* tableland: 2.6 mi., 3 hr. 15 min.
> *to* Thoreau Spring and Hunt Trail junction: 2.8 mi., 3 hr. 20 min.
> *to* Baxter Peak (via Hunt Trail): 3.8 mi. (6 km.), 4 hr. 5 min. (*descending,* 2 hr. 45 min.)

to Katahdin Stream Campground (via Hunt Trail):
9.0 mi. (14.5 km.), *est.* 9 hr.

Roaring Brook Campground

This campground, at about 1480 ft., is on the south bank
of Roaring Brook at the northern terminus of Roaring
Brook Road. It is about 8.1 mi. from Togue Pond Gate
House. Trails to Chimney Pond and Russell Pond start
here. Closer by are Sandy Stream Pond (where hikers
often see moose) and South Turner Mountain.

Roaring Brook Campground

Distances from Roaring Brook Campground

to Chimney Pond (via Chimney Pond Trail): 3.3 mi.
(5.3 km.), 2 hr. 20 min. (*descending,* 1 hr. 40
min.)

to Baxter Peak (via Chimney Pond and Dudley trails
and Knife Edge): 5.7 mi. (9.2 km.), 6 hr. 5 min.
(*descending,* 4 hr. 40 min.)

to Baxter Peak (via Chimney Pond and Saddle trails):
5.5 mi. (8.9 km.), 4 hr. 35 min. (*descending,* 3 hr.
15 min.)

to Baxter Peak (via Taylor Trail and Knife Edge): 4.3
mi. (6.9 km.), 5 hr. 15 min. (*descending,* 3 hr. 10
min.)

to Hamlin Peak (via Chimney Pond, North Basin
Cutoff, and Hamlin Ridge trails): 4.5 mi. (7.2
km.), 4 hr. 15 min.

to North Basin (via Chimney Pond, North Basin Cutoff, and North Basin trails): 3.3 mi. (5.3 km.), 2
hr. 35 min. (*descending,* 1 hr. 50 min.)

to Russell Pond (via Russell Pond Trail): 7 mi. (11.3
km.), 3 hr. 45 min.

to South Turner Mountain summit (via Russell Pond
and South Turner Mountain trails): 2 mi. (3.2
km.), 1 hr. 50 min.

Helon N. Taylor Trail

A lot of this trail follows the route of the old Leavitt Trail. It provides a direct route from the Roaring Brook Campground to Pamola and follows the exposed Keep Ridge. This route provides the best sustained views of any trail starting from a road in the park, but it also exposes the hiker to the weather. *Be careful.* Avoid this trail in bad weather, particularly if you plan to go all the way to Baxter Peak via the Knife Edge. The Taylor Trail does not have dangerous footing, but it does require almost continuous climbing over rocks and boulders, so it is fairly tiring.

The trail, relocated in 1980, begins on the Chimney Pond Trail 0.1 mi. west of Roaring Brook Campground. It climbs 0.5 mi. through mixed growth to a ridgecrest. It then levels off for a short period, passing through scrub and a boulder field. After that it climbs steeply through small birch, enters an old flat burn, and drops to the small Bear Brook, one of the branches of Avalanche Brook. This stream offers the only *water* on the trail.

After Bear Brook, the trail ascends steeply through scrub, a fine stand of conifers, and a boulder field with wide views in all directions. It climbs over and between boulders to Keep Ridge and then along the open ridge, with a spectacular view of the Knife Edge opening up ahead, to the summit of Pamola.

Helon N. Taylor Trail

Distances from Roaring Brook Campground

    to start (via Chimney Pond Trail): 0.1 mi., 5 min.

    to Pamola summit: 3.2 mi. (5.2 km.), 3 hr. 20 min. (*descending,* 2 hr. 15 min.)

    to Baxter Peak (via the Knife Edge): 4.3 mi. (6.9 km.), 5 hr. 15 min. (*descending,* 3 hr. 10 min.)

    to Chimney Pond Campground (via the Knife Edge and Cathedral Trail): 6 mi. (9.7 km.), 4 hr. 55 min.

Chimney Pond Trail

The Chimney Pond Trail begins at the ranger's cabin at Roaring Brook Campground. Following the old Basin Ponds tote road, it climbs west along the south bank of Roaring Brook. After 0.6 mi., it bears gradually away from the brook and climbs more steeply. A brook, the outlet of Pamola Pond, crosses at 1 mi. At 1.9 mi., the trail bears left; 150 ft. to the left is the site of the old Basin Ponds Camp, GNP Camp No. 3, 1921–1936. The trail then bears right and enters an overgrown clearing at 2 mi. At that point Lower Basin Pond comes into view.

The trail follows the southern end of Lower Basin Pond and continues along its southwestern shore. At 2.2 mi. the trail goes left uphill into the woods. At 2.3 mi. the North Basin Cutoff goes off to the right. Stay left to continue on the Chimney Pond Trail. At 2.7 mi. it follows the side of a depression known as Dry Pond, which holds water in the spring and after heavy rains. At 3.0 mi. the North Basin Trail to Hamlin Ridge and North Basin leaves on the right, and at 3.2 mi. there is a cabin on the left. The trail then goes downhill slightly to end at the shore of Chimney Pond.

Chimney Pond Trail

Distances from Roaring Brook Campground

to brook crossing: 1 mi., 35 min.

to North Basin Cutoff junction: 2.3 mi., 1 hr. 20 min.

to Dry Pond: 2.7 mi., 1 hr. 55 min.

to North Basin Trail junction: 3 mi., 2 hr. 10 min.

to Chimney Pond Campground: 3.3 mi. (5.3 km.), 2 hr. 20 min.

Chimney Pond Campground

Magnificently located on Chimney Pond (2910 ft.), this campground is an excellent base for climbing to the highest summits and the tableland area. Because of this campground's heavy use and fragile ecology, the park authority enforces several restrictions. No open fires are allowed; campers must use portable stoves. In addition, campers may not set up tents; overnight visitors must sleep in the bunkhouse or lean-tos. Early reservations are a must at this popular site.

Distances from Chimney Pond Campground

> *to* Roaring Brook Campground (via Chimney Pond Trail): 3.3 mi. (5.3 km.), 1 hr. 40 min.
>
> *to* North Basin (via Chimney Pond and North Basin trails): 1.2 mi. (1.9 km.), 45 min.
>
> *to* Hamlin Peak (via Chimney Pond, North Basin, and Hamlin Ridge trails): 2 mi. (3.2 km.), 2 hr. 30 min. (*descending,* 1 hr. 45 min.)
>
> *to* Davis Pond Lean-to (via Saddle and Northwest Basin trails): 4.4 mi. (7.1 km.), 3 hr. 30 min. (*returning,* 3 hr. 45 min.)
>
> *to* Baxter Peak (via Dudley Trail and Knife Edge): 2.4 mi. (3.9 km.), 3 hr. 45 min. (*returning,* 3 hr.)
>
> *to* Baxter Peak (via Cathedral Trail): 1.7 mi. (2.7 km.), 2 hr. 30 min. (*descending,* 1 hr. 45 min.)
>
> *to* Baxter Peak (via Saddle Trail): 2.2 mi. (3.5 km.), 2 hr. 15 min. (*descending,* 1 hr. 35 min.)
>
> *to* Baxter Peak (via Chimney Pond, North Basin, Hamlin Ridge, and Saddle trails): 4.2 mi. (6.8 km.) 3 hr. 55 min. (*descending,* 3 hr. 5 min.)
>
> *to* Katahdin Stream Campground (via Saddle Trail, Baxter Peak Cutoff, and Hunt Trail): 6.8 mi. (10.9 km.), 5 hr.

Dudley Trail

The Dudley Trail leads from Chimney Pond to Pamola. It runs from the ranger's cabin east across the outlet of the pond, bears right, climbs over huge boulders, and reenters the woods, where the route is well blazed. On the rocks, cairns mark the trail clearly.

At 0.3 mi. from the pond, a side trail to the left marked Pamola Caves leads past ledges, often streaming with water, and climbs to some caves that are about 0.8 mi. from the Dudley Trail. In the caves, hikers must worm their way through small winding passages to reach three remarkably straight, spacious corridors. At the junction of the Dudley Trail and the trail to the caves, there is a *spring* 30 ft. straight ahead.

The Dudley Trail continues nearly due east from the junction, reaches a major cleft in the cliffs, and then climbs rapidly south. The soft granite has eroded into curious forms, and the trail becomes more difficult. Emerging above the timberline, the trail is marked by cairns, blue paint blazes on the rocks, and a well-worn path where it traverses patches of heath and low spruce. The trail bears slightly right (southwest) nearly to the edge of the South Basin. Then it heads south again and on up the long north slope of Pamola. The route's boulders rival the ones on the Hunt Trail, but the constantly changing view of the Great Basin below enhances the climb. After 30 min. among boulders, the going gets smoother and Index Rock (1 mi.) rises ahead. The trail passes just to the right of this landmark and continues less steeply 0.3 mi. to the peak of Pamola (4902 ft.). To reach Baxter Peak and points beyond, continue along the Knife Edge (see below). At Pamola, the Taylor Trail from Roaring Brook Campground comes in over Keep Ridge from the east.

Descending, the left-hand (western) line of cairns should be followed from the summit of Pamola. Stay near the edge of the South Basin and pass just to the left of Index Rock. At 1 mi. from Pamola, the side trail to Pamola Caves goes to the right and the Dudley Trail descends to the left.

Dudley Trail

Distances from Chimney Pond Campground
> *to* side trail to Pamola Caves: 0.3 mi., 15 min.
> *to* Pamola Caves (via side trail): *est.* 1.1 mi., 1 hr.
> *to* Pamola summit: 1.3 mi., 2 hr. (*descending,* 1 hr. 30 min.)
> *to* Baxter Peak (via the Knife Edge): 2.4 mi. (3.9 km.), 3 hr. 45 min. (*descending* back to Chimney Pond, 3 hr.)

The Knife Edge

This narrow, serrated ridge tops the southern wall of the South Basin. Cliffs plummet down on the north, and the walls on the south are only slightly less steep. In places, the ridge narrows to only 2 or 3 ft. This is probably the most spectacular mountain trail in the East. The narrowness of the ridge, combined with the dizzying height and sheer cliffs, gives a sense of extreme exposure.

From the summit of Pamola follow the cairns that lead southwest. The trail drops abruptly into the sharp cleft at the top of the Chimney, then climbs the equally steep rock tower of Chimney Peak. From there the route is fairly obvious. It traverses the Sawteeth, finally climbing South Peak and continuing along the rocks of the summit ridge to Baxter Peak. *Caution:* The Knife Edge is *dangerous in a strong wind. Do not leave the trail.* In recent years, several climbers have had accidents while trying to take unmarked "shortcuts" to the bottom.

The Knife Edge

Distance from Pamola summit
> *to* Baxter Peak: 1.1 mi. (1.8 km.), 1 hr. 45 min.

Cathedral Trail

The three immense Cathedral Rocks extend from the summit ridge and partly separate the South Basin from the Great Basin.

A sign a few feet west of the ranger's cabin at Chimney Pond marks the start of this route to Baxter Peak by way of Cathedral Rocks. The trail climbs through a small, tangled spruce forest and passes into an old evergreen forest. At 0.3 mi., it goes by Cleftrock Pool, on the right. At 0.4 mi., by a large cairn, the trail turns right toward the Cathedrals, crosses a bridge of rock covered with low growth, climbs steeply through boulders to a high point, and from there continues through low trees.

In 1967, a slide wiped out part of the next section of the trail, but with care it is still easy to follow the route. Cairns mark the way around to the right, although ice sometimes sweeps them away. The trail goes around to the right, then up the steep side of the first Cathedral (0.8 mi.). The climb of the second Cathedral (0.9 mi.) is interesting and offers spectacular views of the Chimney and the Knife Edge. The route continues up the ridge to the top of the third Cathedral at 1.1 mi. At 1.2 mi., the trail forks. The right (northwest) fork is the Cathedral Cutoff and leads 0.2 mi. to the Saddle Trail. The Cathedral Trail bears left (southwest) 0.2 mi. over large boulders to the Saddle Trail (1.4 mi.), which it joins 0.8 mi. above the Saddle.

For one of the best circuits of the upper part of Katahdin, go up the Cathedral Trail to Baxter Peak; then either return to Chimney Pond via the Saddle Trail, or take the Knife Edge to Pamola and return to Chimney Pond via the Dudley Trail, or go on to Roaring Brook Campground via the Taylor Trail.

Cathedral Trail

Distances from Chimney Pond Campground
    to second Cathedral: 0.9 mi., 1 hr. 30 min.
    to Saddle Trail junction: 1.4 mi., 2 hr. 20 min.
    to Baxter Peak (via Saddle Trail): 1.6 mi., 2 hr. 30 min.

> *to* Chimney Pond Campground (via Saddle Trail):
> 3.9 mi., 4 hr. 5 min.
> *to* Chimney Pond Campground (via the Knife Edge
> and Dudley Trail): 4.1 mi., 4 hr. 15 min.
> *to* Roaring Brook Campground (via the Knife Edge
> and Taylor Trail): 6 mi. (9.7 km.), 5 hr. 40 min.

Saddle Trail

Climbers have taken this general route out of the basin since the Saddle Slide occurred in 1899. Before that they used an older slide just north of the present one.

The Saddle Trail is the easiest route up Katahdin from Chimney Pond. From the ranger's cabin, the worn trail climbs a rocky path through dense softwoods. Beyond this stand, the trail swings to the right (north) and becomes smoother and flatter as it continues through an evergreen forest. It crosses a brook at 0.8 mi., then climbs steeply over large boulders. At 0.9 mi. the trail bears left up the Saddle Slide and passes through stunted birches. At 1 mi. it emerges from scrub, and there is a scramble for 0.2 mi. up the loose, open slope of the slide. (Be careful of loose rocks.) At 1.2 mi. the trail suddenly reaches the top of the slide and the level, open tableland at the Saddle between the summits of Baxter Peak and Hamlin Peak. Go left (south) to reach Baxter Peak. The Northwest Basin Trail, to the right, leads to Caribou Spring, the Hamlin Ridge Trail, the North (Howe) Peaks Trail, the Northwest Basin, and all points on the northern end of the mountain. About 250 yd. northwest of the head of the slide, there is *water* (unreliable) at Saddle Spring, which flows among the rocks near the edge of the scrub.

The Saddle Trail to Baxter Peak continues south over gentle slopes. Cairns mark the well-worn path.

At 1.7 mi. the trail passes a large boulder. The northern end of the Cathedral Cutoff, which leads to the

Cathedral Trail, is on the left (east); on the right (west) is the eastern end of the Baxter Peak Cutoff, which leads southwest along the base of the summit 0.9 mi. to Thoreau Spring and the Abol and Hunt trails. At 2.0 mi. the Cathedral Trail from Chimney Pond enters on the left. The Saddle Trail continues on to Baxter Peak at 2.2 mi.

Saddle Trail

Distances from Chimney Pond Campground

   to Saddle Slide: 0.9 mi., 40 min.

   to the Saddle and Northwest Basin Trail junction: 1.2 mi., 1 hr. 25 min.

   to Cathedral Trail junction: 2 mi., 1 hr. 55 min.

   to Baxter Peak: 2.2 mi., 2 hr. 15 min.

   to Chimney Pond Campground (via Cathedral Trail): 3.9 mi., 4 hr.

   to Chimney Pond Campground (via the Knife Edge and Dudley Trail): 4.6 mi., 4 hr.

   to Roaring Brook Campground (via the Knife Edge and Taylor Trail): 6.5 mi. (10.5 km.), 5 hr. 25 min.

Baxter Peak Cutoff

This trail makes it possible to go from one side of Katahdin to the other without climbing over the summit, saving 0.7 mi. of distance and about 600 ft. of elevation. It is wise to take this route in bad weather.

The trail leaves the Saddle Trail 1.7 mi. from Chimney Pond. It runs southwest over the open tableland along the base of Baxter Peak and ends at Thoreau Spring, which is on the Hunt Trail, 4.2 mi. from Katahdin Stream Campground. These two trails form the shortest route between Chimney Pond and Katahdin Stream Campground (6.8 mi.).

Baxter Peak Cutoff

Distances from Chimney Pond Campground
- *to* start of cutoff (via Saddle Trail): 1.7 mi., 1 hr. 45 min.
- *to* Thoreau Spring (Hunt Trail/Abol Trail junction): 2.6 mi., 2 hr. 15 min.
- *to* Abol Campground (via Abol Trail): 5.3 mi., 5 hr.
- *to* Katahdin Stream Campground (via Hunt Trail): 6.8 mi. (10.9 km.), 5 hr. 30 min.

North Basin Trail

From Chimney Pond follow the Chimney Pond Trail toward the Basin Ponds. At 0.3 mi. the North Basin Trail starts on the left (north; look for sign). The trail runs through spruce forest to a junction with Hamlin Ridge Trail on the left (west) at 0.7 mi. Then it passes across the foot of Hamlin Ridge to a junction, at 0.9 mi., with the North Basin Cutoff Trail. Signs and a large cairn mark this junction. The North Basin Trail continues to the lip of the North Basin, and then it reaches Blueberry Knoll, a few feet higher than the floor of the basin, where there is a sweeping view of both North Basin and South Basin, as well as the landscape to the east. From Blueberry Knoll, it is possible to bushwhack to the boulder-strewn floor of the North Basin, with its two little ponds. The northern wall is a tremendous sheer cliff.

North Basin Trail

Distances from Chimney Pond Campground
- *to* start (via Chimney Pond Trail): 0.3 mi., 10 min.
- *to* North Basin Cutoff junction: 0.9 mi., 30 min.
- *to* Blueberry Knoll: 1.2 mi., 45 min.
- *to* North Basin Ponds (via bushwhack): 1.4 mi., 55 min.
- *to* Roaring Brook Campground (via North Basin Cutoff and Chimney Pond Trail): 3.9 mi. (6.3 km.), 2 hr. 35 min.

North Basin Cutoff

This trail from the Basin Ponds to Hamlin Ridge and the North Basin forks right (sign) 2.3 mi. from Roaring Brook Campground on the Chimney Pond Trail. It traverses an area of second-growth spruce, runs past several active beaver ponds, then climbs steeply through old growth to a junction with the North Basin Trail (0.7 mi.). Turn left (southwest) to reach Hamlin Ridge, or right (northeast) to reach Blueberry Knoll and the North Basin.

North Basin Cutoff

Distances from Roaring Brook Campground

- *to* start (via Chimney Pond Trail): 2.3 mi., 1 hr. 20 min.
- *to* North Basin Trail junction: 3 mi., 2 hr. 15 min.
- *to* Blueberry Knoll (via North Basin Trail): 3 mi., 2 hr. 25 min.
- *to* Hamlin Ridge Trail (via North Basin Trail): 3.2 mi., 2 hr. 15 min.
- *to* Chimney Pond Campground (via North Basin and Chimney Pond trails): 3.9 mi. (6.3 km.), 2 hr. 45 min.

Hamlin Ridge Trail

The trail climbs, largely in the open, up Hamlin Ridge, which separates the North and South basins. The views are magnificent. From Chimney Pond Campground, follow the Chimney Pond Trail 0.3 mi. to the North Basin Trail, then follow the North Basin Trail for 0.4 mi., to the start of the Hamlin Ridge Trail. The trail reaches the treeline after a climb of about 20 min. Then, after a short stretch of boulder-strewn slope, it rises to the backbone of the ridge. The trail follows the open ridge to Hamlin Peak, and from there it goes on 0.2 mi. west across the open tableland and through a boulder field to Caribou Spring, which usually has *water* in a spring on the right side of the trail near a large cairn. To the right

from Hamlin Peak, the North (Howe) Peaks Trail runs
along the headwall of North Basin and reaches the
Howe Peaks in just under a mile.

Hamlin Ridge Trail

Distances from Chimney Pond Campground

   to start (via Chimney Pond and North Basin trails):
     0.7 mi., 20 min.

   to Hamlin Peak: 2 mi., 2 hr. 30 min.

   to Caribou Spring: 2.2 mi. (3.5 km.), 2 hr. 40 min.

North (Howe) Peaks Trail

This trail offers a route up the northern slope of
Katahdin from the Russell Pond area. It leads first over
the North (Howe) Peaks. (The official name is Howe
Peaks, after Burton Howe, a lumberman who organized
a trip that Percival Baxter made to Katahdin in 1920.)
The trail continues to Hamlin Peak, from which connecting trails lead to other points on the mountain. The
lower end of the North Peaks Trail runs through dense,
mixed growth of small trees. The central section follows
a brook up into a large ravine between Russell Mountain
on the left (east) and Tip Top on the right (west). Then it
climbs the ravine's headwall. Be careful above the treeline when visibility is poor, especially descending.
There is plenty of *water* nearly to the treeline and usually at Caribou Spring.

   The trail leaves the Northwest Basin Trail 1.2 mi.
southwest of Russell Pond Campground. At 1.5 mi. the
trail crosses to the south bank of Wassataquoik Stream.
(***Caution:*** This crossing can be dangerous or impassable
in high water after rain.) It then climbs a short, steep
slope to the top of a little horseback ridge at the mouth
of a brook. When it leaves the ridge (1.6 mi.) the trail
continues along an old road. Then it becomes a narrow
path through thick, young spruce and reaches a brook at
2.7 mi. It crosses the brook about 90 yd. farther on.

At the foot of a steep rise the trail bears right (west) away from the west bank of the brook and gradually curves left (south) on a steep climb. At 2.9 mi. it recrosses to the east bank of the brook near the foot of a lovely waterslide, where the brook runs over sloping ledges. The path parallels the waterslide for a short distance before curving to the left away from the brook and climbing through majestic old trees, which become smaller at the top of the headwall. At 4.4 mi. the trail crosses a spring brook—the last place where there is sure to be *water*. At 4.6 mi. the trail becomes a trench in dense scrub, and at 4.9 mi. it reaches the open northern tableland. Cairns lead up to a minor peak (4182 ft./1275 m.), then down its southern slope and across a level stretch covered with dead scrub. At 5.2 mi. the trail starts its final steep climb to the North Peaks. At 5.6 mi. it reaches the easternmost (4612 ft.) of the high, rocky knobs that make up the summit ridge. (*Caution:* Be careful here in fog. Dangerous cliffs drop off 50 or 60 ft. away, to the southwest [left].) The trail follows the line of the ridge southwest over intervening knobs to a large cairn on the highest peak (4734 ft.), at the southwestern end of the ridge (6.3 mi.). From this point the views out over the country to the north are spectacular. The trail, well-cairned, descends slightly and crosses the tableland.

At 6.5 mi. the trail forks. The North Peaks Trail follows the left (southeastern) fork and climbs gradually to Hamlin Peak, where it ends at 6.9 mi. The right fork is the Hamlin Peak Cutoff that leads to Caribou Spring and the Northwest Basin Trail.

North (Howe) Peaks Trail

Distances from Russell Pond Campground
    to start (via Northwest Basin Trail): 1.2 mi., 35 min.
    to waterslide: 2.9 mi., 2 hr. 5 min.

   to tableland: 4.9 mi., 4 hr. 5 min.

   to first (easternmost) North Peak: 5.6 mi., 4 hr. 55 min.

   to second North Peak: 6.3 mi., 5 hr. 15 min.

   to Hamlin Peak Cutoff junction: 6.5 mi., 5 hr. 25 min.

   to Hamlin Peak: 6.9 mi. (11.1 km.), 5 hr. 40 min.

Hamlin Peak Cutoff

Following a good path along the contour, this trail runs from the North Peaks Trail, at a point in the col between the North Peaks and Hamlin Peak, to the Northwest Basin Trail at Caribou Spring. By traveling north-south along the tableland, it avoids the climb over Hamlin Peak.

Hamlin Peak Cutoff
Distance from North Peaks Trail junction

   to Northwest Basin Trail junction, Caribou Spring: 0.3 mi. (0.5 km.), 8 min.

Northwest Basin Trail

This route climbs from the Russell Pond area to the Saddle through wild and secluded Northwest Basin, with its virgin trees, glacial sheepback rocks, five ponds, waterfalls, and interesting central ridge. The lower end of the trail follows the route of the old Wassataquoik Tote Road.

The trail begins at Russell Pond Campground. It leads southwest from Russell Pond following the Russell Pond Trail for 0.1 mi. It then diverges right and crosses a dam at the foot of the Turner Deadwater at about 0.3 mi. From there it goes on through the woods until it joins the route of the old Wassataquoik Tote Road, at about 0.5 mi. At 1.2 mi. the North Peaks Trail leaves left. With Wassataquoik Stream on the left, the trail stays on the tote road and climbs gradually, crossing Annis Brook about 2.5 mi. from Russell Pond. After passing over a section of corduroy road, the trail crosses a small brook that drains the eastern slope of Fort Mountain. It continues through thick woods and crosses Wassataquoik Stream at 3.6 mi. (*Caution:* Be very careful in high water.)

The trail climbs steadily, soon approaching Northwest Basin Brook. It runs along the brook bed for 300 ft. at about 4.4 mi. (Proceed carefully here; the rocks are very slippery and cairns may be swept away by freshets.) Above the junction of the outlets from the first two ponds, Lake Cowles and Davis Pond, the trail leads steeply up to the northern shore of Lake Cowles. It then turns left and crosses the outlet of Lake Cowles at 4.7 mi. Where it climbs to a heath-covered glacial sheepback rock, the path is becoming overgrown with blueberry bushes but is not hard to follow. From the sheepback there are enjoyable views of the entire basin. The trail continues down to the Davis Pond Lean-to, at 5.1 mi. The shelter, rebuilt in 1987, is located on the north side of Davis Pond.

From the Davis Pond Lean-to, the Northwest Basin Trail passes the so-called disappearing pond. (The fourth pond is 0.3 mi. below and on the outlet of Davis Pond; the fifth is hidden deep in the woods between the outlets of Lake Cowles and Davis Pond.) The trail first goes southwest and then south as it climbs through a steep and rough area up the basin wall.

The trail emerges from the scrub and at 6.2 mi. reaches a large cairn that marks a small peak (4401 ft.) near the western end of the Northwest Plateau. The Northwest Plateau reaches toward the west and is a flat extension of the northern tableland. It lies west of the North Peaks and separates the Northwest Basin from the Klondike Pond Ravine. Its lower slopes push their way far out into the Klondike. At 6.4 mi. an obscure, unmaintained route leads right (south) to the head of a slide down into the Klondike Pond Ravine. The Northwest Basin Trail climbs very gradually across the Northwest Plateau, passing through a belt of scrub at 6.8 mi. Then it continues more to the south across open tableland to Caribou Spring, at 7.3 mi. At the spring, the Hamlin Peak Cutoff leads sharply left to the North Peaks Trail, and the Hamlin Ridge Trail climbs left (east) to Hamlin Peak.

The Northwest Basin Trail descends south toward the Saddle, which it reaches at 8.3 mi. To get to Chimney Pond, descend east on the Saddle Trail.

Keep in mind that poor trail or weather conditions, heavy packs, and different levels of physical conditioning in hiking parties will increase the times given here.

Northwest Basin Trail

Distances from Russell Pond Campground

    to North Peaks Trail junction: 1.2 mi., 35 min.

    to Annis Brook crossing: 2.5 mi., 1 hr. 30 min.

    to Wassataquoik Stream crossing: 3.6 mi., 2 hr. 15 min.

    to Davis Pond Lean-to: 5.1 mi., 3 hr. 15 min.

    to peak of Northwest Plateau: 6.2 mi., 4 hr. 50 min.

    to Hamlin Ridge Trail and Hamlin Peak Cutoff junction, Caribou Spring: 7.3 mi., 5 hr. 35 min.

    to the Saddle and Saddle Trail junction: 8.3 mi. (13.3 km.), 6 hr.

Klondike Pond Ravine

This ravine contains a long, narrow pond that drains into the Klondike. The great slabs of the central gully form the most spectacular route down into the ravine. Rock fields forming an island in dense scrub on the northeastern headwall offer a rough but safe approach to them. (**Caution:** Be careful on the slabs, and avoid wet places on the steeper ones.) At the foot of the headwall, follow the brook 200 yd. to the head of Klondike Pond, where there are impressive views of the ravine.

This trail is *not* officially maintained, and fire poses great danger in this remote area. Therefore, hikers must get permission to enter from park officials.

An unmaintained, seldom-used route leaves the Northwest Basin Trail on the left (south) 0.9 mi. north-west of Caribou Spring (about halfway between the belt of scrub and the peak of the Northwest Plateau). This route continues to the rim of the ravine, and after a short drop, it enters the head of a recent slide. From the bottom of the slide, bear slightly right through brush to reach the head of the pond. The dense scrub and the cliffs discourage any other entry into the ravine from above.

It is possible to hike from Chimney Pond to Klondike Pond and back in one day by starting early, but it makes for a long day.

Russell Pond Trail

This trail runs from Roaring Brook Campground north-ward between Katahdin and Turner Mountain to Russell Pond Campground. It is the principal approach to the Russell Pond area.

After leaving Roaring Brook Campground, the trail crosses Roaring Brook. At 0.2 mi. it turns left (north-west; look for sign). To the right the South Turner Mountain Trail leads to Sandy Stream Pond and South Turner Mountain. In the next half mile the Russell Pond Trail crosses several brooks while gradually climbing the low height-of-land between Sandy Stream Pond and Whidden Pond. The trail descends and passes to the east (right) of the latter, where there is an extensive view of the basins and peaks on the east side of Katahdin. At 1.1 mi. the Sandy Stream Pond Trail comes in on the right. At 1.4 mi. an opening yields good views; after this point the trail moves into denser forest. Between 2.3 mi. and 3.1 mi., it crosses several brooks, and at 3.3 mi. it reaches a junction on the right with the Wassataquoik Stream Trail, which leads 2.5 mi. to the two Wassataquoik Stream Lean-tos and rejoins the Russell Pond Trail at 3.9 mi. At 3.4 mi. the Russell Pond Trail crosses the Wassataquoik South Branch and soon crosses another brook. There are no bridges here; crossing is knee-deep in dry weather, dangerous after rain.

The trail, now on the western side of the valley, passes under an overhanging rock at 3.8 mi. Moving away from Wassataquoik Stream, it passes several brooks and springs and climbs gently for nearly 2 mi. to a spruce grove. Then the trail gradually descends, with the impressive, high, forested slopes of Russell Mountain on the left. At 6.3 mi. it crosses the main branch of Wassataquoik Stream. At 6.5 mi. it crosses the old Wassataquoik Tote Road with the abandoned clearing for New City Camps on the right. A trail on the right leads 1.4 mi. to the two lean-tos on Wassataquoik Stream. Immediately beyond the tote road, the Russell Pond Trail crosses Turner Brook (North Branch of the Wassataquoik).

At 6.9 mi. the Northwest Basin Trail to the Saddle leaves on the left (west). Soon after, the trail reaches Russell Pond.

Russell Pond Trail

Distances from Roaring Brook Campground

> *to* Sandy Stream Pond Trail junction: 1.1 mi., 30 min.
>
> *to* Wassataquoik Stream Trail junction: 3.3 mi., 1 hr. 40 min.
>
> *to* Wassataquoik Tote Road junction: 6.5 mi., 3 hr. 10 min.
>
> *to* Northwest Basin Trail junction: 6.9 mi., 3 hr. 40 min.

to Russell Pond Campground: 7 mi. (11.3 km.), 3 hr. 45 min.

Wassataquoik Stream Trail

Some once called this old route the Tracy Horse Trail or Wassataquoik South Branch Trail. It has been reopened and runs from the Russell Pond Trail along the South Branch of Wassataquoik Stream to the main branch of Wassataquoik Stream. It leaves the right side of the Russell Pond Trail about 3.3 mi. north of Roaring Brook Campground, just before that trail crosses South Branch. It leads to the junction with the main stream and continues along the south bank of the main stream for about 200 yd.

The park authority maintains two lean-tos at the site of the old Hersey Dam (where you can still see spilling at the crossing). Reservations for them can be made as for any campsite.

To reach Russell Pond Campground from the lean-tos, cross to the north side of Wassataquoik Stream upstream from the lean-tos (no bridge) and look for a blue-blazed trail along the old Wassataquoik Tote Road. In the downstream direction, this trail leads 1.6 mi. to a junction with the Grand Falls Trail at Inscription Rock. In the upstream direction, it leads 1.4 mi. to a junction with the Russell Pond Trail just south of the Turner Brook crossing. Turn right on the Russell Pond Trail to reach the campground, which is about 0.4 mi. away.

Wassataquoik Stream Trail

Distances from Roaring Brook Campground

to start of trail to lean-tos (via Russell Pond Trail): 3.3 mi., 1 hr. 40 min.

to lean-tos: 5.8 mi., 3 hr.

to Russell Pond Campground (via Russell Pond Trail): 7.6 mi. (12.2 km.), 3 hr. 45 min.

RUSSELL MOUNTAIN (2801 ft./854 m.)

This mountain is the most northern extension of Katahdin. Its broad, trailless summit area is devoid of recognizable characteristics and so flat and full of boulders that you have to search for the summit cairn. But the summit offers excellent views in all directions. To reach it, bushwhack west from the Russell Pond Trail about 4.5 mi. north of Roaring Brook Campground. Since there is no trail to the mountain and conditions change from year to year, check with the ranger at Russell Pond Campground for the latest information.

Russell Pond Campground

On the southwestern shore of Russell Pond (1333 ft.) in the heart of the wilderness north of Katahdin, this campground is a convenient and interesting hiking base. The wildlife in this remote area is especially intriguing. Facilities include tent sites, lean-tos, and a bunkhouse. The Wassataquoik Lake Cabin and the lean-tos on Wassataquoik Stream, Pogy Pond, and Little Wassataquoik Pond are administered from this campground.

Russell Pond Campground

Distances from Russell Pond

> *to* Roaring Brook Campground (via Russell Pond Trail): 7 mi., (11.3 km.), 3 hr. 45 min.
>
> *to* Hamlin Peak (via North Peaks Trail): 6.9 mi. (11.1 km.), 5 hr. 40 min. (*descending,* 3 hr. 50 min.)
>
> *to* Davis Pond Lean-to (via Northwest Basin Trail): 5.1 mi. (8.2 km.), 3 hr. 15 min. (*descending,* 2 hr. 45 min.)
>
> *to* Wassataquoik Lake (via Wassataquoik Lake Trail): 2.4 mi. (3.9 km.), 1 hr. 15 min.
>
> *to* Little Wassataquoik Lake (via Wassataquoik Lake Trail): 5.2 mi. (8.4 km.), 3 hr. 10 min.
>
> *to* dam at Nesowadnehunk Lake (via Wassataquoik Lake Trail): 11.4 mi. (18.4 km.), 6 hr. 15 min.

to Lookout Ledges (via Pogy Notch and Grand Falls trails): 1.3 mi. (2.1 km.), 50 min.

to Grand Falls (via Grand Falls Trail): 2.8 mi. (4.5 km.), 1 hr. 30 min.

to South Branch Pond Campground (via Pogy Notch Trail): 9.7 mi. (15.6 km.), 4 hr. 40 min.

to Wassataquoik Stream Lean-tos (via Wassataquoik Stream Trail): 1.8 mi. (2.9 km.), 1 hr.

Wassataquoik Lake Trail

This trail connects the Russell Pond Campground with the Wassataquoik Lake area and continues on to the west to the perimeter road and the foot of Nesowadne-hunk Lake. Most of the first part of this route was a logging road prior to 1878, and there is evidence it was cut out before 1845. The area was logged several times afterward. The west end of the trail follows a fairly new logging road built after the park was created. The former owners retained cutting rights for a period after they sold the property to Governor Baxter.

The trail leads north off the Pogy Notch Trail opposite lean-to No. 4 at the northwestern corner of Russell Pond. At 0.6 mi. from Russell Pond take the left fork (the right fork leads to Deep Pond). At 1.7 mi. the trail crosses a dam between two of the Six Ponds. It then crosses a brook at 2.2 mi., and at 2.3 mi. it takes the left fork (the right fork leads to the dam at the foot of Wassataquoik Lake) to a point near the dam (2.4 mi.). On an island near the eastern end of the pond there is a cabin. To reach the island, you can make arrangements at Russell Pond to use a canoe.

To reach the head (western) end of the lake (4.2 mi.), follow the trail along the rocky southern shore. The views are magnificent. About halfway along the southern shore of Wassataquoik Lake, a trail leads left (south) uphill to Green Falls, one of the most beautiful spots in the park. Above the falls, the hiker can pick out a route through a stand of virgin spruce to the summit of Wassataquoik Mountain (2984 ft./910 m.).

Near the head of Wassataquoik Lake, at an old grassy clearing, the trail leaves the lake and leads nearly due north on an old road. After crossing the outlet stream from Little Wassataquoik Lake several times, it reaches the lake itself. Then it follows along the northern shore to the lake's western end (about 5.2 mi.). The trail heads west from the lake toward a col between Wassataquoik Mountain and Lord Mountain. Shortly after leaving the lake, the trail passes the Little Wassataquoik Lake Lean-to. The trail climbs to the col and then descends into the Trout Brook drainage area. From the col, the trail follows an old logging road for about a mile and a half before it leaves the road and turns left at about 6.5 mi. Wet in places, it crosses a brook several times, and at about 7.6 mi. it crosses the South Branch of Trout Brook. Soon after crossing the brook, the trail enters an old logging camp clearing. From here, a tote road that is easy to follow leads for about 4 mi. through a valley between Center Mountain and Strickland Mountain. It reaches a col and then descends to the perimeter road. Turn left for the dam at the foot of Nesowadnehunk Lake.

Wassataquoik Lake Trail

Distances from Russell Pond Campground

   to start (via Pogy Notch Trail): 0.2 mi., 5 min.

   to Deep Pond side trail junction: 0.6 mi., 20 min.

   to dam at Six Ponds: 1.7 mi., 50 min.

   to side trail to dam at foot of Wassataquoik Lake: 2.3 mi., 1 hr. 10 min.

   to Green Falls (via side trail): *est.* 3.3 mi., 1 hr. 45 min.

   to Little Wassataquoik Lake: 5.2 mi., 3 hr. 10 min.

   to left turn off old logging road: 6.5 mi., 3 hr. 50 min.

   to tote road junction: 7.5 mi., 4 hr. 30 min.

to Nesowadnehunk Lake (via tote road): 11.4 mi.
(18.4 km.), 6 hr. 15 min.

Grand Falls Trail

This trail leads from Russell Pond Campground to several interesting locations in the Wassataquoik Valley. The first part coincides with the Pogy Notch Trail.

From the campground, follow the Pogy Notch Trail around the western shore of the pond. The Wassataquoik Lake Trail leaves to the left soon after the start of the route. At 0.2 mi. the Pogy Notch Trail continues north (left) at a junction. The Grand Falls Trail takes the right fork, passes the ranger station, and continues to the next junction (0.4 mi.), where the trail to Lookout Ledges leaves to the left (north). The Grand Falls Trail continues ahead on the right through woods and over relatively level ground toward Wassataquoik Stream. As it nears the Wassataquoik, a side trail to the right leads 50 ft. to the bank of the stream and Inscription Rock, a huge boulder with a notice about logging in the area that was inscribed in 1883. A 1.6-mi. segment of the Wassataquoik Tote Road, from Inscription Rock to the Wassataquoik Stream Lean-tos, was reopened in 1983, so it is now possible to loop back to Russell Pond via the Wassataquoik Stream Trail and the Russell Pond Trail. From this junction, the main trail soon reaches the bank of Wassataquoik Stream near the Grand Falls of the Wassataquoik. These falls drop steeply through high granite walls and are impressive, particularly in high water. The ruins of a logging dam lie just upstream.

Grand Falls Trail

Distances from Russell Pond Campground

to Lookout Ledges Trail junction: 0.4 mi., 10 min.

to Inscription Rock (via side trail): *est.* 2.5 mi., 1 hr. 20 min.

to Grand Falls: *est.* 2.8 mi. (4.5 km.), 1 hr. 30 min.

Lookout Ledges Trail

This high outlook (1730 ft./527 m.) offers views from Traveler Mountain around to Katahdin and is easy to reach from Russell Pond Campground. Follow the Pogy Notch and Grand Falls trails for 0.4 mi. and turn left at the junction. The trail climbs moderately and steadily for nearly a mile to the ledges.

Lookout Ledges Trail

Distances from Russell Pond Campground

> *to* start (via Pogy Notch and Grand Falls trails): 0.4 mi., 10 min.
>
> *to* Lookout Ledges: 1.3 mi. (2.1 km.), 50 min.

THE OWL (3736 ft./1139 m.)

This mountain is the first summit in the long, high range that runs west from Katahdin. Its southern face is especially steep.

The Owl Trail

The blue-blazed Owl Trail leaves the Hunt Trail 1.1 mi. from Katahdin Stream Campground. The trail goes left from the Hunt Trail just before a crossing of Katahdin Stream and then follows the north bank of a tributary. It turns sharp right (southeast) and crosses the tributary at 1.6 mi. (last source of water). The trail climbs gradually through dense spruce and fir and follows the western spur toward the summit. At 2.9 mi. the trail rises steeply through a ravine and then across the upper part of the Owl's prominent cliffs. At 3.2 mi. the trail reaches the first outlook. After a more gradual climb, it reaches the summit at 3.3 mi. Views in all directions are outstanding, especially the ones into the Klondike and across to the tremendous wind-rows in Witherle Ravine and on Fort Mountain.

The Owl Trail

Distances from Katahdin Stream Campground
> *to* start (via Hunt Trail): 1.1 mi., 45 min.
> *to* first outlook: 3.2 mi., 2 hr. 35 min.
> *to* the Owl summit: 3.3 mi. (5.3 km.), 2 hr. 40 min.

BARREN MOUNTAIN (3580 ft. and 3681 ft./ 1091 m. and 1122 m.)

A high wooded ridge, Barren Mountain has two well-defined summits and several lower humps. A blowdown that occurred in 1974 eliminated possible approaches from the south and southwest.

One route goes up the southeast slide of O-J-I and then southeast into the col and up the Barren summit ridge. Scrub growth near the summits of O-J-I and Barren makes this route slow. It is also possible to climb from the Owl-Barren ravine, but blowdowns make this approach very difficult.

MOUNT O-J-I (3410 ft./1039 m.)

Mount O-J-I got its name from three slides on the southwestern slope that suggested the three letters. After a major storm in 1932, however, the slides began to enlarge and the letter shapes have become distorted. A fourth large slide that can be climbed came down in 1954 and is south of the so-called south slide.

Two of the other slides, the north and south slides, offer routes up the mountain. They are connected, which allows a circuit of the mountain in either direction. However, descending the smooth, steep granite slope on the north slide can be very dangerous, particularly in wet weather; so it is better to climb up by the north slide and return by the south slide.

The trail leaves the perimeter road at Foster Field directly opposite the road to Kidney Pond and immediately crosses a brook. At 0.4 mi. the trail forks. Go left to reach the north slide. (The right fork leads to the south slide.) The trail follows an old road and immediately crosses two small brooks. At 1.1 mi. the road ends in a small open area covered with slide gravel and cut by a stream bed that is usually dry. (About 45 yd. north of this point watch for a huge boulder off the trail on the left. The boulder is approximately 73 ft. long, 48 ft. wide, and 25 ft. high.) From the small open area, the trail parallels the stream bed without crossing it and leads directly (approximately 200 yd.) to a large open wash at the foot of the north slide and then to the top of the lower ledges. Many sections of this route traverse smooth granite, sometimes covered by gravel; so *be careful,* particularly if the rock is wet. Climb to the head of the slide and then go through brush to the summit ridge. There the trail heads to the western summit, where a trail leads left to the Old Jay Eye Rock, a fine observation point. From the summit ridge a trail leads right to the south slide.

To follow the south slide route, go right at the fork 0.4 mi. from Foster Field. The route follows an old road and at 1.8 mi. continues on a narrow trail. As the gravel wash from the slide becomes noticeable on the forest floor, the trail bears right and soon reaches the open wash (2 mi.). Climb to the head of the slide and through brush and scrub to the summit ridge. Then go northwest to the summit (2.9 mi.).

Another route is to approach the mountain by climbing the Mount Coe slide. The O-J-I Link Trail, cleared in 1983, runs 0.5 mi. from the Mount Coe slide across the col to a junction with the O-J-I south slide trail 0.2 mi. from the summit.

Mount O-J-I

Distances from perimeter road at Foster Field

    to fork in trail: 0.4 mi., 10 min.

    to foot of north slide (via left fork): 1.2 mi., 45 min.

    to foot of south slide (via right fork): 2 mi., 1 hr. 10 min.

    to O-J-I summit (via north slide): 2.7 mi., 3 hr.

    to O-J-I summit (via south slide): 2.9 mi., 3 hr. 15 min.

    to perimeter road (via north slide–south slide circuit): 5.6 mi. (9 km.), 6 hr.

MOUNT COE (3764 ft./1147 m.)

This peak, just north of Mount O-J-I, has excellent views into the Klondike and is well worth the challenge of the climb.

Follow the Marston Trail to the sign 1.2 mi. from the perimeter road. Turn right, and follow the trail 0.2 mi. to the bottom of the Mount Coe slide (it follows a stream). The climb is steady but moderate at first, then steep. At 2.6 mi. the trail bears left and begins to climb the left center of a wide slide area at 2.8 mi. (The O-J-I Link Trail leads right 0.5 mi. to the O-J-I South Slide Trail. It is 0.7 mi. to the summit of O-J-I via this trail.) At 3.1 mi. the trail enters scrub growth. At 3.3 mi. you will reach the summit.

An extension of the Mount Coe Trail, cleared in 1983 and further extended in 1987, rejoins the Marston Trail at a point 0.8 mi. from the summit of North Brother.

The trail descends the east ridge of Mount Coe and proceeds toward South Brother. At 4.2 mi. pass two clearings with fine views of Mount Coe. At 4.4 mi. the South Brother Side Trail leads right 0.3 mi. to the summit of South Brother. At 5.1 mi. reach the junction with the

Marston Trail. Ahead it is 0.8 mi. to the summit of North Brother. To the left it is 2.9 mi. to the perimeter road.

Mount Coe

Distances from perimeter road at Slide Dam

> *to* start of Mount Coe Trail (via Marston Trail): 1.2 mi., 50 min.
>
> *to* foot of Mount Coe slide: 1.4 mi., 1 hr.
>
> *to* start of scrub: 2.9 mi., 3 hr. 40 min.
>
> *to* Mount Coe summit: 3.3 mi., 4 hr. (*descending,* 2 hr.)
>
> *to* junction South Brother Side Trail: 4.4 mi., 4 hr. 45 min.
>
> *to* junction Marston Trail: 5.1 mi. (8.2 km.), 5 hr. 15 min.

THE BROTHERS (North 4143 ft./1263 m. and South 3930 ft./1198 m.)

North and South Brother are open peaks that offer splendid views in several directions. (*Caution:* Early in the season, in late May and the first half of June, climbers should expect to find deep snow from the head of the slide all the way to the ledges at the summit of North Brother—a distance of 1.5 mi.)

Marston Trail

The Marston Trail, the best approach for exploring the area, was relocated in 1987.

The trail leaves the perimeter road at Slide Dam, 5.9 mi. north of Katahdin Stream Campground and 3.6 mi. south of Nesowadnehunk Campground. The trail starts from the road, nearly opposite the picnic shelter, and follows the northern bank of Slide Brook to an open, sandy area. At 0.2 mi., the trail bears left into a wooded area and over a slight rise into the drainage area of a second brook. The trail, climbing steadily, follows this brook closely for the next mile. At 0.8 mi. it crosses, and there are several more crossings in the next 0.4 mi. before the trail reaches the junction with the Mount Coe trail at 1.2 mi.

The Marston Trail leads to the left and climbs gradually through extensive blowdown. A small pond with fine views is reached at 2 mi. At 2.1 mi. the pond's outlet is reached (last *water*). The trail then climbs steeply, passing several viewpoints. The trail levels off at 2.7 mi. and reaches the upper junction with the Mount Coe Trail at 2.9 mi. To the left, it is 0.8 mi. to North Brother. To the right, the Mount Coe Trail leads (1 mi. to South Brother via South Brother Side Trail) 5.1 mi. to the perimeter road. After crossing this fairly level valley, it passes a *spring* at 3.1 mi. and then climbs steeply. At 3.6 mi. the trail leaves the scrub and continues among open boulders, reaching the summit of North Brother at 3.7 mi. Note particularly the view of the west slopes of Katahdin and, in the opposite direction, of the Nesowadnehunk Lake region and the interesting valley of Little Nesowadnehunk Stream.

Marston Trail

Distances from perimeter road at Slide Dam

   to Mount Coe Trail first junction: 1.3 mi., 50 min.
   to Pond: 2.0 mi., 1 hr. 10 min.
   to Mount Coe Trail, second junction: 2.9 mi., 2 hr.
   to North Brother summit: 3.7 mi. (6 km.), 3 hr.
      (*descending,* 2 hr.)

FORT MOUNTAIN (3861 ft./1177 m.)

This mountain, with its 0.5-mi. summit ridge, is northeast of North Brother. A high saddle connects the two. The best and easiest route to Fort Mountain is a trail leading left into the bush from the summit of North Brother. The trail is rough, unmarked, and obliterated in sections by blown-down trees, and keeps to the southern side of the North Brother–Fort ridge most of the way. It emerges on the northwestern end of the Fort ridge. The distance is less than 1 mi.

Before trying to take this route, keep in mind that it comes at the end of a very tiring climb to North Brother.

Fort Mountain

Distances from perimeter road at Slide Dam

> *to* North Brother summit (via Marston Trail): 3.7 mi., 3 hr.
>
> *to* Fort Mountain northwestern summit: *est.* 4.7 mi. (7.6 km.), 4 hr. (*descending,* 2 hr. 45 min.)

Daicey Pond Campground

When the BSP Authority terminated the private leases still existing in the park in the late 1960s, it decided to continue operations on a modified scale at the former Twin Pines Camps at Daicey Pond. There are ten cabins for rent. Users must provide their own cooking equipment. Canoes may be rented. To reach Daicey Pond, follow the perimeter road for 2.7 mi. beyond Katahdin Stream Campground and turn left (south). It is 1.5 mi. to the camps, which have beautiful views of the western side of Katahdin and the mountains to the west. From a canoe on the pond, you can get an excellent view of Doubletop.

The Appalachian Trail passes within a short distance of the campground and skirts the shore opposite the camp for 0.3 mi. Hikers entering the park from the south along the Appalachian Trail must register at Daicey Pond. Katahdin Stream Campground is 1.9 mi. northeast on the Appalachian Trail. South of Daicey Pond, the Appalachian Trail passes an old dam on Nesowadnehunk Stream and Little and Big Niagara Falls. All are worth seeing and are within 1.3 mi. of the campground. The Appalachian Trail then leads out of the park to the West Branch of the Penobscot (see the MATC *Guide to the Appalachian Trail in Maine* for details).

Daicey Pond is a good starting point for the climb to Sentinel Mountain. Trails also lead to the Kidney Pond area, and a lovely trail of about 1 mi. leads from the canoe landing on Daicey Pond, across from the cabins, to Lost Pond.

Kidney Pond Campground

Formerly a private enterprise, the Kidney Pond Campground reopened under park management in 1990 for day-use fishing, canoe rental on some of the surrounding ponds, and cabin rental for family groups and hikers. The campground is reached off the Perimeter Road, with day-use parking available.

Draper Pond Trail leads north for 0.5 mi. to a canoe landing on the pond's south shore. A short trail connects the east shore with the campground access road and the trail to Slaughter Pond and Doubletop Mountain. Rocky Pond Trail (0.6 mi.) to the northwest reaches the pond where park canoes can be rented. A 100-yd. portage leads to Little Rocky Pond. From the west shore the Polly Pond Trail runs 0.9 mi. to just outside the park border. From a canoe landing on the west shore of Kidney Pond the Celia and Jackson Pond Trail reaches Celia Pond at 0.9 mi. At 1.1 mi. Little Beaver Pond Trail starts south for 0.7 mi. Jackson Pond, with park canoes, is reached at 1.3 mi.

Kidney Pond is girded east and south by its Outlet Trail (1.8 mi.) which heads east, then south along Nesowadnehunk Stream and branches, left to Daicey Pond Campground and right (west) to connect with Sentinel Mountain Trail.

South of Kidney Pond, Lily Pad Pond Trail goes to a canoe landing on a stream, which reaches the pond in .25 mi. From Lily Pad Pond's south landing, the 1-mile-long Windy Pitch Pond Trail heads south to the pond, passing Little and Big Niagara Falls.

SENTINEL MOUNTAIN (1837 ft./560 m.)

This low mountain rises over the northern bank of the West Branch of the Penobscot River and offers the finest view of the western side of Katahdin. From Kidney Pond Road, skirt the western side of Kidney Pond, or paddle across it to the canoe landing (Sentinel Landing) on the southern side of the cove on the right (west).

From Daicey Pond, cross Nesowadnehunk Stream and branch left (west) from the trail to Kidney Pond at a point 300 yd. from that pond. The trail goes around the southwestern side of the pond to Sentinel Landing, which is about 0.7 mi. from Daicey Pond. (*Caution:* Be careful to avoid several branch trails that are almost as clear as the main trail; some of them lead from a landing the main trail passes before it gets to Sentinel Landing.)

From Sentinel Landing, the blue-blazed trail to Sentinel Mountain leads southwest. At 0.3 mi. (sign) the trail bears right onto a section that was relocated to avoid beaver flow. At 0.7 mi. you will have to cross Beaver Brook on stepping stones. The trail climbs the northeastern side of the mountain along a brook, which crosses the trail at 1.1 mi. and furnishes water nearly to the open summit ledges. The trail reaches the ledges at 2.2 mi. Follow the ledges to the right (north) to the actual summit (2.3 mi.).

From the actual summit at the western end of the summit ridge, the trail continues back along the southern side of the ridge, with an outlook over the West Branch, to form a loop. It rejoins the main trail about halfway between the first ledges and the true summit.

Sentinel Mountain Trail

Distances from Sentinel Landing

    to Beaver Brook crossing: 0.7 mi., 20 min.

    to second brook crossing: 1.1 mi., 40 min.

    to Sentinel summit: 2.3 mi. (3.7 km.), 1 hr. 30 min.

DOUBLETOP MOUNTAIN (North Peak 3488 ft./ 1063 m.)

Doubletop's steep, slide-scarred eastern slopes make it easy to identify from many points in the Katahdin region. The views from its two peaks are impressive and are particularly helpful to anyone planning to climb South Brother, Mount Coe, O-J-I, or Barren Mountain, or to hike into the Klondike.

Doubletop Mountain Trail, Southern Approach

To approach Doubletop from the south, take the road to Kidney Pond, which intersects the perimeter road at Foster Field. Follow it for 0.8 mi. across a bridge over Nesowadnehunk Stream. There is parking for several cars in a gravel pit on the right immediately after a bridge crossing.

From the bridge, the Doubletop Mountain Trail starts on the right and follows the general course of Nesowadnehunk Stream for about 0.5 mi. Then it crosses Slaughter Pond Brook, bears left, climbs slowly, and leads more or less directly to the eastern side of Deer Pond. It follows the old Deer Pond Trail to the Slaughter Pond Tote Road, which leads to the old Camp 3 clearing (at about 1.3 mi.).

At the far end of the Camp 3 clearing, the trail to Doubletop forks right (north), leaving the clearing near its northwest corner.

(*Watch carefully;* this turn is hard to see. Straight ahead [west] an old road continues to Slaughter Pond. Turn right [north] before reentering the woods or leaving the clearing.) The trail follows an old road northwest up a valley and crosses a stream four times. The stream and the trail run together for a while, which makes the route extremely wet and muddy. The trail passes close under the cliffs on Squaw's Bosom, the peak west of Doubletop, and then turns northeast at about 2.3 mi. Just after crossing the headwaters of the stream, it reaches uncut spruce woods and passes a spring at 3.1 mi. Turning north again, the trail climbs the saddle west of Doubletop. Then it slabs up a steep timbered slope on the western side of the mountain to South Peak (4 mi.), which is above the timberline. The trail continues from South Peak 0.2 mi. to North Peak. From North Peak the trail descends and leads north to Nesowadnehunk Campground.

Doubletop Mountain Trail, Southern Approach

Distances from Kidney Pond road

    to old Camp 3 clearing: 1.3 mi., 45 min.

    to spring in spruce woods: 3.1 mi., 2 hr. 15 min.

    to South Peak: 4 mi., 3 hr. 20 min.

    to North Peak: 4.2 mi., 3 hr. 30 min.

    to Nesowadnehunk Campground: 7.3 mi. (11.7 km.), 6 hr. 30 min.

Doubletop Mountain Trail, Northern Approach

The approach from the north leads south from the last lean-to at Nesowadnehunk Campground. Initially it parallels Nesowadnehunk Stream, which lies to the east. For the first mile, it follows a fairly level course, and then it turns southwest and ascends gradually in the valley of the brook draining the area between Veto Mountain on the northwest and Doubletop on the southeast. After about 1.5 mi. the trail swings generally south once more to follow the northern ridge of Doubletop as it climbs more steeply and steadily to North Peak.

Doubletop Mountain Trail, Northern Approach

Distances from Nesowadnehunk Campground

    to North Peak: 3.1 mi., 2 hr. 45 min.

    to South Peak: 3.3 mi., 3 hr.

    to Kidney Pond Camps road: 7 mi. (11.3 km.), 6 hr. 30 min.

Nesowadnehunk Campground

This campground on Nesowadnehunk Stream, although beautiful, is not a major hiking center. It is the base for the approach to Doubletop from the north. It is also a control point for entering the park from the west. Fishermen find this campground a convenient base.

MULLEN MOUNTAIN (3450 ft./1052 m.)

This rock-capped peak is north of the Brothers and south of Wassataquoik Mountain. The climb starts in the vicinity of Mullen Pond. Virgin spruce cover the northern slope, and the hiking is smooth.

The old Mullen Brook Tote Road, up Mullen Brook to Mullen Pond, provides an approach from the Russell Pond area. (This route is not official—check for permission and trail conditions with the Russell Pond Campground ranger.) The old Mullen Brook Tote Road leaves the Northwest Basin Trail on the north, opposite where the Northwest Basin Trail joins the old Wassataquoik Tote Road, about 0.5 mi. from Russell Pond. The old Mullen Brook Tote Road is overgrown and hard to see from the Northwest Basin Trail. Beavers have dammed ponds along the route, so the trail skirts them and is often difficult to follow. Soon after leaving the Northwest Basin Trail, the route follows the edge of a swamp and then turns sharply left, skirts another swamp, crosses a brook, and returns to the Mullen Brook Tote Road. The tote road climbs gradually and then more steeply to Mullen Pond, about 3.5 mi. from the Northwest Basin Trail. To bushwhack to the summit, from the eastern shore of the pond turn left (south) and pass through open spruce woods to a collar of thick dwarf birches just below the open, rocky summit.

Mullen Mountain

Distances from Russell Pond Campground

   to old Mullen Brook Tote Road junction (via North-
      west Basin Trail): 0.5 mi., 25 min.

   to Mullen Pond: *est.* 4 mi., 2 hr. 15 min.

   to Mullen Mountain summit: *est.* 5 mi. (8 km.), 4 hr.
      30 min.

WASSATAQUOIK MOUNTAIN (2984 ft./910 m.)

Hikers can climb this broad, wooded mountain from the
southern shore of Wassataquoik Lake. (See the description of Wassataquoik Lake Trail for the approach to the
start of the route.) The trail up Wassataquoik is not officially maintained. It starts west of the outlet brook of
Green Falls, crosses the brook, and climbs steeply east
of the falls. After several more crossings, it leaves the
brook and climbs on up the mountain. Near the top, it is
obscured by raspberry bushes and debris from a fire in
1959. From the southern and more precipitous edge of
the summit, there is a good view of Mullen Mountain
and the country beyond.

Wassataquoik Mountain

Distances from Russell Pond Campground

   to start of trail to Green Falls (via Wassataquoik
      Lake Trail): *est.* 3.2 mi., 1 hr. 35 min.

   to Green Falls: *est.* 3.3 mi., 1 hr. 45 min.

   to Wassataquoik summit: *est.* 5 mi. (8 km.), 4 hr.

STRICKLAND MOUNTAIN (2400 ft./732 m.)

It is best to climb this low, wooded summit from Camp
Phoenix on Nesowadnehunk Lake. Camp Phoenix, on
the eastern side of Nesowadnehunk Lake, is an enclave
of privately owned land surrounded by BSP and the
lake. From the eastern side of the barnyard in the rear of

the camps, cross the perimeter road and follow logging roads over the gentle slope to where it starts to get steeper. Beyond, there are no trails, but you can hike through mostly open, pleasant woods to the summit, from which there are good views toward Center Mountain and the Brothers. Take a compass bearing on Camp Phoenix before descending.

BURNT MOUNTAIN (1793 ft./547 m.)

There is a firetower on this low summit in the northwestern section of the park. Trees are gradually blocking what were once excellent views from the summit. Burnt Mountain Trail begins at the Burnt Mountain picnic area, 13.8 mi. west of Matagamon Gate or 8.8 mi. north of Nesowadnehunk Gate.

Burnt Mountain Trail

Distances from Burnt Mountain picnic area
   to Burnt Mountain summit: 1.3 mi. (2.1 km.), 50 min.

South Branch Pond Campground

This campground is at the eastern end of the Lower (northern) South Branch Pond (981 ft.). The South Branch Ponds have perhaps the most spectacular surroundings of any in Maine, except the ones near Katahdin. They lie in a deep valley between Traveler Mountain to the east and the South Branch Mountains (Black Cat Mountain) to the west. The campground, the usual base for hiking in the Traveler area, has choice views of Traveler's peaks and ridges, of the pond, and of the South Branch Mountains. Facilities include openfront shelters, tenting space, a bunkhouse, and rental canoes.

South Branch Campground

Distances from South Branch Campground

    to Middle Fowler Pond: 4.0 mi. (6.5 km.), 2 hr. 30 min.

    to North Traveler summit (via North Traveler Trail): 2.5 mi. (4 km.), 2 hr. 20 min.

    to Peak of the Ridges (via Pogy Pond and Center Ridge trails): *est.* 3.5 mi. (5.6 km.), 2 hr. 50 min.

    to southern end of Upper South Branch Pond (via Pogy Notch Trail): 1.9 mi. (3.1 km.), 1 hr.

    to Russell Pond Campground (via Pogy Notch Trail): 9.7 mi. (15.6 km.), 4 hr. 40 min.

Pogy Notch Trail

This trail leads from South Branch Pond Campground around the eastern shores of the ponds, then south through Pogy Notch. It passes west of Pogy Pond and continues southwest to Russell Pond Campground. The trail offers fairly easy access to the center of the park and the trails on Katahdin, and nice views enhance the hike.

From South Branch Pond Campground enter woods on the trail toward the eastern shore of the pond. The North Traveler Trail diverges left at 0.2 mi. At 1.0 mi. the trail reaches the delta of Howe Brook and the Howe Brook Trail, which leaves to the west. Soon it enters some woods, where it follows a brook route at first and then bears right (south) away from the brook. At 1.3 mi. the trail climbs over the end of the cliff between the Lower and the Upper South Branch Pond. The Center Ridge Trail goes left at 1.4 mi. The Pogy Notch Trail descends and passes an old campsite at the southeastern corner of the upper pond. The South Branch Mountain Trail comes in on the right at the old campsite (1.9 mi.). The Pogy Notch Trail continues south, passing through an alder swamp and beaver works at 2.8 mi. It crosses several brooks and rises and falls moderately in the next 0.5 mi. At 3.3 mi. the trail forks. Straight ahead is the old route to Traveler Pond; the Pogy Notch Trail turns right, climbs gradually, and passes through Pogy Notch.

Bear left at 3.9 mi. into a sparsely grown old burn. The trail then crosses a beaver canal and descends into the Pogy Pond watershed. It crosses a brook several times while passing out of the notch area and descending toward Pogy Pond. Then it crosses several other brooks and reaches the head of Pogy Pond at 6.0 mi. (There are clear views of Traveler, Turner, and Katahdin mountains from the shore of the pond.)

The trail bears right, uphill, and at 6.1 mi. a side trail to the left leads in 0.2 mi. to the Pogy Pond Lean-to. The main trail descends nearly to the pond (6.2 mi.), then bears right, away from the pond. (Be careful you don't take a wrong turn onto a short spur trail to the west, and watch carefully for blazes, which are scarce in this area.) The main trail rises gradually, then descends through an old burn, traverses a series of shallow rises, and bears right. At 6.7 mi. the trail drops into the gully of the western tributary of Pogy Brook. It crosses the brook and climbs up the opposite slope. Then it runs through a swampy hollow, climbs a rocky rise, and descends gradually to cross another brook (7.3 mi.). Immediately after the brook the trail bears right and climbs gradually through sparse mixed growth. It crosses a beaver meadow, reaches a rough boulder field at 7.8 mi., and descends through it. The trail descends toward Russell Pond, and at 9.4 mi. the trail to Grand Falls and Lookout Ledges leaves to the left. Just before Russell Pond Campground, the Wassataquoik Lake Trail leaves to the right.

Pogy Notch Trail

Distances from South Branch Pond Campground

   to North Traveler Trail junction: 0.2 mi., 5 min.

   to Howe Brook Trail junction: 1 mi., 30 min.

   to Center Ridge Trail junction: 1.4 mi., 45 min.

to South Branch Mountain Trail junction: 1.9 mi., 1 hr.

to Pogy Pond: 6 mi., 3 hr.

to Grand Falls Trail junction: 9.3 mi., 4 hr. 30 min.

to Russell Pond Campground: 9.7 mi. (15.6 km.), 4 hr. 40 min.

SOUTH BRANCH (BLACK CAT) MOUNTAIN
(north summit 2599 ft./792 m. and south summit 2585 ft./788 m.)

South Branch Mountain (Black Cat Mountain on USGS maps) is across the ponds from Traveler Mountain. It offers extraordinary views of Traveler Mountain as well as the region immediately to the west, and the climb can help hikers pick out routes up Traveler Mountain.

South Branch Mountain Trail
The South Branch Mountain Trail runs from South Branch Pond Campground over both summits and down to the Pogy Notch Trail, which it joins at the southern end of the upper pond.

The trail (blue blazes) starts at the northwestern corner of Lower South Branch Pond, across the outlet brook from the canoe rack (sign). The trail parallels a small brook, staying from 100 to 200 yd. away from it, for 0.3 mi. and then follows a ridge for 0.8 mi. to nearly flat lookouts with vistas of the ponds and the Traveler range. After contouring for 0.3 mi., the trail turns abruptly right and climbs more steeply to the northern peak.

The southern peak is 0.5 mi. farther—an easy hike along the high saddle connecting the two summits. The trail from the south peak was relocated in 1983. It descends over gentle meadows and rock fields to open ledges on the south side of the mountain. At about 3 mi.

it swings eastward and descends through mixed forests. There is a short, steep climb of about 0.1 mi., then the trail rejoins the old trail at about 4 mi. At 4.3 mi. it passes a side trail to the upper South Branch Lean-to, and at 4.5 mi. it crosses a brook with beaver works before joining the Pogy Notch Trail at the southern end of the upper pond. Turn left (north) for South Branch Pond Campground and right (south) for Pogy Notch and Russell Pond Campground.

South Branch Mountain Trail

Distances from South Branch Campground

> *to* lookouts: 1.1 mi., 45 min.
>
> *to* South Branch Mountain northern peak: 2 mi., 2 hr.
>
> *to* South Branch Mountain southern peak: 2.5 mi., 2 hr. 15 min.
>
> *to* Pogy Notch Trail junction: *est.* 4.5 mi., 4 hr.
>
> *to* South Branch Campground (via Pogy Notch Trail): *est.* 6.4 mi. (10.3 km.), 5 hr.

TRAVELER MOUNTAIN (3541 ft./1079 m.)

Traveler Mountain is a great, starfish-shaped mountain with four high ridges sprawling out south, west, northwest, and north, and four shorter spurs between them.

Fires have ravaged the mountain, the last one in 1902, so that while the lower parts support hardwoods of some size, the upper slopes are mostly bare, and good for climbing. The bareness of these higher slopes makes for a uniform landscape that can be highly confusing in fog or darkness. Although the mountain's altitude is quite a bit lower than Katahdin's, the routes up Traveler from the South Branch Pond Campground are longer, partially without trails, and equally exposed; so treat the mountain with respect, start early, and allow a full day for the climb. Estimate time, distance, and the roughness of the terrain generously.

There are four main routes up Traveler from South Branch Pond Campground. Three of them follow trails for part of the climb. The following sections describe the routes in order, from north to south.

North Traveler Trail

From South Branch Pond Campground follow the Pogy Notch Trail 0.2 mi. to the North Traveler Trail, which diverges left. The North Traveler Trail climbs through open woods to the crest of North Ridge, which it follows over bare ledges in places. The view improves until the trail enters birch woods. After that the trail passes through lovely alpine meadows and fine old woods that alternate with steep ledges. At about 1.6 mi., in one of the wooded sections, a side trail leaves left to a good *spring*. After emerging from the last section of woods, the trail continues in the open up the ridge to the summit at 3144 ft./958 m. The views are impressive.

North Traveler Trail

Distances from South Branch Pond Campground
>   *to* start (via Pogy Notch Trail): 0.2 mi., 5 min.
>   *to* side trail to spring: *est.* 1.6 mi., 1 hr. 30 min.
>   *to* North Traveler summit: 2.5 mi. (4 km.), 2 hr. 20 min.

Howe Brook Trail

The Howe Brook Trail begins at the southeastern corner of Lower South Branch Pond, where the rocky, fanlike delta of Howe Brook merges with the pond. This inlet is 1 mi. south along the Pogy Notch Trail from the campground. The trail follows the route of the brook to the first chutes and potholes. (Howe Brook is noted for its many pools, rock- and water-formed potholes, slides, and chutes, which continue for quite a distance up the valley.) The trail crosses the brook a number of times before it ends at a beautiful waterfall.

Howe Brook Trail

Distances from South Branch Pond Campground
    to start (via Pogy Notch Trail): 1 mi., 30 min.
    to waterfall: *est.* 3 mi. (4.8 km.), 1 hr. 45 min.

Center Ridge Trail

This route starts at the foot of Center Ridge at the northeastern corner of the upper pond, 1.4 mi. south on the Pogy Notch Trail from South Branch Pond Campground. The Center Ridge Trail runs to the Peak of the Ridges. Diverging left (east) from the Pogy Notch Trail, it climbs steadily through woods and then across open ledges. There are excellent views of the Howe Brook valley and North Traveler. After climbing over many rocky knobs, the trail reaches the Peak of the Ridges (about 3200 ft./975 m.), where it ends. There the route up Pinnacle Ridge comes in on the right.

Center Ridge Trail

Distances from South Branch Pond Campground
    to start (via Pogy Notch Trail): 1.4 mis., 45 min.
    to Peak of the Ridges: *est.* 3.5 mi. (5.6 km.), 2 hr. 50 min.

Loop Route over Traveler and North Traveler

Only strong parties can make a circuit of Traveler Mountain. Climbers who attempt this trip, which takes at least 12 hours, should be well supplied with food and water and should carry a good compass. It is possible to follow the route by ascending North Traveler first, but the description goes in the other direction.

Climb to Peak of the Ridges on the Center Ridge Trail. To climb Traveler, continue northeast along the ridge from Peak of the Ridges to the point where you can see clearly down into the meadow in the col on the way to Traveler. From there, use binoculars to carefully study the animal yards and rock slides on the way to Traveler summit. There are three animal yards. An almost straight line of animal trails going up the slope (east) connects them to the meadow. You should keep a little to the right of the center of each animal yard to find the path to the next one above. Near the top of the third yard, turn almost 90° to the right (south) and look for an exit out onto the rock slide. There is at least one that is almost completely open. Traverse horizontally and possibly drop down a little to get around the end of the heavy brush. Keep close to the brush and angle up as soon as possible. There are several breaks in the trees through which you can angle up until you come out into the open below one of the western peaks of Traveler. Continue up toward the peak. The rock slope is somewhat loose but stable enough for safe passage. Traveler's summit is about 1.7 mi. from the Peak of the Ridges.

To reach North Traveler from Traveler, first go as far northeast as possible in the open (there is a cairn on the last outcrop). From there take a compass bearing on the several outcrops visible on the way to North Traveler. Study the areas between these outcrops and between them and the one you are on. The thick woods make it necessary to follow a compass bearing carefully to come out on the first outcrop. (The strongest member of the party might want to break through the trees, guided by the compass carrier following 5 to 10 yd. behind.) The trees are so dense that you may not be able to see the next outcrop from the first one. Correct the compass bearing based on your earlier observation and go down into the trees again. Follow the compass to come out on the next outcrop. The next leg of the bushwhack will also have to be on a compass course, and then you will be able to stay in the open until you pass over the top of a subsidiary northern peak of Traveler. Then you should take a compass bearing for a spot just above the ever-green growth in the col between there and North

Traveler. Lucky climbers may find animal trails that will make hiking easier, but be careful not to go too far to the right (northeast) and get into the evergreen growth. By staying to the left you will also avoid a deep cut at the bottom of the col.

Hard bushwhacking will continue up the slope of North Traveler. Again you should watch the compass and, at the same time, take advantage of animal trails. Be careful again not to get too far off course, and you will come out into the open and be able to continue to the top of North Traveler. The distance is a very tiring 3 mi. from the Traveler summit.

From North Traveler, descend to South Branch Pond Campground via the North Traveler Trail.

Loop Route over Traveler and North Traveler
Distances from South Branch Pond Campground
> *to* Center Ridge Trail (via Pogy Notch Trail): 1.4 mi., 45 min.
> *to* Peak of the Ridges: 3.5 mi., 2 hr. 50 min.
> *to* Traveler summit: *est.* 5.2 mi., 4 hr.
> *to* North Traveler summit: *est.* 8.2 mi., 10 hr.
> *to* South Branch Pond Campground (via North Traveler Trail): *est.* 10.7 mi. (17.2 km.), 12 hr.

Pinnacle Ridge Route

This is the most spectacular of the four routes up Traveler, but there is no trail beyond the Pogy Notch Trail. From the southern end of the south pond, follow the Pogy Notch Trail about 0.8 mi. to a knoll where the slide on the Pinnacle is plainly visible. Turn left (east) through pleasant woods and across older slides, and you will reach the Pinnacle slide. Climb up on the left to avoid the cliffs above. From the top of the Pinnacle, a steady climb through open brush brings you to the Peak of the Ridges. The distance from the Pogy Notch Trail to the Peak of the Ridges is about 2 mi.

Do not descend the Pinnacle Ridge. If you are caught by bad weather as you climb up on the upper slope, there is an emergency way off via the so-called Escape Route down the broad gully between Pinnacle and Center ridges. It gets climbers off the exposed ridge quickly and allows them to follow the little stream and skirt the low cliffs near the bottom to the Pogy Notch Trail near the southern end of the upper pond.

Pinnacle Ridge Route

Distances from South Branch Pond Campground

> *to* turn off Pogy Notch Trail: *est.* 2.7 mi., 1 hr. 25 min.
>
> *to* Peak of the Ridges: *est.* 4.7 mi., 3 hr.
>
> *to* Pogy Notch Trail (via Center Ridge Trail): *est.* 5.8 mi., 3 hr. 35 min.
>
> *to* South Branch Campground (via Pogy Notch Trail): *est.* 7.2 mi. (11.6 km.), 4 hr. 20 min.

Trout Brook Farm Campground

The newest campground in BSP, Trout Brook Farm is on the site of an old farm that served logging operations. The campground is on the north side of the perimeter road, about 27 mi. west of Patten and 2.6 mi. west of Matagamon Gate House. It is 4.7 mi. east of the Crossing Lunchground, where the perimeter road crosses Trout Brook and where the road to South Branch Campground leads south. Trout Brook Farm has only tent sites. It is a starting point for many trips in the park, including canoe trips and hikes to Traveler Mountain and other outlying mountains and hikes along the new trail system in the northern and northeastern sections of the park. Trails north of Trout Brook Farm Campground are, for the most part, not on the map that accompanies this book. In addition to a handout, *Outlying Campsites,* available from BSP, hikers are referred to *A Guide to Baxter Park and Katahdin,* by Stephen Clark, and to

DeLorme's Map and Guide of Baxter State Park and Katahdin (DeLorme Publishing Co., PO Box 298GS, Freeport ME 04032).

Webster Lake and Freezeout Trails

Combined, these trails make a delightful two- or three-day circuit, which is the longest linear backpacking trip in the park. The many tent sites along the route permit flexibility in planning the trip. Although it does not involve mountain travel, it offers streams and ponds and access to good fishing areas.

The Webster Lake and Freezeout trails traverse a section of the park known as the Scientific Forest Management Area. This 28,000-acre parcel was specifically designated by Governor Baxter as an area to be managed by the "most modern methods of forest controls," and further as a "showplace for those interested in forestry" and forest management operations.

Caution: Ask at Park Headquarters or any facility in the northern end of the park for locations of the latest timber-harvesting operations. If you run into any equipment working in the woods, don't get too close. Questions and comments are invited; write the Park Forester at Park Headquarters.

The Webster Lake Trail leaves the perimeter road at the Black Brook Farm site, 8.8 mi. west of Trout Brook Farm. It leads northwest along the route of the old Wadleigh Tote Road until it reaches the east bank of Thissell Brook, which it follows for some distance. Then it turns northeast to the shore of Webster Lake. The Webster Lake Trail ends there at its junction with the Freezeout Trail.

The Freezeout Trail parallels the entire length of Webster Stream, which under the right conditions can be a challenging white water experience (see the *AMC River Guide: Maine*).

The trail leaves the Webster Lake Trail at the southern shore of Webster Lake. It follows the shore around to the outlet, where there is a good tent site. From here, the trail generally descends toward Matagamon Lake, paralleling Webster Stream. It sometimes bears away from the stream, but it always returns. At 5.2 mi. it passes Webster Stream Lean-to and at 9.5 mi. it passes Little East Branch Lean-to, opposite the confluence of the East Branch of the Penobscot and Webster Stream. (To use lean-tos and tent sites, make arrangements with park officials in Millinocket or at one of the campgrounds.) From there, the trail makes a sharp right turn onto the remains of the old Burma Road, an improved tote road last used in 1950. Follow it for the remaining distance to Trout Brook Farm.

Webster Lake and Freezeout Trails

Distances from perimeter road, Black Brook farm site

> *to* Freezeout Trail junction (via Webster Lake Trail): 7.2 mi., 3 hr. 50 min.
>
> *to* Webster Lake outlet tent site (via Freezeout Trail): 8.1 mi., 4 hr.
>
> *to* Webster Stream Lean-to: 13.4 mi., 6 hr. 45 min.
>
> *to* Little East Branch Lean-to: 15.9 mi., 8 hr.
>
> *to* Trout Brook Farm Campground: 21.8 mi. (35.1 km.), 10 hr. 55 min.

FOWLER PONDS AREA

In conjunction with the development of Trout Brook Farm Campground, some new official routes have been opened to several lakes in the area south of the perimeter road, west of Horse Mountain, and northeast of the South Branch Ponds area. Between Barrell Ridge and Billfish Mountain are the three Fowler Ponds; in the next valley to the northeast are Billfish and Round ponds (which drain to the east) and High and Long ponds (which drain into Fowler Brook). Further north, at the head of Littlefield Brook, is Littlefield Pond. For years, fishermen kept routes to these ponds open from the perimeter road to the east and north. Official campsites are on the northern shore and outlet of Lower Fowler Pond and at the outlet and southern end of Middle Fowler Pond. See the ranger at Trout Brook Farm or South Branch Pond Campground for camping and trail information. The Clark guide and the BSP handout mentioned above under Trout Brook Farm would be most useful.

The Fowler Brook Trail leads south from the perimeter road about 2 mi. west of Trout Brook Farm Campground. It generally follows Fowler Brook and leads to the northern end of Lower Fowler Pond.

A second trail leaves the southern side of the perimeter road 1 mi. west of the entrance to Trout Brook Farm Campground. It leads generally south for about 1.8 mi., after which it forks. (The left fork is a side trail leading to High and Long ponds.) After crossing a second brook, the main trail climbs a crest and reaches a second junction. The trail to the left goes to the Middle Fowler Pond outlet and its campsites; to the right, the trail reaches the northeastern shore of Lower Fowler Pond at about 2.5 mi.

A third route leaves south from the perimeter road on the west side of Littlefield Brook, about 0.9 mi. east of the Trout Brook Farm Campground entrance. It leads south 1.5 mi. up the valley of Littlefield Brook to Littlefield Pond.

In 1982, a new route was opened from Littlefield Pond to High Pond via Billfish and Round ponds. There are new tent sites at Littlefield, Billfish, Round, and Long ponds.

In 1987 a new route was opened from South Branch Pond to Middle Fowler Pond. It is considered to be an extension of the Middle Fowler Pond Trail, connecting the South Branch Pond and Trout Brook Farm Campground.

The trail leaves the north end of the campground and follows the Ledges Trail for the first 0.3 mi. The trail climbs gradually, following a small brook until open ledges are reached at 1.7 mi. From here the trail proceeds through the gap between Big Peaked and Little Peaked mountains. The trail then traverses the north slope of Traveler Mountain and provides occasional views. At 3 mi. the Barrell Ridge Side Trail leads 0.3 mi. to the open summit of Barrell Ridge. The summit has very fine views, especially of Traveler Mountain. From this point the trail descends, and it reaches Middle Fowler Pond at 4 mi. (sign). To the left it is 3.3 mi. to the perimeter road via the Middle Fowler Pond and Fowler Brook trails. To the right it is 0.2 mi. to the south campsite on Middle Fowler Pond.

Fowler Ponds Area

Distances from perimeter road

> *to* Littlefield Pond: *est.* 1.5 mi., 45 min.
>
> *to* Lower Fowler Pond, northern end (via Fowler Brook Trail): 1.5 mi., 1 hr.
>
> *to* Lower Fowler Pond, northeastern shore (via High and Long ponds): *est.* 2.5 mi. (4 km.), 1 hr. 15 min.

Distance from South Branch Pond

> *to* Middle Fowler Pond: 4 mi. (6.4 km.), 2 hr. 30 min.

HORSE MOUNTAIN (1589 ft./484 m.)

In the northeastern corner of BSP, this mountain rises above the western shore of First Grand (Matagamon) Lake. There is an abandoned MFS firetower on the summit, which is easy to reach from the perimeter road.

The trail leaves the southern side of the perimeter road 2.5 mi. west of the bridge over the East Branch of the Penobscot and just west of the Matagamon Gate House. It rises at an easy rate and near the top turns sharp right (west) to the summit and tower.

Horse Mountain

Distance from perimeter road

   to Horse Mountain summit: 1.4 mi. (2.3 km.), 1 hr. 5 min.

TURNER MOUNTAIN (north summit 3323 ft./ 1013 m. and south summit 3122 m./952 m.)

This mountain northeast of Katahdin is low compared with the great mountain. However, Turner offers magnificent views of Katahdin, particularly of the basins. You can approach South Turner from Roaring Brook Campground. The hike involves a moderate climb up the southwestern slide. North Turner is trailless. The two summits are more than 2 mi. apart and are separated by a deep saddle.

South Turner Mountain Trail

This trail starts out across Roaring Brook at Roaring Brook Campground and coincides with the Russell Pond Trail. (At 0.2 mi. the Russell Pond Trail goes left.) The Sandy Stream Pond Trail goes straight to Sandy Stream Pond. At 0.4 mi. it turns right, crosses the outlets, and continues around the southeastern shore of the pond. (This section is often wet and muddy during rainy seasons.) Along the trail near the southeastern shore of the pond, a number of side paths lead left to the shore. Moose frequent the pond. The trail follows the right fork at 0.7 mi. (The left fork is the Sandy Stream Pond Trail, which leads northwest 0.9 mi. to Whidden Pond and a junction with the Russell Pond Trail 1.1 mi. north of Roaring Brook Campground.) The South Turner

Mountain Trail enters a small boulder field at 0.9 mi. and follows cairns and paint blazes on the rocks as it climbs. At 1.1 mi. it turns left and rises steeply. At 1.5 mi. it passes a side trail right to a spring, bears left and continues. At 1.8 mi. the trail leaves the scrub and starts over open ledges. It follows cairns and paint blazes to the summit at 2 mi.

South Turner Mountain Trail

Distances from Roaring Brook Campground
> *to* start (via Russell Pond Trail): 0.2 mi., 5 min.
> *to* Whidden Pond Trail junction: 0.7 mi., 20 min.
> *to* South Turner summit: 2 mi. (3.2 km.), 1 hr. 50 min.

MOUNT CHASE (2440 ft./849 m.)

This mountain north of Patten has an abandoned MFS firetower. There are extensive views from the summits. Looking northeast from Katahdin, it is the very prominent mountain in the distance. Refer to the USGS Island Falls Quadrangle, 15-minute series.

The approach road diverges left (west) from ME 11 6.5 mi. north of Patten, 1.5 mi. north of the Penobscot-Aroostook border, and 9.5 mi. south of Knowles Corner. Follow the approach road to the west for 2.3 mi. from ME 11.

The trail leaves the right (northern) side of the road, proceeds first west and then almost due north, following a jeep road to the warden's cabin, which it reaches in about 0.8 mi. Beyond the cabin, the trail climbs steadily north to the summit. *There is no water* on the trail. The firetower cab has been removed.

Mount Chase

Distances from ME 11

   to start (via approach road): *est.* 2.3 mi., 1 hr. 10 min.

   to firewarden's cabin: *est.* 3.1 mi., 1 hr. 50 min.

   to Mount Chase summit: *est.* 3.8 mi. (6.1 km.), 2 hr. 35 min.

SECTION 2
Aroostook

Aroostook County, with an area of 6453 square miles, sprawls along Maine's northern and northeastern boundary. It is larger in area than Connecticut and Rhode Island combined. Aroostook's greatest north-south dimension is about 120 mi. and its greatest east-west dimension is 104 mi.

The mountains of Aroostook County are widely scattered. There are no ranges or compact mountain areas except two small clusters of hills—the Deboullie Mountain region west of Eagle Lake and east of the Allagash territory, and the hills west of Bridgewater and around Number Nine Lake. Solitary Mars Hill (1660 ft.), which rises from almost level country near the county's eastern boundary, is probably the best-known mountain. Peaked Mountain (2260 ft./689 m.), a trailless summit in the wilderness west of Ashland, is the county's highest.

See page xviii in the introduction to this guide for information on the North Maine Woods Association and its control policies in the western part of Aroostook County.

NUMBER NINE MOUNTAIN (1638 ft./499 m.)

This peak is west of Bridgewater in the small group of mountains around Number Nine Lake. The lake has an interesting MFS campsite. Refer to the USGS Howe Brook quadrangle, 15-minute series, or Number Nine Lake quadrangle, 7.5-minute series.

At the southern end of Bridgewater turn west off US 1 onto Boutford Road (West Road) which leaves in front of the Bridgewater Grammar School. This road runs west, northwest, and then west again into a wilderness area. At about 11 mi. take the left fork (south) toward Number Nine Lake (1084 ft.), which is less than 1 mi. farther. The road, partly paved, turns left across the outlet, follows the south side of a logged area, and climbs 1.5 mi. to the summit, where there is a helopad and an abandoned radar installation with antennas. A few steps are missing, but the tower gives a grand 360° view.

Number Nine Mountain

Distance from US 1 in Bridgewater
   to Number Nine Lake: *est.* 12 mi. (19.2 km.)

Distance from lake outlet
   to Number Nine summit: 1.5 mi. (2.4 km.), 1 hr. 15 min.

MARS HILL (1660 ft./506 m.)

This monadnock rises abruptly from an almost level area of farms and woodland in the eastern section of the town of the same name. Refer to the USGS Mars Hill quadrangle, 15-minute series or 7.5-minute series.

The mountain runs north-south for 3 mi. and parallels the Canadian border, which is about 1 mi. to the east. The southern peak is the highest and is being developed as a recreation area (with picnicking and tenting) by the Mars Hill Junior Chamber of Commerce. There is also a ski area on the mountain. A rough road climbs up this peak, rising slightly more than 1000 ft. in 1.6 mi. The views from the summit extend across the potato fields in all directions to other mountains in the county, and on to Katahdin to the southwest and across the St. John River valley into New Brunswick to the east.

From Mars Hill Village, take US 1A north for 0.4 mi. Then turn right (east) on Boynton Road. The pavement ends 1.7 mi. from US 1A. Turn right and then take the first left (toward Mars Hill and the ski area). For the south (highest) peak, turn right and then take the first left to the ski area. The trail goes up the left side of the main ski slope. For the north peak, turn left instead. Drive 1.7 mi., passing the country club. The posted road at power pole S 23/20 heads up the mountain.

Mars Hill

Distance from start of access road
   to Mars Hill summit: 1.6 mi. (2.6 km.), 1 hr. 15 min.

QUAGGY JO (1213 ft./370 m.)

Quaggy Jo (also called Quoggy Joe and Quaquajo) dominates Aroostook State Park from the southwestern corner of Presque Isle. The 1700-acre state park offers swimming, boating, camping, and picnicking. A side road runs west to the park from US 1 (sign) 4 mi. south of Presque Isle and 10.5 mi. north of Mars Hill village. Refer to the USGS Presque Isle quadrangle, 15-minute series, or Echo Lake quadrangle, 7.5-minute series.

The mountain, which rises 600 ft. above Echo Lake, has two peaks. On the higher, southern peak there are four radio transmitters and an aircraft beacon. The slightly lower, northern peak has better views to the northwest and east.

The trail to the summit starts just south of the playground area and soon joins the Quaquajo Trail and climbs quickly to the northern peak. From the northern peak a trail leads south to the true summit on the southern peak.

Quaggy Jo

Distances from parking area
   to summit of northern peak: 0.8 mi., 40 min.
   to summit of southern peak: 1.5 mi. (2.4 km.), 1 hr. 5 min.

DEBOULLIE MOUNTAIN (1981 ft./604 m.)

Deboullie Mountain is the highest of a small cluster of mountains in the wilderness south of St. Francis and southwest of Eagle Lake. Refer to the USGS Fish River Lake quadrangle, 15-minute series, and Gardner Pond and Deboullie Pond quadrangles, 7.5-minute series.

The views, only available from the unmanned MFS firetower on Deboullie's summit, take in Long, Eagle, and Square lakes. From one spot, Quebec Province can be seen beyond the strip of New Brunswick that runs north of Fort Kent. Other mountains in the area include Black Mountain (1901 ft.) to the east, and Gardner Mountain (1817 ft.) and Whitman Mountain (1810 ft.) to the south. Interspersed between the mountains are small but picturesque lakes and ponds. There are also a warden's cabin, unused since 1984, and a helopad on the summit.

In 1975 the state of Maine, through a land exchange, took ownership of 15,000 acres on and around the mountain. The Bureau of Public Lands plans to manage the land as a protected area with primitive recreation.

The present access to the township is from St. Francis Road and checkpoint (fee), which turns left off ME 161 about 6.5 mi. southwest of St. Francis and soon heads south and then east for some 20 mi., ending at a parking area at Pushineer Pond. The hiking trail starts west, skirts the north edge of Deboullie Pond (1128 ft.), crosses an intermittent rockslide, and at its western end heads steeply up to the summit.

Deboullie Mountain

Distance from end of auto road at Pushineer Pond
   to Deboullie summit: 2.5 mi. (4 km.), 1 hr. 35 min.

HEDGEHOG MOUNTAIN (1594 ft./486 m.)

This mountain is in T 15 R 6 just off ME 11 between Winterville and Portage. (T and R stand for *township* and *range*. The state of Maine uses this system to designate unincorporated areas.) The mountain, which runs north-south, falls off steeply on its eastern side. Refer to the USGS Winterville quadrangle, 15-minute series or 7.5-minute series.

The trail up Hedgehog starts on the west side of ME 11, 3.5 mi. south of Winterville and 12.8 mi. north of Portage. There are also a picnic site, campsite, a good *spring,* and a parking area at the start. The trail begins at the picnic area. The summit has a radio antenna but no views.

Hedgehog Mountain

Distance from warden's cabin

to Hedgehog summit (via left fork): 0.6 mi. (1 km.), 30 min.

ROUND MOUNTAIN (2174 ft./654 m.)

This mountain is west of Ashland and south of the American Realty Road, which serves as an access road. Peaked Mountain (2260 ft.), 2 mi. to the southwest, is the highest point in Aroostook County, but there is no trail up it. Refer to the USGS Mooseleuk Lake quadrangle, 15-minute series, or Round Mountain quadrangle, 7.5-minute series.

At the western end of the bridge over the Aroostook River in Ashland, turn west off ME 11 onto a paved road. In 0.6 mi. go straight ahead on American Realty Road, which is private but open to the public for a fee paid at a tollgate about 6 mi. west of Ashland. The road runs west and, about 14 mi. from ME 11, it goes over a pass (1280 ft.) between Greenlaw Mountain and Orcutt

Mountain. Then it descends and crosses Machias (Aroostook) River in another 2 mi. It reaches the start of the trail to Round Mountain about 22 mi. from ME 11 and about 0.3 mi. west of the line between T 11 R 8 and T 11 R 9.

The trail starts out south, crosses the outlet of Rowe Lake, and runs along the southwestern shore. Beyond, it passes to the west of Round Mountain Pond and skirts the northwestern base of the mountain, then climbs steadily to the summit where there is a radio shack and helopad.

Round Mountain

Distances from American Realty Road
    to warden's camp: *est.* 3.3 mi., 1 hr. 40 min.
    to Round Mountain summit: 4 mi. (6.4 km.), 2 hr. 20 min.

HORSESHOE MOUNTAIN (2084 ft./635 m.)

Horseshoe Mountain is part of the Rocky Brook Range, which has some surprisingly rugged terrain for this part of the state. Refer to the USGS Mooseleuk Lake quadrangle, 15-minute series.

The road to the trail leaves the left side of the American Realty Road (see the preceding description) about 41 mi. west of Ashland and 2.5 mi. before the Upper McNally Pond Campsite (MFD Campsite #45). About 1 mi. from the American Realty Road, the road to the trail turns sharply left up over a hill. The trail begins on the right at this corner, where there is a small sign on a tree.

At first the trail is an obscure road that leads in about 0.3 mi. to a firewarden's cabin. The trail passes directly behind the cabin, and after another 200 yd. it reaches a side trail on the right. (The side trail goes 0.8 mi. to the very picturesque Horseshoe Pond.) About 0.5 mi. from the cabin the main trail gets increasingly steeper and in another 0.5 mi. it reaches the summit, which is flat. The Katahdin area is 40 mi. to the south.

Horseshoe Mountain

Distances from road

   to firewarden's cabin: 0.3 mi., *est.* 20 min.

   to Horseshoe summit: 1.3 mi. (2.1 km.), 1 hr. 10 min.

PRIESTLY MOUNTAIN (1900 ft./579 m.)

Priestly Mountain, in northern Piscataquis County, near the Aroostook boundary, rises west of the Allagash River about 60 mi. west of Ashland. Its summit bears a steel firetower, a cabin, a helopad, and an Allagash Wilderness Waterway repeater.

   Drive to a point on the Churchill Dam Road about 7.5 mi. before the American Realty Road (see the section on Round Mountain) 67 mi. west of Ashland and west and south of Umsaskis Lake. Refer to the USGS Umsaskis Lake quadrangle, 15-minute series, or Umsaskis Lake West quadrangle, 7.5-minute series.

   The trail (small sign on a tree) leaves the west side of Churchill Dam Road (left when going northwest from Churchill Dam) on a hill. At first it is an old road and flat. It runs generally southwest for 1.3 mi. and crosses Drake Brook, the outlet of Priestly Lake. The trail turns south near the northwestern side of Priestly Lake. About 0.3 mi. from the brook it reaches a firewarden's cabin, where it turns abruptly right (west) uphill to the right of the cabin. It then rises moderately for 0.5 mi. to the summit. The firetower has a long stretch of excellent views, particularly of the Allagash Wilderness Waterway.

Priestly Mountain

Distances from Churchill Dam Road

   to firewarden's cabin: 1.5 mi.

   to Priestly summit: 2 mi. (3.2 km.), 1 hr. 25 min.

SECTION 3
Mount Desert Island and Acadia National Park (including Isle Au Haut)

Mount Desert Island is connected to the mainland about 10 mi. southeast of Ellsworth by a short bridge and causeways. The island is about 15 mi. long and 13 mi. wide, roughly heart shaped, and is divided into east and west sides by Somes Sound, often described as the only true fjord on the East Coast. A mountain chain of 17 peaks, with elevations from 200 to about 1500 ft., runs through the island from the southwest to the northeast. The southerly thrust of glacial action created deep valleys between the mountains that may require descent almost to sea level to go from one peak to the next. Acadia National Park, created in 1916, includes much of Mount Desert Island. With the sections on Schoodic Point and Isle au Haut, it now has an area of approximately 35,000 acres.

Hiking and walking on Mount Desert Island are very rewarding. Approximately 120 mi. of maintained and marked trails provide a unique network of mountain, lakeshore, and seaside paths. A 50-mi. system of carriage paths, barred to automobiles, permits pleasant walking, easy snowshoeing and cross-country ski routes, and clear horseback trails. The National Park Service (NPS) encourages their use. The fine-grained gravel surface on the carriage roads around Eagle Lake and Witch Hole Pond makes them suitable for bicycles with small-diameter tires. Other carriage roads tend to have a softer, looser surface suitable for non-motorized mountain bikes. Bicycles (including mountain bicycles), however, are not allowed on any hiking trails within the park. The descriptions within this guide are limited to trails reserved only for hiking, and so do not cover the carriage paths. However, the carriage roads are marked on the map.

The traveler on Mount Desert Island should be prepared for the changeable weather of the northern New England seashore. Changes can be swift, but because the maximum elevation, Cadillac Mountain, is only 1530 ft., problems will generally involve discomfort and not danger. These trails are all within a few miles of roads or houses. The terrain is often sharp and precipitous, so the climber who explores off marked trails risks uncomfortable going and even dead ends at cliffs and ravines. The hiker can find paths of any desired degree of difficulty, from the mildest lakeside paths to challenging "ladder" trails with iron rungs driven into rock as the tread. (Novice hikers should consult a park ranger for specific advice on how difficult a trail to attempt.) Most of the summits are treeless and open. Trails on MDI's treeless peaks often have rock cairns to guide hikers. In the event of heavy fog, the hiker must make certain to locate the next cairn before leaving the last when above treeline.

There are NPS camping facilities inside the National Park. A complete selection of hotels, motels, tourist homes, and private campgrounds is also available on the island. Park campsites, shown on the map, are at Blackwoods (by reservation from June 15–Sept. 15, call 1-800-365-CAMP; first-come, first-served for the rest of the year) and Seawall (first-come, first-served from late May to late September). For detailed park campground information, write: Acadia National Park, PO Box 177, Bar Harbor ME 04609 (or phone 207-288-3338). If park campgrounds are filled, you will be referred to private campgrounds on the island. Camping in Acadia is limited to established NPS and private sites. No backcountry camping is permitted because of space limitations within the park.

Hiking, camping, and tourist information is readily available on the island. The Thompson Island Information Center, located just after the causeway at the entrance to Mount Desert Island, is jointly operated by the National Park Service and the island-wide Chamber of Commerce. Acadia National Park Visitor Center, on ME 3 at Hulls Cove near Bar Harbor, offers current information, including an NPS map and descriptive material. Of particular interest will be "Acadia Beaver Log" (summer and fall only) which announces guided naturalist walks, hikes, and boat cruises. The villages of Bar Harbor, Northeast Harbor, and Southwest Harbor maintain offices that provide help to visitors.

Public excursion boats for local trips depart from the town dock areas of Bar Harbor, Northeast Harbor, Southwest Harbor, and Bass Harbor. Bar Harbor is the western terminus of a ferry (autos carried) that departs in the early morning for Yarmouth, Nova Scotia. Plan to stay overnight if you go; round trip, this ferry makes for a long day with no appreciable time for sightseeing in Yarmouth.

Most of the larger lakes are public water supplies and thus closed to swimming, but freshwater swimming is available at a public beach, maintained by the NPS, at the south end of Echo Lake. The NPS also offers Sand Beach, a saltwater beach with fine sand and traditionally cold Maine sea bathing.

The following descriptions do not cover *all* the trails in the park. Some areas, around Northeast Harbor for example, are honeycombed with local woodland paths. Those selected for detailed treatment here are well marked, offically recognized and maintained paths that give access to all of the preferred summits on Mount Desert Island and Isle au Haut (the Schoodic Peninsula, with five short, forested trails, is excluded). For the most part, you can reach the individual summits in comfortable half-day walks. Longer or more strenuous excursions can be planned easily by including as many peaks as desired. To simplify reference and to conform with Acadia National Park nomenclature, the island is divided into an eastern district and a western district. The NPS maintains all trails described, and markings include signs, cairns, blue painted blazes, and metal markers. In addition to the map in this guide, refer to USGS Mount Desert and Bar Harbor quadrangles, 15-minute series.

Last, the National Park Service has recently rated each trail in the park by its relative difficulty. The ratings are determined by the following criteria:

Easy: Fairly level ground.

Moderate: Uneven ground with some steep grades and/or gradual climbing. Footing may be difficult in places.

Strenuous: Steep and/or long grades; steady climbing or descending. Sometimes difficult footing, difficult maneuvering.

Ladder: Iron-rung ladders and handrails placed on steep grades or difficult terrain. These trails are very difficult.

EASTERN DISTRICT
(EAST OF SOMES SOUND)

CHAMPLAIN MOUNTAIN (1058 ft./322 m.) **AREA**

Champlain Mountain is the easternmost summit on the island. Its east face is sharp, with the Precipice Trail climbing on ladder rungs in some parts. The Bear Brook Trail offers easier access up the north ridge. From the west and the Sieur de Monts Spring area, the Beachcroft Path traverses Huguenot Head en route to the summit. To the south is the Bowl (415 ft.), a delightful mountain pond, and the Beehive (520 ft.), a sharp promontory above Sand Beach. A pleasant excursion is possible following any route up Champlain and proceeding to Sand Beach via the Bowl and the Beehive. Gorham Mountain (525 ft.) is another summit south of the Beehive.

Precipice Trail
NPS rating: Ladder

This trail starts from the Precipice Trail parking area, located 1.75 mi. beyond the Sieur de Monts Spring entrance on Park Loop Rd. at the foot of Champlain Mountain. The trailhead is located just before the entrance-fee station on Park Loop Road.

Following a rugged talus slope full of big boulders, the trail ascends northwest about 0.4 mi. Here, the right fork runs under the east face of the mountain to connect with the Bear Brook Trail 0.5 mi. from the summit on the north ridge. From the fork, the Precipice climbs southwest, rising steeply to a point directly west of the parking area. The direction is now west-northwest. Along this section of the trail, ladders and iron rungs help hikers negotiate precipitous vertical drop-offs. The final 500 ft. to the summit follow gentle slopes and ledges. People afraid of heights should *not* climb the

Precipice Trail. In addition, hikers under 5 ft. tall may have difficulty reaching some handholds. *Caution:* It's most important that Precipice Trail hikers remain on the designated trail. Wandering off the trail can quickly lead hikers onto cliffs that require technical mountain-climbing skills and equipment.

Note: The Precipice Trail can be closed for an undetermined amount of time each spring and summer because of the reintroduction of peregrine falcons to the park. Since they are an endangered species, their nesting success is critical. The trail will thus be closed to all hikers until the falcons have established a new population. Violators of the closure are subject to a $10,000 fine. Those wishing the experience of a ladder trail should consider the nearby Beehive Trail, the Dorr Mountain Ladder Trail, the Jordan Cliffs Trail, Giant Slide Trail, or the Beech Cliffs Trail.

Precipice Trail

Distances from Park Loop Rd.

    to right fork to Bear Brook Trail: 0.4 mi., 15 min.

    to Champlain summit: 0.8 mi. (1.3 km.), 1 hr.

Bear Brook Trail
NPS rating: Moderate

This trail begins on the Park Loop Rd., 0.2 mi. east of the entrance to the Bear Brook Picnic Area. The trail ends at the northern terminus of the Gorham Mountain Trail, located at the south end of the Bowl.

This trail climbs gradually from the parking area through a mixed forest of birch, pine, and spruce to a junction on the north slope of Champlain with the Champlain East Face Trail entering left at 0.5 miles. Continuing left, the Bear Brook Trail steadily emerges from the forest canopy giving outstanding views of Frenchman Bay and Schoodic Peninsula on the mainland to the east.

At 1 mi. the trail reaches the open, rocky summit of Champlain. *Descending,* it meets the Precipice Trail, entering left at 1.1 mi., then descends into the Bowl and terminates at the Gorham Mountain Trail.

Bear Brook Trail

Distances from Park Loop Rd.

>*to* junction with the Champlain East Face Trail: 0.5 mi., 30 min.

>*to* Champlain summit: 1.0 mi., 55 min.

>*to* junction with the Precipice Trail: 1.1 mi., 1 hr.

>*to* Gorham Mt. Trail: 2.6 mi. (4.2 km.), 1 hr. 45 min.

Beachcroft Trail
NPS rating: Moderate

This is a convenient route between Champlain Mountain and the area to the west. For the most part, the trail is entirely open. While the ascent to Hugenot Head from ME 3 is gradual and easily traveled, the character of the trail becomes more difficult on the actual ascent of Champlain.

The trail leaves ME 3 close to the north end of the Tarn and begins with a flight of granite steps on the east side of the highway. (There is parking above the north end of the Tarn off the west side of the highway.) It then runs southeast, often on carefully placed stone stairs. Following switchbacks and stone steps, it rises up and across the west face of Huguenot Head. The trail passes to the south of (not over) the summit of Huguenot Head at about 0.4 mi. A brief, gradual descent into the gully between Huguenot Head and Champlain Mountain is followed by a sharp, difficult ascent over rocks up the northwest slope of Champlain Mountain to the summit at 0.8 mi.

Beachcroft Trail

Distances from ME 3

>*to* shoulder of Huguenot Head: 0.4 mi., 25 min.

>*to* Champlain summit: 0.8 mi. (1.3 km.), 55 min.

Bowl Trail

NPS rating: Moderate

This trail leaves from opposite the Sand Beach parking area, located 3.25 miles beyond Sieur de Monts Spring on the Park Loop Rd. Using this trailhead means paying an entrance fee on the Park Loop Road.

The Bowl Trail is a gently sloping path that offers access to the Beehive Trail and the Gorham Mountain Trail. It connects Sand Beach to the Bowl, a lovely lake at the base of Halfway Mountain. At the Bowl a connector trail to the Beehive bears right.

Bowl Trail

Distances from Sand Beach Parking area

> *to* junction with the Beehive Trail: 0.2 mi., 5 min.
>
> *to* the Bowl and junction with the Beehive and Gorham Mt. trails: 0.6 mi. (1 km.), 25 min.

Beehive Trail

NPS rating: Ladder

This trail begins 0.2 mi. up the Bowl Trail from the Sand Beach parking area. Take a sharp right at the sign marked Beehive. For 0.3 mi., the trail rises abruptly via switchbacks and iron ladders over steep ledges to the summit of the Beehive. This trail is challenging and not for those who are uneasy on precipitous heights. The views of the Frenchman Bay–Sand Beach–Otter Cliff area are magnificent.

The trail continues down the northwest slope of the Beehive and dips steeply to the south for 0.2 mi. to a junction with the Gorham Mountain and Bowl trails. Take the left fork for 0.6 mi. to return to Park Loop Road.

Beehive Trail

Distances from Park Loop Rd.

> *to* the Beehive: 0.5 mi., 25 min.

to complete loop back to the Sand Beach area (via Bowl Trail): *est.* 1.3 mi. (2.1 km.), 50 min.

Gorham Mountain Trail
NPS rating: Moderate (Cadillac Cliffs Loop: Strenuous)

The trail starts at the Gorham Mountain Trail parking area (also known as the Monument Cove parking area) on Park Loop Rd. (fee) 1 mi. past Sand Beach. It rises gently over open ledges 0.3 mi. to a junction with the Cadillac Cliffs Trail [(NPS rating: Strenuous). The Cadillac Cliffs Trail is a loop that leads right and rejoins the Gorham Mountain Trail 0.5 mi. later, after passing under ancient sea cliffs and by an ancient sea cave.] The Gorham Mountain Trail continues 0.3 mi. over easy open granite ledges to where the Cadillac Cliffs loop rejoins the main trail.

The main trail continues north over the Gorham Mountain summit, which is open and bare, with some of the finest panoramas on Mount Desert Island. *Descending,* the trail reaches a junction with the Bowl Trail in another 0.7 mi. For the Bowl, go left 0.2 mi. To reach the Beehive, turn right, then left at the next junction, about 0.1 mi. farther. (Continuing straight ahead at this junction will bring you to Park Loop Rd. at Sand Beach.)

Gorham Mountain Trail

Distances from trailhead parking area

   to summit of Gorham Mt.: 1.0 mi., 45 min.

   to the Bowl: 1.7 mi., 1 hr. 5 min.

   to Park Loop Rd. in Sand Beach area: *est.* 2.3 mi. (3.7 km.), 1 hr. 30 min.

Great Head Trail
NPS rating: Moderate

The Great Head Trail is a scenic, short walk that passes largely along cliffs directly above the sea. From the

Sand Beach parking area on Park Loop Rd. (fee), cross
Sand Beach to the east end. Near the seaward end of the
interior lagoon, look for a trailhead post and a series of
granite steps with a hand rail ascending a high bank.
The trail quickly reaches a huge millstone, where the
trail turns sharply right (south) switchbacking up the
cliff. The path continues to the extremity of the peninsula, then turns northeast along the cliff to the high point,
Great Head (145 ft.), where there are ruins of a stone
teahouse. The trail descends northwest to a junction at
which the right path returns more quickly to the east end
of Sand Beach. The path that leads north reaches an
abandoned service road in about 0.3 mi. Turn left on the
road, and follow it south for about 0.3 mi. to the east
side of Sand Beach.

Great Head Trail

Distances from east side of Sand Beach

> *to* south end of peninsula (via millstone): 0.5 mi., 15
> min.
>
> *to* teahouse ruins: 0.8 mi., 20 min.
>
> *to* junction with Schooner Head Rd./Sand Beach
> paths: 1.3 mi., 35 min.
>
> *to* start (via service road): 1.6 mi. (2.6 km.), 55 min.

Ocean Trail (also called Shore Path)

NPS rating: Easy

Park at the large, lower Sand Beach parking area on the
Park Loop Rd. (fee). From the parking area, follow the
asphalt trail about 50 ft. toward the beach. Where the
staircase descends to the left, turn right to begin the
Ocean Trail. As of publication date, the trailhead was *not*
marked. The trail leads uphill several hundred yards,
crosses through a small, paved upper parking area, and
continues south to Otter Point, paralleling Park Loop Rd.
1.8 mi. The Ocean Trail offers spectacular shoreline

scenery and follows a level grade. Of interest en route
are Thunder Hole, Monument Cove, and the Otter Cliffs.

Ocean Trail

Distance from Sand Beach
  to Otter Point: 1.8 mi. (2.9 km.), 55 min.

DORR MOUNTAIN (1270 ft./387 m.)

Dorr Mountain lies immediately west of Sieur de Monts
Spring. Two routes up the mountain are possible from
Sieur de Monts Spring. Trails also ascend from the
north and south over long ridges. The east and west
slopes are steep. With properly placed cars, a party can
have a good climb leaving from Sieur de Monts Spring,
traversing Dorr, and continuing west to the summit of
Cadillac Mountain (1530 ft.). The route descends to
about 1000 ft. between the two summits. There is parking both at the nearby Tarn and on Cadillac's summit.
(Hikers are encouraged not to park at the very congested
Sieur de Monts Spring parking area. There is a connecting path between the Tarn and the spring parking areas
for hikers wishing to visit or begin a hike at the spring.)

Dorr Mountain Trail
NPS rating: Moderate (East Face Trail: Strenuous)

Follow the paved walkway from the Nature Center
Parking Area at Sieur de Monts Spring toward the
Springhouse. At the rock inscribed Sweet Waters of
Acadia, turn right on a walkway that remains paved for
a few feet. The trail continues, following a series of
switchbacks up the northeast shoulder of Dorr Mountain. The first half has many stone steps. At 0.5 mi., the
trail is joined by the Dorr Mountain East Face Trail,
entering left, which comes directly up from the north
end of the Tarn, a lovely mountain lake. At 1.1 mi. is a

junction on the left with a short trail leading to the Dorr Mountain Ladder Trail, which comes directly up from the south end of the Tarn. Much of the next 0.4 mi. to the summit is steep and exposed.

Dorr Mountain Trail

Distances from Sieur de Monts Spring

> *to* Dorr Mountain East Face Trail junction: 0.5 mi., 30 min.
>
> *to* link to Dorr Mountain Ladder Trail: 1.1 mi., 1 hr.
>
> *to* Dorr summit: 1.5 mi. (2.4 km.), 1 hr. 20 min.

Dorr Mountain Ladder Trail
NPS rating: Ladder

This trail climbs from the south end of the Tarn up the eastern side of Dorr Mountain. The first half is steep, climbing many stone steps and over iron rungs. At 0.3 mi. the trail bears right to join with the Dorr Mountain Trail. Much of the next 0.4 mi. to the summit is steep and exposed.

Dorr Mountain Ladder Trail

Distance from south end of the Tarn

> *to* Dorr Summit: 0.6 mi. (1 km.), 50 min.

Dorr Mountain North Ridge Trail
NPS rating: Moderate

This trail begins on the south side of Park Loop Rd. about 1 mi. after the road becomes one-way. It climbs south over the summit of Kebo Mountain (407 ft.), traverses a second hump, and ascends the burned-over ledges of the north ridge to reach the summit of Dorr Mountain.

Dorr Mountain North Ridge Trail

Distance from Park Loop Rd.

> *to* Dorr summit: 1.9 mi. (3.1 km.), 1 hr. 25 min.

Dorr Mountain South Ridge Trail
NPS rating: Moderate

This trail diverges right from the Canon Brook Trail 0.6 mi. from ME 3 at the southern extremity of Dorr Mountain. It rises with moderate grade over rocky ledges and through evergreen forest. Views of Champlain, Cadillac, and the ocean are frequent during the ascent of the south ridge to the summit.

Dorr Mountain South Ridge Trail
Distances from ME 3
>   *to* start (via Canon Brook Trail): 0.6 mi., 20 min.
>   *to* Dorr summit: 1.9 mi. (3.1 km.), 1 hr. 25 min.

Dorr Mountain Notch Trail
NPS rating: Strenuous

This short trail links the summits of Dorr and Cadillac mountains. From the summit of Dorr Mountain, go north on the North Ridge Trail about 0.1 mi. Then turn left (west) on the Dorr Mountain Notch Trail, which drops quickly and in another 0.3 mi. reaches junctions with the Gorge Path and the A. Murray Young Path in the valley between the two mountains. Cross these and continue southwest, ascending to reach the summit of Cadillac.

The start of the trail at the summit of Cadillac may be difficult to see. Walk counterclockwise along the paved trail on the summit to the interpretive sign about Bar Harbor. Look for cairns and paint marks on the granite indicating the beginning of the trail leading to the notch. About 0.3 mi. south of the Park Loop Rd., the trail turns left to cross a brook; be careful to avoid an old wood road that goes straight ahead.

Dorr Mountain Notch Trail

Distances from Dorr Summit

> *to* junction with the Gorge and A. Murray Young
> paths: 0.4 mi., 15 min.
>
> *to* Cadillac summit: 0.9 mi. (1.4 km.), 40 min.

A. *Murray Young Path*
NPS rating: Moderate

Ascending the narrow valley between Dorr and Cadillac
mountains from the south, this trail leaves the Canon
Brook Trail 0.7 mi. west of ME 3. It climbs gradually to
the Gorge Path near its junction with the Dorr Mountain
Notch Trail. This point affords relatively quick (if strenuous) access to the summit of either mountain.

A. Murray Young Path

Distances from ME 3

> *to* start (via Canon Brook Trail): 0.7 mi., 25 min.
>
> *to* Dorr Mountain Notch Trail: 1.9 mi., 1 hr.
>
> *to* Dorr summit (via the Dorr Mt. Notch Trail): 2.3
> mi., 1 hr. 20 min.
>
> *to* Cadillac summit (via the Dorr Mt. Notch Trail):
> 2.4 mi. (3.9 km.), 1 hr. 25 min.

Jessup Path
NPS rating: Easy

A pleasant, level woodland walk, this path begins on
Park Loop Rd. opposite the first road on the left after the
beginning of the one-way section of Park Loop Rd. It
follows the west margin of Great Meadow, where it may
be flooded as a result of beaver activity. The path passes
through a mixed forest of hemlock and hardwood to
Sieur de Monts Spring at 0.6 mi. Located here are the
Abbe Museum, which has displays of ancient Indian
culture; the Wild Gardens of Acadia, a formal garden of
native plants; and the Nature Center, with a book-sales

area and natural history exhibits. The trail terminates 0.3 mi. farther at the north end of the Tarn.

Jessup Path

Distances from Park Loop Rd.
    to Sieur de Monts Spring: 0.6 mi., 20 min.
    to north end of the Tarn: 0.9 mi. (1.4 km.), 30 min.

The Tarn Trail (Kane Path)
NPS rating: Moderate

This path leads from the north end of the Tarn south to the Canon Brook Trail, and links the Sieur de Monts Spring area to the southern trails of Dorr and Cadillac mountains, while avoiding ME 3. At its start the path runs south, over a rocky talus slope directly along the west side of the Tarn. After reaching the south end of the Tarn, the trail continues south past a beaver pond at 0.5 mi., then gently climbs until its junction with the Canon Brook Trail.

The Tarn Trail

Distance from north end of the Tarn
    to Canon Brook Trail: 1.4 mi. (2.3 km.), 45 min.

Canon Brook Trail
NPS rating: Strenuous

From a pullout on ME 3 about 0.5 mi. south of the south end of the Tarn and about 2 mi. north of Otter Creek Village, the Canon Brook Trail runs west to join the Pond Trail in the valley south of Bubble Pond. It gives access (via the Pond Trail) to the Jordan Pond area, as well as to the trails running north to Dorr and Cadillac mountains.

From the highway, the trail descends west to Otter Creek and intersects the Tarn Trail at 0.3 mi. Turn left (south) at the intersection and follow the Tarn Trail in the valley of Otter Creek. After a brief, sharp rise from the valley, the trail reaches a junction with the Dorr Mountain South Ridge Trail, which diverges right at 0.6 mi. The trail descends to a junction with the A. Murray Young Path, which goes right at 0.7 mi. Then the trail runs steeply westward up the south bank of Canon Brook for about 0.5 mi. At this point, the trail swings away from the brook, passes a beaver pond at 1.3 mi, and ascends to a small pond known as the Featherbed, where it joins the Cadillac Mountain South Ridge Trail and the Pond Trail.

Canon Brook Trail

Distances from ME 3

> *to* the Tarn Trail junction: 0.3 mi., 10 min.
> *to* Dorr Mountain South Ridge Trail junction: 0.6 mi., 25 min.
> *to* A. Murray Young Path junction: 0.7 mi., 30 min.
> *to* junction with the Cadillac Mountain South Ridge Trail and the Pond Trail: 1.5 mi. (2.4 km.), 1 hr. 5 min.

CADILLAC MOUNTAIN (1530 ft./466 m.)

This peak is the highest point on the island. There is an automobile road to the summit, which has parking, a small gift shop, and bathrooms. Accessibility by car makes this summit the busiest in the park. Its height offers commanding views.

Trails approach the Cadillac Mountain summit from all four directions. The long South Ridge Trail begins from ME 3 near the NPS Blackwoods Campground. A short connector accesses the trail from the campground. The steep West Face Trail begins at the north end of Bubble Pond. The North Ridge Trail, beginning on Park Loop Rd., can be connected with the Gorge Trail by the Dorr Mountain Notch Trail, which ends on Park Loop Rd. about 0.5 mi. east of the North Ridge trailhead, creating a pleasant loop up and down Cadillac.

Cadillac South Ridge Trail
NPS rating: Moderate

A relatively long hike for Mount Desert Island, this trail starts on the north side of ME 3, about 50 yd. west of the entrance to the NPS Blackwoods Campground (a flat, 0.7-mi. connector links the campground to the trailhead). It climbs generally north. At 1.0 mi. a short loop trail on the right leads to Eagle Crag, which has good views to the east and southeast. The loop trail rejoins the main trail in 0.2 mi. After leaving the woods, the South Ridge Trail rises gently over open ledges. It crosses the Canon Brook Trail about 2.3 mi. from ME 3, in a slight col at the Featherbed. Continuing in the open, it passes close to a switchback in the Summit Rd. and ends at the summit parking area.

Cadillac South Ridge Trail

Distances from ME 3

> *to* junction with the Eagle Crag Spur: 1.0 mi., 40 min.

> *to* Cadillac summit: 3.5 mi. (5.6 km.), 2 hrs. 30 min. (*descending* Cadillac summit to ME 3, subtract 45 min.)

Cadillac West Face Trail
NPS rating: Strenuous

This steep trail, which starts at the north end of Bubble Pond, is the shortest route to the summit. Begin where Park Loop Rd. passes north of Bubble Pond, using the short spur road off Park Loop Rd. to reach the pond and trailhead. The trail rises steeply through woods and over open ledges to a junction with the Cadillac Mountain South Ridge Trail 0.5 mi. from the summit. For the summit turn left (north).

Cadillac West Face Trail

Distances from north end of Bubble Pond

   to Cadillac South Ridge Trail junction: 0.9 mi., 1 hr.
   5 min.

   to Cadillac summit: 1.4 mi. (2.3 km.), 1 hr. 25 min.

Cadillac North Ridge Trail
NPS rating: Moderate

This trail follows the north ridge of Cadillac, quickly
rising through the stunted evergreens onto open ledges.
In winter, the North Ridge Trail is often clear of snow
when Summit Rd. and trails on the other parts of the
mountain are blocked. To reach the trailhead follow
Park Loop Rd. south from the Visitor Center. Take the
third left turn (about 3 mi.), following the sign for Sand
Beach and Park Loop Rd. Park at a paved pull-off on
the north side of the road 0.6 mi. beyond the intersection. The trail starts on the south side of the road. It
climbs steadily, always keeping to the east of the automobile road, although it closely approaches road switchbacks on two occasions. For much of the distance both
sides of the ridge are visible. The views of Bar Harbor,
Eagle Lake, Egg Rock, and Dorr Mt. are excellent.

Cadillac North Ridge Trail

Distance from Park Loop Rd.

   to Cadillac summit: *est.* 1.8 mi. (2.9 km.), 1 hr. 30 min.

Gorge Path
NPS rating: Moderate

Follow Park Loop Rd. south from the Visitor Center.
Take the third left turn (about 3 mi.), following the sign
for Sand Beach and Park Loop Rd. The Gorge Path
starts from a gravel pullout on the south side of Park
Loop Rd. 0.8 mi. beyond the intersection. The trail rises
south up the gorge between Cadillac and Dorr mountains for 1.3 mi. to the narrow notch between the two

mountains. The trail ends at this notch at junctions with the Dorr Mountain Notch Trail and the A. Murray Young Path.

Gorge Path

Distances from Park Loop Rd.

> *to* Dorr-Cadillac notch: 1.3 mi., 1 hr. 5 min.
>
> *to* Cadillac summit (via Dorr Mt. Notch Trail): 1.8 mi. (2.9 km.), 1 hr. 35 min. (in reverse direction, Cadillac summit to Park Loop Rd., subtract about 40 min.)

JORDAN POND and SOUTHERN TRAILS AREA

Jordan Pond (274 ft.) is a central trailhead to the eastern side of Mount Desert Island. Located in the valley between Pemetic Mountain on the east and Penobscot and Sargent mountains on the west, the Bubbles to the north, The Triad and Day Mountain to the southeast, and Eliot Mountain and the Thuya Gardens to the southwest, Jordan Pond offers access to all of these places. The view from the Jordan Pond House across the pond to the Bubbles is justifiably famous.

Jordan Pond Shore Trail
NPS rating: Moderate

This circuit around Jordan Pond is level most of the way, but crosses a rocky slope with occasional loose boulders at the pond's northeastern shore. It is 3.3 mi. long; directions here are for traveling the east shore first. Park at the Jordan Pond parking area, located off the west side of Park Loop Rd., about 0.1 mi. north of the Jordan Pond House. Follow the boat-launch road to the south shore of the pond.

When you reach the pond, turn right to start the circuit. The trails listed below all diverge to the right,

because the route described is counterclockwise around
the lake.

Along the west side of the pond, the trail runs under
the sharp Jordan Cliffs and loses the sun early in the day.
The trail along the west shore also has many wet spots
and exposed tree trunks. An alternative route is a carriage road that runs along the pond uphill from the trail.
Use the Deer Brook Trail to reach the carriage road. The
circuit is completed at the south end of Jordan Pond.

Jordan Pond Shore Trail
Distances from Jordan Pond parking area

> *to* Pond Trail (to Canon Brook Trail): 0.1 mi., 5 min.
> *to* Jordan Pond Carry Trail (to Eagle Lake): 1.0 mi.,
> 30 min.
> *to* South Bubble Mountain Trail (to gap between
> North and South Bubble): 1.1 mi., 35 min.
> *to* Bubble Gap Trail (to Bubble Gap): 1.5 mi., 45
> min.
> *to* Deer Brook Trail (to Penobscot Mountain): 1.6
> mi., 50 min.
> *to* Jordan Pond parking area: 3.3 mi. (5.3 km.), 1 hr.
> 40 min.

Jordan Stream Trail
NPS rating: Moderate

This walk along the outlet of Jordan Pond passes
through pleasant cedar, maple, and spruce woods. The
trailhead is reached by a short connecting path from the
Jordan Pond House. The path essentially parallels a carriage road, which can be hiked for a return trip.

At 0.7 mi., the trail passes under a cobblestone
bridge and continues descending along the stream. The
trail takes a sharp left from the stream at 1.3 miles and
rises to end at a carriage road at the base of Lookout
Ledge, close to Long Pond.

Jordan Stream Trail
Distances from the Jordan Pond House
   to trailhead: 0.1 mi., 5 min.
   to cobblestone bridge: 0.7 mi., 20 min.
   to carriage road: 1.4 mi. (2.3 km.), 45 min.

Jordan Pond Seaside Trail
NPS rating: Easy

The Jordan Pond Seaside Trail offers an easy, level walk between the Jordan Pond House and Seal Harbor. Starting from the south side of the Jordan Pond House, the trail passes through an evergreen forest. After crossing a carriage road at 0.2 mi., the trail continues on a level course to a private driveway just west of Seal Harbor. Follow the driveway south to ME 3 and Seal Harbor. Parking on the southern terminus of the trail is best found at the entrance to the Park Loop Rd. at Seal Harbor.

Jordan Pond Seaside Trail
Distance from the Jordan Pond House
   to Seal Harbor: *est.* 2.0 mi. (3.2 km.), 1 hr.

Asticou Trail
NPS rating: Easy

The Asticou Trail is reached by the short connecting path from the west side of the Jordan Pond House. This trail follows a level course for most of its distance, yet gains some elevation to reach the Asticou Ridge Trail. It provides an important link to Eliot Mountain as well as a potential leg of a loop over Sargent and Penobscot mountains.

Leaving from the trailhead, the trail goes through a mixed forest of birch, maple, white pine, and spruce. At 0.8 mi., the trail crosses a carriage road. At 0.9 mi., it crosses another carriage road. Access to the Amphitheater Trail leaves right from this second carriage road.

Gradually descending from this point, the trail crosses
Harbor Brook at 1.1 mi. The Harbor Brook Trail leaves
left at this point. The trail then begins to climb up the
Asticou Ridge. At 1.5 mi., the Asticou Ridge Trail
leaves left, and the trail levels once again. The Asticou
Trail follows straight ahead to a junction with the Sargent Mountain South Ridge Trail at 1.8 mi. At 2.0 mi.,
the trail ends at a private drive. *Note:* the private drive is
not open to the public. It is recommended that hikers
turn back or take other trails leading from the Asticou
Trail to reach public areas.

Asticou Trail

Distances from the Jordan Pond House

> *to* start of the Asticou Trail: 0.1 mi., 5 min.
>
> *to* junction with the Amphitheater Trail: 0.9 mi., 30
> min.
>
> *to* junction with the Harbor Brook Trail: 1.1 mi., 35
> min.
>
> *to* junction with the Asticou Ridge Trail: 1.5 mi., 50
> min.
>
> *to* junction with the Sargent Mountain South Ridge
> Trail: 1.8 mi. (2.9 km.), 1 hr.

Asticou Ridge Trail
NPS rating: Moderate

This trail is reached by following the Asticou Trail for
1.5 mi. Traversing a ledgy ridge, this trail climbs over
Eliot Mt., offering views to the south and east of the
ocean, Day Mt., and The Triad. Gradually descending
from the summit, the trail reaches a monument to
Charles William Eliot, one of the founders of the park,
at 0.9 mi. Descending into the woods, the trail reaches a
junction with a side trail to ME 3 (0.4 mi. in length).
Keeping right, the trail descends into the beautiful
Thuya Gardens.

Asticou Ridge Trail
Distance from junction with the Asticou Trail
   to summit of Eliot Mt.: 0.8 mi., 25 min.
   to monument: 0.9 mi., 30 min.
   to junction with ME 3 spur trail: 1.1 mi., 35 min.
   to Thuya Gardens: 1.4 mi. (2.3 km.), 45 min.

Amphitheater Trail
NPS rating: Moderate
The Amphitheater Trail is a spur trail into the basin of Penobscot Mountain. It leaves right from the Asticou Trail and follows a carriage path for 0.5 mi., where it cuts right (north) off the carriage path to follow Little Harbor Brook to the Amphitheater. The Amphitheater is an impressive rim with the longest carriage-path bridge in Acadia National Park.

Amphitheater Trail
Distances from the Jordan Pond House (via Asticou Trail)
   to beginning of trail: 0.9 mi., 30 min.
   to Little Harbor Brook: *est.* 1.4 mi., 45 min.
   to Amphitheater Bridge: *est.* 2.0 mi. (3.2 km.), 1 hr. 5 min.

Harbor Brook Trail
NPS rating: Moderate
The Harbor Brook Trail connects the Asticou Trail with a point on ME 3 between Bracy Cove and Northeast Harbor. Following the brook for its entire length, the trail passes through beautiful cedar groves, as well as mixed forest. At 1.1 mi., a connector to Eliot Mountain and the Asticou Ridge Trail leaves west. The trail ends on ME 3 at 2.0 mi.

Harbor Brook Trail
Distance from the Asticou Trail
   to ME 3: 2.0 mi. (3.2 km.), 1 hr.

THE BUBBLES (North Bubble 872 ft./266 m. and South Bubble 766 ft./ 233 m.)

These two finely shaped, almost symmetrical hills rise above the north end of Jordan Pond. Formerly covered with heavy evergreen growth, they were swept by fire in 1947, leaving many open views.

Trails honeycomb the area, and the best access is from the Bubble Rock parking area about 1.1 mi. south of Bubble Pond on the west side of Park Loop Rd. From the parking area, follow the Bubble-Pemetic Trail west for 0.2 mi. to a junction with the Jordan Pond Carry Trail and the North Bubble Trail.

North Bubble Trail
NPS rating: Strenuous

Following the Bubble-Pemetic Trail west from the Bubble Rock parking area, this trail rises sharply for 0.2 mi. to a junction with the South Bubble Mountain Trail and Bubble Gap Trail. From the Bubble-Pemetic Trail, the North Bubble Trail leaves to the right and continues over the North Bubble summit at 0.4 mi. Beyond the summit, the trail descends to reach Eagle Lake at 1.9 mi. (To complete an excellent loop, go right on the Eagle Lake Trail, following the southwest shore to the junction with the Jordan Pond Carry Trail, entering right, which you can follow south back to the start of the North Bubble Trail.)

North Bubble Trail

Distances from the Bubble Rock parking area

> *to* beginning of the North Bubble Trail (via the Bubble-Pemetic Trail): 0.2 mi., 10 min.
>
> *to* summit of North Bubble Mountain: 0.6 mi., 20 min.
>
> *to* Eagle Lake: 1.9 mi., 1 hr.
>
> *to* complete loop (via the Eagle Lake Trail): *est.* 3.7 mi (6.0 km.), 1 hr. 55 min.

South Bubble Trail
NPS rating: Moderate

From the junction of the Jordan Pond Carry and North Bubble trails, follow the Jordan Pond Carry Trail south for 0.4 mi. to the Jordan Pond Shore Trail. Turn right (north) and follow the Jordan Pond Shore Trail for less than 0.1 mi. to the start of the South Bubble Trail. The South Bubble Trail traverses South Bubble to the gap between South and North Bubble. There, 0.3 mi. from the Jordan Pond Shore Trail, it meets the Bubble Gap Trail in the gap between the two summits.

South Bubble Trail

Distances from the Bubble Rock parking area

    to beginning of the South Bubble Trail: 0.5 mi., 15 min.

    to summit of the South Bubble Mountain: 0.7 mi., 30 min.

    to junction with the Bubble Gap Trail: 0.8 mi. (1.3 km.), 35 min.

Bubble Gap Trail
NPS Rating: Moderate

This trail diverges from the Jordan Pond Shore Trail, about 0.4 mi. north of the South Bubble Trail, near the northern edge of Jordan Pond. The Bubble Gap Trail rises through the gap between North and South Bubble mountains, offering a link between these mountains and the Jordan Pond Shore Trail. Rising through mixed forest, it meets a junction with the South Bubble and North Bubble trails at 0.2 mi.

Bubble Gap Trail

Distance from Jordan Pond Shore Trail:

    to junction with the North and South Bubble Trails: 0.2 mi. (0.3 km.), 10 min.

PEMETIC MOUNTAIN (1248 ft./380 m.) **AREA**

Pemetic Mountain is located roughly in the center of the eastern district of the island and offers some of Mount Desert Island's best views. Trails up the west side are short and relatively steep, while routes from the north and south are more gradual and wooded. For the trails from the south, climbers park at the Jordan Pond parking area. This will give access to The Triad and Day Mountain as well as Pemetic. From the north, there is parking at Bubble Pond. From the west, parking is located at Bubble Rock, where the Park Loop Rd. crosses the Bubble-Pemetic Trail.

Pemetic Mountain Trail
NPS rating: Strenuous

This trail traverses the length of the mountain north to south. The views of Jordan Pond, the Bubbles, Sargent Mountain, and Eagle Lake are outstanding.

From the north, the trail leaves from the Bubble Pond parking area at the north end of Bubble Pond. It quickly climbs through spruce-fir forest to a junction with the Bubbles-Pemetic Trail at 1.1 mi. The trail reaches the summit of Pemetic Mountain at 1.3 mi. There are excellent views of The Triad, Cadillac Mountain, and Jordan Pond from the summit. The trail then descends gradually to a junction with the West Cliff Trail. Go left to continue on the Pemetic Mountain Trail.

Steeply descending after the junction with the West Cliff Trail through delightful mixed forest, the trail meets the Pond Trail at the notch between Pemetic and The Triad. After crossing the Pond Trail, the trail climbs for 0.6 mi. to the summit of The Triad (698 ft.), giving views to the south and west. The trail then descends over ledges to a carriage path at the base of Day Mountain.

Pemetic Mountain Trail
Distances from Bubble Pond parking area
   to Bubble-Pemetic Trail junction: 1.1 mi., 55 min.
   to Pemetic summit: 1.3 mi., 1 hr. 5 min.
   to West Cliff Trail junction: 1.9 mi., 1 hr. 20 min.
   to Pond Trail: 2.2 mi., 1 hr. 30 min.
   to summit of The Triad: 2.8 mi., 2 hrs.
   to carriage road: 3.1 mi. (5 km.), 2 hrs. 10 min.

Bubble-Pemetic Trail
NPS rating: Strenuous
This trail begins at the Bubble Rock parking area, on the west side of Park Loop Rd. about 1.1 mi. south of Bubble Pond.

   The path enters the woods east of Park Loop Rd. and climbs in almost constant cover. Sometimes following a rocky stream bed, the trail ends at a junction with the Pemetic Mountain Trail about 0.1 mi. north of the summit.

Bubble-Pemetic Trail
Distances from Bubble Rock parking area
   to Pemetic Mountain Trail junction: 0.4 mi., 35 min.
   to Pemetic summit (via Pemetic Mountain Trail): 0.5 mi. (0.8 km.), 40 min.

Pond Trail
NPS rating: Moderate
This slightly graded path leaves from the southeast shore of Jordan Pond to the valley south of Bubble Pond, where the Pond Trail meets the west end of the Canon Brook Trail.

   The Pond Trail leaves the shore of Jordan Pond, traveling east, and crosses Park Loop Rd. at 0.1 mi. There is a small parking area at this crossing. Continuing through heavy woods and by easy grades, the path swings in the valley between The Triad and Pemetic

Mountain. It crosses the Pemetic Mountain Trail at 0.8 mi., continues northeast to cross a carriage road at 1.1 mi. Continuing to climb, the trail joins the Canon Brook Trail and Cadillac South Ridge Trail at the Featherbed, a pond in the col on the south shoulder of Cadillac.

Pond Trail

Distances from Jordan Pond
>   *to* Pemetic Mountain Trail: 0.8 mi., 25 min.
>   *to* carriage road: 1.1 mi., 40 min.
>   *to* the Featherbed: 2.3 mi. (3.7 km.), 1 hr. 35 min.

Pemetic West Cliff Trail
NPS rating: Strenuous

This very steep trail directly links the Pond Trail to the Pemetic Trail just south of the summit of Pemetic Mountain. Leaving from the Pond Trail, the trail quickly ascends through the forest onto a rocky slope. Occasionally, there are views of Jordan Pond from the cliffs. The climb to the summit of Pemetic Mountain along the Pemetic Mountain Trail is gradual.

Pemetic West Cliff Trail

Distances from Pond Trail parking area on Park Loop Rd.
>   *to* beginning of West Cliff Trail: 0.4 mi., 15 min.
>   *to* junction with the Pemetic Mountain Trail: 1.0 mi.
>   (1.6 km.), 45 min.

Day Mountain Trail
NPS rating: Moderate

The Day Mountain Trail starts on the north side of ME 3 approximately 1.5 mi. south of the Blackwoods Campground. The parking area is located on the south side of the highway.

The Day Mountain Trail climbs moderately through the forest for its entire length. Periodically crossing carriage roads, the trail offers beautiful views of Hunter's Beach and Seal Harbor from ledges 0.6 mi. from the trailhead. At 0.9 mi., the summit of Day Mountain is reached. (There is a carriage road which also rises to the summit of Day.) Then descending into the forest quickly, the trail reaches another carriage road at 1.4 mi., across from the Pemetic Mountain Trail. (Cross a cobblestone carriage path bridge to reach the trailhead for the Pemetic Mountain Trail.)

Day Mountain Trail
Distances from ME 3
> *to* summit of Day Mountain: 0.9 mi., 35 min.
> *to* carriage road: 1.4 mi. (2.3 km.), 50 min.

Triad–Hunter's Brook Trail
NPS rating: Strenuous
This trail begins on the Park Loop Rd. near the southern overpass of ME 3. It follows along Hunter's Brook, passing through a canopy of cedar, maple, and spruce. At 1.25 mi. the trail bears west from the brook and climbs to a carriage road at 1.5 mi. Crossing the carriage path, the trail continues to climb to a junction with the Pemetic Mt. Trail near The Triad. Then the trail descends for 0.3 mi. to end at The Triad Pass Trail.

Triad-Hunter's Brook Trail
Distances from Park Loop Rd.
> *to* carriage path: 1.5 mi., 45 min.
> *to* junction with the Pemetic Trail: *est.* 2.2 mi., 1 hr. 15 min.
> *to* Triad Pass Trail: *est.* 2.5 mi. (4.0 km.), 1 hr. 25 min.

SARGENT MOUNTAIN (1373 ft./418 m.)
PENOBSCOT MOUNTAIN (1194 ft./364 m.)

Penobscot Mountain and Sargent Mountain are open summits about 1 mi. apart. Sargent Pond, a pleasant mountain pond, lies between the two summits. From the south, the preferred starting point is Jordan Pond parking area. From here, hikers can climb both Penobscot and Sargent without retracing steps. The longer route up Sargent is from St. James Church on ME 3/198 via the Giant Slide Trail.

The outlying territory to the southwest contains an interesting maze of trails and carriage roads around Bald Peak (974 ft.) and Parkman Mountain (941 ft.). Ample parking is available at two areas: One is on the west side of ME 3/198 and about 0.3 mi. north of Upper Hadlock Pond (reservoir, no swimming); and the other, Parkman Mountain parking area, is on the east side of ME 3/198, about 0.5 mi. north of Upper Hadlock Pond. Upper Hadlock Pond is approximately 2.5 mi. south of where ME 3/198 splits from ME 233.

Penobscot Mountain Trail
NPS rating: Strenuous

This trail starts from the west side of Jordan Stream (outlet of Jordan Pond) about 0.1 mi. west of the Jordan Pond House and is reached by a short connecting path starting from the house.

The trail runs west and, after crossing a carriage road, rises abruptly to the south end of Jordan Ridge, about 0.5 mi. from Jordan Pond House. The trail then swings north, climbing gradually over open granite ledges to the summit of Penobscot Mountain, where it terminates at the Sargent Pond Trail.

For Sargent Pond and the summit of Sargent Mountain, go left on the Sargent Pond Trail 0.2 mi. Sargent Pond (at about 1060 ft.) is a delightful spot nestled between Penobscot and Sargent mountains. From the pond, the Sargent Mountain South Ridge Trail offers easy access to the summit.

Penobscot Mountain Trail

Distances from Jordan Pond House

- *to* Penobscot summit: *est.* 1.5 mi., 1 hr. 10 min.
- *to* Sargent Pond (via Sargent Pond Trail): *est.* 1.7 mi., 1 hr. 15 min.
- *to* Sargent Mountain summit (via Sargent Pond and Sargent Mountain South Ridge trails): *est.* 2.5 mi. (4 km.), 1hr. 50 min.

Jordan Cliffs Trail
NPS rating: Ladder

Take the Penobscot Mountain Trail to reach the Jordan Cliffs Trail. This challenging yet scenic trail leaves the Penobscot Mountain Trail 0.4 mi. west of the Jordan Pond House, just northeast of the junction of the Penobscot Trail and a carriage road. Bearing right soon after crossing the carriage road, the trail to Jordan Cliffs heads north and rises up the east shoulder of Penobscot Mountain in gradual pitches to the cliffs at 0.8 mi. The trail traverses the Jordan Cliffs, via ladders and handrails, to a junction with the Penobscot East Trail. Turn left on the Penobscot East Trail to reach the summit of Penobscot Mountain. While very steep, the trail is spectacular, with views of the Bubbles, Pemetic, and Jordan Pond.

Continuing straight past the East Face Trail, the Jordan Cliffs Trail traverses the cliffs above Jordan Pond to cross the Deer Brook Trail. It ends on the summit of Sargent Mountain.

Jordan Cliffs Trail

Distances from Jordan Pond House

- *to* Jordan Cliffs Trail (via Penobscot Mountain Trail): 0.4 mi., 15 min.
- *to* Jordan Cliffs: 1.2 mi., 55 min.
- *to* Penobscot summit (via Penobscot East Trail): 1.7 mi., 1 hr. 20 min.

to junction with the Deer Brook Trail: *est.* 1.6 mi., 1 hr. 15 min.

to summit of Sargent Mountain: *est.* 2.0 mi. (3.2 km.), 1 hr. 30 min.

Deer Brook Trail
NPS rating: Strenuous

This is a steep, quick ascent of 0.8 mi. to Sargent Pond from the Jordan Pond Shore Trail at the north end of Jordan Pond. The route is entirely wooded and follows the course of Deer Brook. This trail joins the Sargent Pond Trail in the valley between Sargent and Penobscot.

Deer Brook Trail

Distance from Jordan Pond Shore Trail

to Sargent Pond Trail junction: 0.8 mi. (1.3 km.), 45 min.

Sargent Mountain South Ridge Trail
NPS rating: Moderate

This trail starts from a carriage path leaving from a mansion known as the Gate House. The trailhead is located about 1 mi. south of Upper Hadlock Pond, on the east side of ME 3/198. Follow the carriage path east, always bearing right at junctions for about 0.7 mi. There, the trail begins on the north side of the carriage path.

The Sargent Mountain South Ridge Trail rises over the wooded shoulder and passes just southeast of the summit of Cedar Swamp Mountain. A spur trail bears left to the summit. It drops to cross Little Harbor Brook at 1.2 mi. The trail then leaves the woods and rises sharply 0.4 mi. to a junction with the Sargent Pond Trail, which comes in from the right. The trail continues north over open granite ledges to the summit of Sargent, past junctions to the left with the Hadlock Brook Trail at 1.8 mi. and the Maple Spring Trail at 2.1 mi.

Sargent Mountain South Ridge Trail

Distances from the Gate House

  to Sargent Pond Trail: *est.* 0.7 mi., 30 min.
  to Hadlock Brook Trail: *est.* 2.5 mi., 1 hr. 55 min.
  to Maple Spring Trail: *est.* 2.8 mi., 2 hr. 5 min.
  to Sargent summit: *est.* 3.1 mi. (5.0 km.), 2 hr. 15 min.

Giant Slide Trail
NPS rating: Ladder

This trail is the approach to the Sargent Mountain area from the northwest. The trail starts at St. James Church, a small stone chapel located on the east side of ME 198, about 0.3 mi. north of the intersection with ME 3 and 1.1 mi. south of the northern intersection with ME 233. The trail leads east 0.4 mi. to the Acadia National Park boundary and continues through woods up a gradual slope to a carriage road, at 0.7 mi. The trail turns sharply right (south) and, following Sargent Brook, rises steeply over the tumbled boulders of Giant Slide. At 1.8 mi., the Parkman Mountain Trail diverges right and the Sargent Mountain North Ridge Trail leaves left. The Giant Slide Trail continues through the notch between Parkman Mountain and Gilmore Peak at 2.4 mi. and descends to end at a junction with the Maple Spring Trail at 2.8 mi.

Giant Slide Trail

Distances from the St. James Church on ME 198

  to carriage road crossing: 0.7 mi., 25 min.
  to Parkman Mountain Trail–Sargent Mountain North
    Ridge Trail junction: 1.8 mi., 1 hr. 10 min.
  to Maple Spring Trail junction: 2.8 mi. (4.5 km.), 1
    hr. 45 min.

Sargent Mountain North Ridge Trail
NPS rating: Moderate

Leaving the Giant Slide Trail 1.8 mi. from ME 198, this trail ascends east and crosses a carriage road at 0.2 mi.

Continuing essentially east, it rises over slanting pitches another 0.6 mi. to a sharp right (south) turn. The final 0.4 mi. to the summit of Sargent is over open ledges offering spectacular views.

Sargent Mountain North Ridge Trail
Distance from Giant Slide Trail
> *to* Sargent summit: 1.2 mi. (1.9 km.), 1 hr.

Hadlock Brook Trail and Maple Spring Trail
NPS rating: Strenuous

These are the principal routes to Sargent Mountain from the west. From the east side of ME 198 just north of Upper Hadlock Pond and opposite the Norumbega Mountain parking area, the Hadlock Brook Trail runs east 0.4 mi. to a junction, where the Maple Spring Trail leaves left and the Hadlock Brook Trail forks right. From here, there is little difference between the two trails. They are basically parallel, wooded, steep, and rugged, and terminate on the Sargent Mountain South Ridge Trail, south of the summit.

Hadlock Brook Trail and Maple Spring Trail
Distances from ME 198
> *to* junction with the Bald Peak Trail: 0.3 mi., 10 min.
> *to* Sargent summit (via either route): 2 mi. (3.2 km.), 1 hr. 35 min.

Grandgent Trail
NPS rating: Strenuous

This trail runs between the summit of Sargent Mountain and the Giant Slide Trail. From the summit of Sargent, the trail leaves west and steeply descends into a saddle at the base of Gilmore Peak. After a short climb of 0.2 mi., the trail reaches Gilmore Peak. Then it gradually descends for 0.3 mi. to end at the Giant Slide Trail.

Grandgent Trail

Distances from the summit of Sargent Mountain

> *to* saddle between Gilmore Peak and Sargent Mountain: 0.5 mi., 15 min.
>
> *to* Gilmore Peak: 0.7 mi., 25 min.
>
> *to* junction with the Giant Slide Trail: 1.0 mi. (1.6 km.), 35 min.

Parkman Mountain Trail
NPS rating: Moderate

The Parkman Mountain Trail starts out with the Hadlock Brook Trail but soon diverges north (left) to lead 1 mi. through woods and over a series of knobs to the summit of Parkman Mountain. The trail crosses a carriage road three times on the way to the summit. The Bald Peak Trail joins the trail from the right at 0.9 mi. At the summit, a trail that leaves right (east) connects with the Giant Slide Trail in the gap between Parkman Mountain and Gilmore Peak. The Parkman Mountain Trail continues north over open ledges, then through the woods, crossing a carriage road 0.5 mi. beyond the summit. The trail ends 0.2 mi. farther, at the junction of the Giant Slide Trail and the Sargent Mountain North Ridge Trail.

Parkman Mountain Trail

Distances from ME 198

> *to* Parkman summit: 1 mi., 50 min.
>
> *to* Giant Slide Trail-Sargent Mountain North Ridge Trail junction: 1.7 mi. (2.7 km.), 1 hr. 10 min.

Bald Peak Trail
NPS rating: Moderate

This trail connects the Hadlock Brook Trail to the Parkman Mountain Trail. The trail is reached by following the Hadlock Brook Trail for 0.3 mi. At this point, the Bald Peak Trail leaves left. Gradually climbing through the forest, the trail reaches the open Bald Peak at 0.8 mi.

The trail reaches the Parkman Mountain Trail shortly beyond the summit of Bald Peak.

Bald Peak Trail

Distances from ME 198 (via the Hadlock Brook Trail)
    to beginning of Bald Peak Trail: 0.3 mi., 10 min.
    to summit of Bald Peak: 0.8 mi., 30 min.
    to Parkman Mountain Trail: 0.9 mi. (1.5 km.), 35 min.

NORUMBEGA MOUNTAIN (852 ft./260 m.)

Norumbega rises just east of Somes Sound. It is most often climbed from the parking area just north of Upper Hadlock Pond (reservoir, no swimming). You can then descend over the longer south ridge to Lower Hadlock Pond (also a reservoir), and from there walk back to the highway. This summit is wooded, but the blueberries on the north slope make it attractive and appealing in season. The trail offers very good views of Somes Sound and the mountains west of the sound. *Note:* This area is honeycombed with abandoned and unoffical paths. Pay careful attention to trail markers and maps.

Norumbega Mountain Trail
NPS rating: Strenuous

This trail leaves the parking lot on the west side of ME 198 about 0.3 mi. north of Upper Hadlock Pond. It ascends quickly and steeply through woods to granite ledges, then swings south to the summit. The trail descends the south ridge through a particularly fine softwood forest to Lower Hadlock Pond. There, it turns north, following the shore of the pond and Hadlock Brook to Upper Hadlock Pond and ME 198.

Norumbega Mountain Trail

Distance from ME 198 north of Upper Hadlock Pond
    to ME 198 at Upper Hadlock Pond outlet: 2.5 mi. (4 km.), 1 hr. 35 min.

WESTERN DISTRICT
(WEST OF SOMES SOUND)

ACADIA MOUNTAIN (681 ft./208 m.)

Acadia is the only summit on Mount Desert Island with an east-west ridge trail along the top. The views of Somes Sound are noteworthy. Some prefer to climb from the west, dropping down to Somes Sound from the east promontory. Flowing into Somes Sound at the base of the mountain is Man o' War Brook, where nine-teenth-century frigates renewed their water supplies, taking advantage of the deep-water anchorage close to the shore.

Acadia Mountain Trail
NPS rating: Strenuous

Parking is located at the Acadia Mountain parking area on the west side of ME 102, 3 mi. south of Somesville and 3 mi. north of Southwest Harbor (please do not block the fire road gates on the east side of ME 102). The Acadia Mountain Trail begins on the east side of ME 102, across the road from the parking area. Go left at the fork 0.1 mi. down the trail.

The trail ascends the west slope, soon leaving woods for open rocks and frequent views. It passes over the highest summit and reaches the east summit, with views of the sound, at about 1 mi. The trail then descends southeast and south very steeply to cross Man o' War Brook. A junction about 50 yd. beyond the stream marks the end of the Acadia Mountain Trail. To return to ME 102 via the fire road, go west (right) at the junction and proceed past trails to St. Sauveur and Valley Cove, which diverge left about 100 yd. east of the stream. Go through a field for 200 yd. to the east end of the Man o' War Brook fire road. Follow the fire road west over gradual grades about 1 mi. back to ME 102, 50 yd. north of the parking area (you will cross the Acadia Mountain Trail shortly before ME 102; turn left onto the trail to reach the parking lot directly).

Acadia Mountain Trail

Distances from ME 102

> *to* Acadia Mountain, east summit: *est.* 1 mi. (45 min.)
>
> *to* Man o' War Brook: *est.* 1.5 mi. (1 hr.)
>
> *to* ME 102: *est.* 2.5 mi. (4 km.), 1 hr. 30 min.

St. Sauveur Mountain (679 ft./207 m.)

This mountain can be climbed from the north via the Man o' War Brook fire road (NPS fire service road from ME 102), from ME 102 on the west, and from the Fernald Cove Road on the south. There are good views of Somes Sound from Eagle Cliff, just east of the summit.

St. Sauveur Trail
NPS rating: Moderate

This trail is an easy route to the summit of St. Sauveur Mountain from the north. Follow the Acadia Mountain Trail description to reach the parking lot and trailhead. Start 0.1 mi. down the Acadia Mountain Trail, and go right at the fork.

The path runs south through evergreens and over open slopes, rising constantly for 1 mi. to a junction with the Ledge Trail entering on the right. From there it is 0.3 mi. to the summit, where the St. Sauveur Trail joins the Valley Peak Trail.

St. Sauveur Trail

Distances from ME 102

> *to* Ledge Trail junction: 1 mi., 40 min.
>
> *to* St. Sauveur summit: 1.3 mi. (2.1 km.), 55 min.

Ledge Trail
NPS rating: Moderate

This trail begins at St. Sauveur parking area on the east side of ME 102 about 0.2 mi. north of the entrance road to the NPS swimming facilities at the south end of Echo Lake. The parking area is also about 0.2 mi. south of the access road to the AMC Echo Lake Camp (contact the AMC for information: 617-523-0636; 5 Joy St., Boston MA 02108).

The path enters the woods and rises over ledges to its end. It meets the St. Sauveur Trail 0.5 mi. from the highway and about 0.3 mi. northwest of the summit.

Ledge Trail

Distances from ME 102
    to St. Sauveur Trail junction: 0.5 mi., 25 min.
    to St. Sauveur summit: 0.8 mi. (1.3 km.), 40 min.

Valley Peak Trail
NPS rating: Strenuous

This trail leaves the west side of the Valley Cove truck road a few yards north of the parking area at Fernald Cove. It rises steeply northwest through shady woods over Valley Peak (the south shoulder of St. Sauveur Mountain). The trail then skirts the top of Eagle Cliff, with outstanding views of Valley Cove below and the mountains to the east of Somes Sound. On the summit of St. Sauveur, at 0.8 mi., the St. Sauveur Trail merges from the left. The Valley Peak Trail continues fairly steeply down the northeast shoulder of St. Sauveur to end at a junction with the Acadia Mountain Trail near Man o' War Brook and the east terminus of the Man o' War Brook fire road.

Valley Peak Trail

Distances from the Valley Cove truck road
    to St. Sauveur summit: 0.8 mi., 45 min.
    to Acadia Mountain Trail junction: 1.6 mi. (2.6 km.),
        1 hr. 10 min.

FLYING MOUNTAIN (284 ft./87 m.)

Guarding the entrance to Somes Sound, this low peak offers perhaps the greatest reward on the island for a small effort. A few minutes' climb to the open top gives a fine panorama of the sound, Southwest Harbor, Northeast Harbor, and the islands to the south—the Cranberries, Greening, Sutton, Baker, and Bear.

Flying Mountain Trail
NPS rating: Moderate

This scenic trail over tiny Flying Mountain leaves the east side of the parking area at the Fernald Cove end of the Valley Cove truck road and rises quickly and steeply through spruce woods. At the edge of Valley Cove, the trail follows the shore north over rock slides and under forbidding Eagle Cliff to end at a junction with the Acadia Mountain Trail at Man o' War Brook.

At Valley Cove, the north terminus of the truck road can be located up the bank about 75 yd. south from the water's edge. For an easy return to the Fernald Cove parking area, follow the road south for about 0.5 mi.

Flying Mountain Trail

Distances from Fernald Cove parking area

  to Flying Mountain summit: 0.3 mi., 15 min.
  to Fernald Cove parking area (via truck road from Valley Cove): *est.* 1.2 mi. (1.9 km.), 45 min.
  to Acadia Mountain Trail junction: 1.5 mi. (2.4 km.), 1 hr.

BEECH MOUNTAIN (839 ft./256 m.)

Beech Mountain lies between Echo Lake and Long Pond (Great Pond on some maps). Its summit is easy to reach from either the Beech Cliff parking area (located at the end of Beech Hill Rd., in the notch between

Beech Cliff and Beech Mountain) or the pumping station area at the foot of Long Pond. To reach the pumping station, follow Seal Cove Road west from Southwest Harbor. Take the first right (toward the landfill) and follow this road until it ends at the pumping station. Beech Mountain can also be climbed on its southwest flank, beginning at the south end of Long Pond. An added attraction near Beech Mountain is the Beech Cliff–Canada Cliff area just to the east of the Beech Cliff parking area. These rugged cliffs offer spectacular views of Echo Lake.

Canada Cliff Trail
NPS rating: Moderate (Beech Cliffs Trail: Ladder)
This trail offers access to the top of Beech Cliff via a ladder trail (not recommended for those uneasy about heights). It starts at the Beech Cliff parking area located at the end of Beech Hill Road. To reach this trailhead, follow ME 102 south through Somesville and take Pretty Marsh Rd., the first right after the fire station. Follow Pretty Marsh Rd. west for about 0.5 mi., where the Beech Hill Rd. intersects from the left. Follow Beech Hill Rd. south until it ends at the trailhead.

The trail leaves east and climbs quickly via switchbacks and ladders to a junction with the Canada Ridge Trail on the left. Follow the Canada Ridge Trail north to the Beech Cliff Trail and proceed out on the top of Beech Cliff for the views of Echo Lake, the ocean, and islands to the south. This route also provides access from the east to Beech Mountain and Long Pond.

Canada Cliff Trail
Distance from Beech Cliff parking area
>   *to* Beech Cliff (via Canada Ridge and Beech Cliff trails): 0.5 mi. (0.8 km.), 30 min.

Beech Mountain Trail
NPS rating: Moderate

The trail leaves the northwest side of the Beech Cliff parking area and forks in 0.1 mi. The trail to the right (northwest) is 1 mi. long and provides a beautiful vista of Long Pond before climbing to the summit. The trail to the left (south) is 0.6 mi. long and climbs more steeply to the summit of Beech Mountain, with its fire-tower. The two trails can be combined to form a scenic loop hike.

From the summit, the Beech Mountain West Ridge and South Ridge Trails depart to the southwest and south, respectively.

Beech Mountain Trail
Distances from Beech Cliff parking area
> *to* Beech Mountain summit (via north fork): 1.1 mi., 45 min.
>
> *to* Beech Cliff Parking area (via north fork, then south fork): 1.8 mi. (2.9 km.), 1 hr. 15 min.

Valley Trail
NPS rating: Moderate

This graded path is a convenient link between the Long Pond area and the Beech Cliff parking area, which is located in the notch between Beech Cliff and Beech Mountain. It also permits a circuit or one-way trip over Beech Mountain, since it provides direct access to the South Ridge Trail.

The trail enters the woods on the east (right) side of the service road that skirts the east shore of the south end of Long Pond. The entrance is about 0.3 mi. north of the junction with the road to the pumping station. (Or, park at the pumping station. Take the trail east, go right at a fork in 40 or 50 yd. and cross the service road in about 0.3 mi.)

By easy grades over wooded slopes, the trail runs north briefly and then swings east (right) before entering a series of switchbacks on the south slopes of Beech Mountain. At about 0.3 mi., the South Ridge Trail to Beech Mountain leaves left. Continuing east the Valley Trail soon swings north to maintain altitude as it runs up the valley separating Beech Mountain and Canada Cliff. At about 1 mi., are the remains of the old road to Southwest Harbor and the Canada Ridge Trail comes in from the right. Continue directly ahead (north) 0.2 mi. to the Beech Cliff parking area.

Valley Trail

Distances from service road at Great Pond

> *to* Beech Mountain South Ridge Trail junction: 0.3 mi., 10 min.
>
> *to* Old Southwest Harbor Rd. and Canada Ridge Trail junction: 1 mi., 40 min.
>
> *to* Beech Cliff parking area: 1.2 mi. (1.9 km.), 50 min.

Beech Mountain South Ridge Trail
NPS rating: Moderate

This well-marked trail diverges left from the Valley Trail about 0.3 mi. east of the service road and steadily ascends the south ridge to the summit along open ledges, offering views to the south.

Beech Mountain South Ridge Trail

Distances from service road at Long Pond

> *to* start (via Valley Trail): 0.3 mi., 10 min.
>
> *to* summit of Beech Mountain: 0.9 mi. (1.5 km.), 45 min.

Beech Mountain West Ridge Trail
NPS rating: Moderate

Leaving from the east side of the Long Pond pumping station, this trail skirts the edge of Long Pond for 0.3 mi. At this point the trail begins to climb from the shore. Rising steeply at times, there are ledges which offer good views of the pond and Mansell Mountain. It reaches the Beech Mountain Loop Trail at 0.9 mi.

Beech Mountain West Ridge Trail
Distances from pumping station

> *to* junction with the Beech Mountain Loop Trail: 0.9 mi. (40 min.)

> *to* summit of Beech Mountain (via the Loop Trail): 1.0 mi. (1.6 km.), 45 min.

WESTERN MOUNTAINS

BERNARD MOUNTAIN (1071 ft./326 m.)
MANSELL MOUNTAIN (949 ft./289 m.)

This area has two main summits: Bernard to the west and Mansell to the east. Both summits are wooded, and extensive views are rare. There is access from the north via the Western Trail into Great Notch. From the south, there are many choices: Long Pond Trail, Perpendicular Trail, Sluiceway Trail, South Face Trail, Razorback Trail, and the Cold Brook Trail. You can reach all of the southern approaches from the parking area at the foot of Long Pond near the pumping station. To reach the pumping station, follow Seal Cove Road west from Southwest Harbor. Take the first right (toward the landfill) and follow this road until it ends at the pumping station.

Western Trail
NPS rating: Moderate

This is the only trail providing access to the western mountains from the north. There are no open vistas. To reach the trailhead, go about 1 mi. east from the western loop of ME 102 on the Long Pond (sometimes called Great Pond) fire road. Parking is available here. The fire road crosses ME 102 just north of Seal Cove Pond. The Western Trail starts on the southeast side of the road about 0.1 mi. beyond the Pine Hill turnaround and parking area.

The trail trends southeast and rises by easy grades to a junction with the Long Pond Trail (entering left) 1.9 mi. from the fire road. It ends in Great Notch at 2.3 mi. The Great Notch gives access to both western mountain peaks.

Western Trail

Distances from Great Pond fire road
> *to* Long Pond Trail junction: 1.9 mi., 1 hr. 5 min.
> *to* Great Notch: 2.3 mi. (3.7 km.), 1 hr. 25 min.

Long Pond (Great Pond) Trail
NPS rating: Easy

This excellent footpath starts at the pumping station at the foot of Long Pond (sometimes called Great Pond). It follows the west shore of the pond for 1.5 mi., then bears west away from it. Turning south, the trail passes through a beautiful birch forest and follows Great Brook to a junction with the Western Trail. This route to the Western Trail leads to the complex of trails on Bernard and Mansell and completes a circuit back to the pumping station.

Long Pond Trail

Distances from pumping station
> *to* junction with Perpendicular Trail: 0.2 mi., 5 min.
> *to* Western Trail junction: 2.9 mi. (4.7 km.), 1 hr. 40 min.

Perpendicular Trail
NPS rating: Strenuous

This trail, ascending Mansell Mountain, leaves left from the Long Pond Trail on the west shore of Long Pond, 0.2 mi. north of the pumping station. It follows a steep course up the east slope of Mansell, crossing a rock slide. The trail is very steep, much of it passing over stone steps. There are a few iron rungs and one iron ladder along the course of the trail. The upper portion has an excellent view southeast. At an open ledge near the top, watch for a sign marked Path, where an abrupt turn left leads down sharply into woods and marsh before the trail goes up to the actual summit. The summit is wooded.

Perpendicular Trail

Distances from pumping station

    to start (via Long Pond Trail): 0.2 mi., 5 min.

    to Mansell summit: 1.2 mi. (2.6 km.), 1 hr. 10 min.

Sluiceway Trail
NPS rating: Strenuous

This trail starts at Mill Field on the western-mountain fire road. To reach Mill Field, follow Seal Cove Rd. west from ME 102 in Southwest Harbor. The pavement ends at the Acadia Park border. Take the first right off the dirt road, bear right at the first fork, and left at the second fork. The road ends at Mill Field. The trail runs north 0.6 mi. to a junction with the Great Notch Trail. At this junction, the Sluiceway Trail swings northwest and climbs rather steeply, to a junction with the South Face Trail 0.4 mi. farther. To reach Bernard Peak, follow the South Face Trail left (south) for 0.2 mi.

Sluiceway Trail

Distances from western-mountain fire road

    to Great Notch Trail junction: 0.6 mi., 25 min.

    to South Face Trail junction: 1 mi., 50 min.

    to Bernard summit (via South Face Trail): 1.1 mi. (1.8 km.), 1 hr.

Bernard Mountain South Face Trail
NPS rating: Strenuous

This trail also starts at Mill Field on the western-mountain fire road. (For directions to Mill Field, see the Sluiceway Trail description.) As do many of the trails on the western mountains, it runs through a magnificent spruce-fir forest and affords fine views of western Mount Desert Island and Blue Hill Bay. It leads west 0.5 mi. and then rises north to Bernard peak at 1.7 mi. and ends in Little Notch at the junction with the Sluiceway Trail 0.2 mi. beyond.

Bernard Mountain South Face Trail
Distances from western-mountain fire road
> *to* Bernard summit: 1.7 mi., 1 hr. 20 min.
> *to* Little Notch: 1.9 mi. (3.1 km.), 1 hr. 25 min.

Razorback Trail
NPS rating: Strenuous

The Razorback Trail leaves from the Great Notch Trail, which in turn begins at Gilley Field. To reach Gilley Field, follow Seal Cove Rd. west from ME 102 in Southwest Harbor. The pavement ends at the Acadia Park border. Take the first right off the dirt road, bear right at the first fork, and right at the second fork. The road ends at Gilley Field. Follow the Great Notch Trail for 0.2 mi., where the Razorback Trail bears right.

This hike moderately climbs the western side of Mansell, offering views of the Great Notch and Bernard. The trail climbs over ledges and through softwood forest, to connect with the Mansell Mountain Trail between the summit and Great Notch.

Razorback Trail
Distances from Gilley Field
> *to* start of Razorback Trail (via Great Notch Trail): 0.2 mi., 5 min.
> *to* junction with Mansell Peak Trail: 0.9 mi. (1.5 km.), 35 min.

Cold Brook Trail
NPS rating: Easy

This trail is an important link betweeen the Long Pond pumping station trailhead and the western mountains. Running between the Long Pond Trail and Gilley Field, this trail is an easy hike, following the lowlands around Mansell Mountain. It provides access to the Mansell Mountain Trail. More importantly, it is a natural beginning or finish to a circuit hike over both Mansell and Bernard and is a lovely woodlands walk.

Cold Brook Trail
Distances from pumping station
    to start of trail: 0.1 mi., 5 min.
    to Gilley Field: 0.4 mi. (0.6 km.), 20 min.

Great Notch Trail
NPS rating: Moderate
This trail, leaving from Gilley Field, offers a pleasant walk through the notch separating Bernard and Mansell mountains. Gradually rising from the trailhead, the Great Notch Trail provides access to the Razorback Trail, Knight's Nubble, the Little Notch, and the summits of Bernard and Mansell.

Great Notch Trail
Distances from Gilley Field
    to Razorback Trail junction: 0.1 mi., 5 min.
    to Great Notch: 1.1 mi. (1.8 km.), 45 min.

Mansell Mountain Trail
NPS Rating: Moderate
This trail leaves from Gilley Field and offers a beautiful hike up Mansell Mountain. Gradually climbing from the trailhead, this trail passes through softwood forest. It continues to climb onto ledges, giving views to the east and south of Southwest Harbor, Beech Mountain, Long Pond, and Northeast Harbor. It meets the Perpendicular Trail at the summit of Mansell.

Mansell Mountain Trail
Distances from Gilley Field
    to outlook spur trail: 0.7 mi., 30 min.
    to Mansell summit: 0.8 mi. (1.3 km.), 35 min.

ISLE AU HAUT

This island, about 5 mi. south of Stonington, was an early landmark for sailors. Samuel de Champlain, a seventeenth-century French explorer, named it High Island. A range of mountains extends for 6 mi., the length of the island. Mount Champlain (543 ft.), near the north end, is its highest summit. Farther south along the ridge are Rocky Mountain (500 ft.), Sawyer Mountain (480 ft.), and Jerusalem Mountain (440 ft.). Near the southwest tip is Duck Harbor Mountain (314 ft.).

The island is reached by mail boat from Stonington (45 min.). The schedule should be checked locally.

About half of the island is within Acadia National Park. The NPS maintains a camping area at Duck Harbor, on the southwest side of the island and about 4 mi. from Isle au Haut Village. There are five lean-tos (no tent sites), which are available by reservation only. The NPS has established daily limits on the number of people allowed to visit Isle au Haut. For the latest information and reservations (available no earlier than April 1 for the following calendar year), call the park headquarters on Mount Desert Island (207-288-3338), or write to Acadia National Park, PO Box 177, Bar Harbor ME 04609.

The 12-mi. road around the island is partly paved. Some sections of the road, however, are very rough and not recommended for bike riding. The road passes the foot of Long Pond, where there is a place to swim.

Numerous trails offer opportunities to explore wild and rocky shoreline, heavily wooded uplands, marshes, and mountain summits. For current hiking information, write to Acadia National Park, stop at the park Visitor Center in Hulls Cove, or pick up a map from the mailboat operators. From mid-May to mid-October, park rangers will meet the mail boat and provide you with detailed hiking information.

Goat Trail
NPS rating: Moderate

This trail runs from the southern portion of the main road to the Western Head Rd. It parallels the shoreline and offers spectacular views of Head Harbor, Merchant Cove, Barred Harbor, Squeaker Cove and Deep Cove.

The trail begins in a marshy lowland and gradually rises to the coastal ridge. Passing through an evergreen forest, at 0.6 mi. the trail emerges onto a rocky beach. Shortly thereafter, the trail climbs again and passes the southern terminus of the Median Ridge Trail (0.9 mi.). Once again, the trail passes intermittently through both beaches and highlands offering a variety of perspectives on the southern coast of Isle au Haut.

Goat Trail
Distances from main road

- *to* junction with Median Ridge Trail: 0.9 mi., 30 min.
- *to* junction with Duck Harbor Mountain Trail: 1.8 mi., 1 hr.
- *to* junction with Western Head Rd.: 2.2 mi. (3.5 km.), 1 hr. 15 min.

Cliff Trail
NPS rating: Moderate

This trail leaves from the Western Head Rd. It offers the shortest possible route to the Western Ear, which is a small island accessible only during low tide. It begins by climbing steeply (50 ft.) to reach the coastal ridge. Then, it follows the ridge, passing through an evergreen forest. At 0.6 mi. the trail passes through a rocky beach, offering views of Deep Cove and the coast.

Cliff Trail

Distances from Western Head Rd.

> *to* junction with Western Head Trail: 0.7 mi., 40 min.
> *to* Western Ear: 0.8 mi. (1.3 km.), 45 min.

Western Head Trail
NPS rating: Moderate

This trail follows the western shore of Western Head. It offers spectacular views of the ocean from oceanside cliffs. Included in these views are rock outcroppings in the Western Bay. Combined with the Cliff Trail, the Western Head Trail offers a very nice loop around Western Head. The trailheads are a short walk apart on the Western Head Road.

The trail begins in lowlands. At 0.2 mi., it begins to gradually climb to a shoreline ridge. Shortly thereafter, it crosses an active stream. While continuing to ascend through an evergreen forest upon a ledge, views of the coast are evident to the west. At 0.4 mi., the trail descends onto a rocky beach. The terrain continues to follow along the coast, ascending and descending between ridge and beach.

Western Head Trail

Distances from Western Head Rd.

> *to* view of rock outcroppings in the Western Bay: 0.7 mi., 45 min.
> *to* cliffs: 1.2 mi., 1 hr.
> *to* junction with Cliff Trail: 1.6 mi. (2.6 km.), 1 hr. 15 min.

Duck Harbor Trail
NPS rating: Moderate

This trail begins at the park ranger station on the north end of the island. As a major connector, this trail offers hiking access to Duck Harbor, Moore's Harbor, Eli

Creek, the Bowditch Trail, the Nat Merchant Trail, and the park campground.

Following the marshy lowlands, this trail passes through mature stands of softwoods. At 0.9 mi., a small pond will appear to the left. At 1.5 mi., the Bowditch Trail bears to the left. Shortly thereafter, another junction with the town road cuts off to the right. The trail crosses a sandy beach at 1.9 mi., offering views of the western coast. At 2.2 mi., a park service cabin will be visible. A small side trail which offers views of Deep Cove bears off to the right at 2.7 mi. After crossing the road, the trail offers outstanding views of the ocean and harbor.

Duck Harbor Trail

Distances from park ranger station

   to junction with Bowditch Trail: 1.5 mi., 45 min.
   to junction with town road: 1.5 mi., 45 min.
   to park service cabin: 2.3 mi., 1 hr. 10 min.
   to junction with side trail to Deep Cove: 2.7 mi., 1 hr. 20 min.
   to second junction with road: 3.0 mi., 1 hr. 30 min.
   to views of harbor and ocean: 3.7 mi., 1 hr. 50 min.
   to Duck Harbor and road: 3.9 mi. (6.2 km.), 2 hrs.

Duck Harbor Mountain Trail
NPS rating: Strenuous

This trail begins on the Western Head Rd. and is one of the most physically challenging trails on Isle au Haut. It climbs over Duck Harbor Mountain, offering terrific views of the harbor as well as the southern end of the island. The trail begins on rapidly ascending ledges. At 0.2 mi., the trail briefly crests. Then, at 0.3 mi., after a short descent, the trail again ascends steeply. It passes through a mixture of softwood forest and open ledge to the summit of Duck Harbor Mountain.

After the summit, this trail continues along the ridge. It goes over the Puddings, offering more views, and descends rapidly through softwood forest and ledges down to a junction with the Goat Trail.

Duck Harbor Mountain Trail

Distances from Western Head Rd.

> *to* summit of Duck Harbor Mountain: 0.4 mi., 35 min.
>
> *to* junction with Goat Trail: 1.2 mi. (1.9 km.), 1 hr. 30 min.

Median Ridge Trail
NPS rating: Moderate

The trailhead is located on the main road in the southern part of the island. This trail has two spurs, north and south, from this point. The south spur connects quickly (0.3 mi.) with the Goat Trail by following low marshlands. The north spur quickly ascends to the ridge. At 0.3 mi., a blue blaze appears on trees. The trail follows the ridge into a Japanese garden, offering views to the east. At 0.7 mi., excellent views can be seen from a ledge area surrounded by small conifers. The trail then descends into a bog. At 1 mi., it crosses the Nat Merchant Trail. The trail continues through marsh, evergreens, and a cedar bog to a junction with the Long Pond Trail.

Median Ridge Trail

Distances from main road

> *to* junction of south spur with the Goat Trail: 0.3 mi., 25 min.
>
> *to* junction of north spur with the Nat Merchant Trail: 1 mi., 45 min.
>
> *to* junction of north spur with the Long Pond Trail: 1.6 mi. (2.5 km.), 1 hr. 30 min.

Nat Merchant Trail
NPS rating: Moderate

The Nat Merchant trailhead is located on the main road on the western shore of the island. This trail begins by entering low marshlands covered in cedar and pine. It crosses several intermittent streams until it meets with the Median Ridge Trail (0.8 mi.). After this junction, the trail begins to climb gradually. It passes over a boulder field and crests at the top of this field offering fine views. Once this ridge is crested, the trail passes through a softwood forest. The trail ends at the main road on the island's eastern side.

Nat Merchant Trail

Distances from main road
   to junction with Median Ridge Trail: 0.8 mi., 25 min.
   to junction with road: 1.2 mi. (1.9 km.), 45 min.

Long Pond Trail
NPS rating: Strenuous

This trailhead is located on the main road on the western portion of the island. While this trail is relatively flat to begin, once on the loop the change of elevation is quite severe. Despite the difficult climb, this trail offers wonderful views of the largest pond on Isle au Haut, not to mention access to the summit of Bowditch Mountain, the Bowditch Trail, and the Median Ridge Trail. The trail forms a nice loop for a day hike.

Beginning at the road, the trail follows a low, wet area for 0.4 mi., where the trail meets the Median Ridge Trail (entering right) and splits into its two legs of the loop. The southern loop follows along an old stream bed for quite some time. At 1.1 mi., the trail passes over the old foundation of a building, follows along a stone wall, and then gradually climbs onto a ridge. At 1.7 mi., you will see Long Pond. The trail follows Long Pond north for a short time, bears west and climbs gradually through evergreens to the summit of Bowditch Mountain. At the summit, the Bowditch Trail enters from the right. The Long Pond Trail continues straight ahead and returns to the junction with the southern leg and the Long Pond Trail.

Long Pond Trail

Distances from main road

   to junction with the Median Ridge Trail: 0.4 mi., 15 min.

   to foundation of old building: 1.1 mi., 35 min.

   to Long Pond (via south leg): 1.7 mi., 55 min.

   to summit and junction with Bowditch Trail (via south leg): 2.4 mi., 1 hr. 30 min.

   to complete the Long Pond Loop: 3.2 mi. (4.6 km.), 2 hrs.

Bowditch Trail
NPS rating: Moderate

This trail runs between the Duck Harbor Trail and the Median Ridge Trail. If offers spectacular views from Bowditch Mountain.

   Beginning from the Duck Harbor Trail, this trail follows low marshlands for its first 0.8 mi., where it crosses an active stream and turns onto an old firebreak. After following the firebreak, the trail begins to climb gradually, offering wonderful views of the ocean to the west. It continues to climb through a softwood forest over wet ledge for 1.1 mi., where it reaches the summit of Bowditch Mountain. At this point, it connects with the Median Ridge Trail.

Bowditch Trail

Distances from junction with Duck Harbor Trail

   to sign marking trail: 1.1 mi., 40 min.

   to ledges with views to the west: 1.6 mi., 1 hr.

   to summit and junction with Median Ridge Trail: 2.0 mi. (3.2 km.), 1 hr., 30 min.

SECTION 4
East of the Penobscot

This section describes the mainland area east of the
Penobscot River and south of Aroostook County,
between the Penobscot River plain on the west and the
coastal rivers, including the Union, Narraguagus,
Machias, and St. Croix, on the south and east. In this
region the country rolls up into low, mostly widely scattered mountains. Lead Mountain (1475 ft.) and Passadumkeag Mountain (1463 ft.) are the highest, and several
others are over 1000 ft. In general, extensive views
characterize the mountains, and some have attractive
open summits and ledges. This section describes the
mountains to the south and west first, and then those to
the north and east.

TUNK MOUNTAIN (1157 ft./353 m.)

This mountain is located in T 10 S D (T stands for
township). It is northeast of Schoodic Mountain. There
is no trail on the upper part, but bushwhacking is fairly
easy. Refer to the USGS Tunk Lake quadrangle, 15-
minute series, and Tunk Mountain quadrangle, 7.5-
minute series.

Take US 1 east from Ellsworth for 6 mi. and bear
left on ME 182. At about 7.5 mi. east of ME 200 in
Franklin, park at the entrance of a road on the left that is
0.2 mi. east of the eastern end of Fox Pond and 2.7 mi.
west of the outlet of Tunk Lake.

The trail leads north, first ascending steeply, easing
up through the woods, then requiring a scramble up a
series of ledges on the way to and along the partially

127

wooded, five-peaked summit ridge. The whole southern face of the mountain consists of cliffs and steep ledges. Views are limited but interesting, particularly the ones of Spring River Lake and the Black Hills.

Tunk Mountain

Distance from entrance of road off ME 182
  to Tunk summit: 1.5 mi. (2.4 km.), 1 hr. 30 min.

SCHOODIC MOUNTAIN (1069 ft./326 m.)

Of the small group of mountains northeast of the head of Frenchman's Bay, Schoodic is the most popular for climbing. It is located in T 9 S D. Refer to the USGS Tunk Lake quadrangle, 15-minute series, and Sullivan quadrangle, 7.5-minute series.

A good trail to the abandoned firetower on the summit starts 2.2 mi. south of Franklin Village and 4 mi. north of Sullivan. It leaves the east side of ME 200 between two bridges at the foot of a steep hill in East Franklin. Park in the space just north of the north bridge. Take the paved road east and follow the right fork up a hill. At about 0.5 mi., the road (which possibly can be driven to this point) crosses a large brook, the last sure source of *water* on the trail. At about 1 mi. the road crosses a railroad. Turn right and follow the road beside the railroad for a short distance until it swings away to the left. Pass through a logged area, keeping straight at the next left fork. About 20 min. farther take the well-worn path to the left (cairn), which is a shortcut to a warden's cabin site. The trail then climbs steeply but presents no difficulties. The top of the mountain is bare and flat and offers views in all directions. Those of Mount Desert and Frenchman's Bay are very scenic.

Another, easier approach to the mountain, except during very wet weather, begins in East Sullivan. At the junction of US 1 and ME 183, follow ME 183 north. It crosses railroad tracks at 4.4 mi. At 4.5 mi. turn left on a dirt road, which is rough and no good after long rains. Also, road signs for the tower are not always present at key junctions. At 0.7 mi. from ME 183, continue straight ahead, and at 1.3 mi. take the right fork. Follow it to another fork 1.8 mi. from ME 183 and turn left on Western Road. Park and take the trail (north-northwest) at 2.3 mi. from ME 183. Follow for 0.5 mi., where it meets the trail junction described in the preceding paragraph.

Schoodic Mountain

Distances from ME 200

    to large-brook crossing: *est.* 0.5 mi., 15 min.

    to railroad tracks: 1 mi., 30 min.

    to warden's cabin site: 2 mi., 1 hr.

    to Schoodic summit: 2.8 mi. (4.5 km.), 1 hr. 40 min.

Distances from Western Road

    to warden's cabin site: 0.6 mi., 20 min.

    to Schoodic summit: 1.4 mi. (2.3 km.), 1 hr.

BLUE HILL (934 ft./285 m.)

This isolated mountain rises just north of the town of the same name. There is a MFS firetower as well as a microwave tower on the summit. Refer to the USGS Blue Hill quadrangle, 15-minute series and 7.5-minute series.

    Opposite the Blue Hill Fair Grounds, 13 mi. from Ellsworth on ME 172, go right on a road that heads west. An excellent MFS trail leaves this road on the right (north) 0.8 mi. from ME 172. (You can also reach the start of the trail by turning east from ME 15, 1 mi. north of Blue Hill Village and 11 mi. south of the junction with US 1 between Orland and East Orland. The trail is on the left [north] 0.5 mi. from ME 15.) Not far from the start it branches right and runs through a fine stand of spruce to the summit. Extensive views take in the Mount Desert mountains and Blue Hill Bay. See *A Hiker's*

Guide to Blue Hill Mountain, by Alison Dibble, sponsored by the Blue Hill Heritage Trust. This pamphlet will be available in local stores and inns for a $2 donation.

Blue Hill

Distance from road between ME 172 and ME 15
to Blue Hill Summit: 1 mi. (1.6 km.), 45 min.

GREAT HILL (1038 ft./316 m.)

Great Hill appears on the USGS Orland quadrangle, 7.5-minute series. It is also called Great Pond Mountain, and is known locally as Old Baldy. It is in the town of Orland, northeast of Alamoosook Lake.

Leave US 1 in East Orland 6 mi. east of Bucksport and 14 mi. west of Ellsworth at Toddy Pond Outlet (sign reading Craig Brook National Fish Hatchery). Take the road to the north for 1.3 mi. Drive through the hatchery grounds and bear right before the picnic ground. Park at 0.9 mi., within sight of a private gate. Take wood-road trail up to the left. The trail climbs through woods and soon emerges onto spacious open ledges where you can see from Mount Desert to Penobscot Bay. The wooded summit, about 100 ft. higher with an open ledge, offers views to the northeast and east.

Be careful to note where the trail leaves the woods, so you can find it again on the way down; there are no markers on the ledges.

Great Hill

Distance from parking area
to Great Hill summit: 1.8 mi. (2.9 km.), 1 hr. 15 min.

BALD MOUNTAIN (1234 ft./376 m.)

This interesting mountain (also known as Dedham Bald Mountain) is in the town of Dedham, and a MFS trail in good condition leads to a tower and radio towers on the summit. The Bald Mountain Ski Area used to occupy the western side of the mountain. After it closed, the lifts and other equipment were removed. Refer to the USGS Green Lake quadrangle, 7.5-minute series.

From US 1A in East Holden, 9 mi. from Bangor and 18 mi. from Ellsworth, turn south onto the paved Upper Dedham Rd.; do *not* take ME 46. In 2.7 mi. take a left at the fire station. Then, 6.3 mi. from US 1A, where the road bears right, continue straight on FR 62 for 100 yds. and park the car on ledges to the left. The trail starts at the parking area and is easy to follow. It leads through open fields and over ledges to the tower, which the MFS maintains for communication. From the tower, you can see to the north and northwest from Katahdin to Bigelow, and the nearby ledges on the northern side of the mountain look out over beautiful Phillips Lake, now known as Lucerne-in-Maine. The eastern side offers views of the Mount Desert Island mountains.

An alternative route follows the old ski trail, which is easy to see from the approach road. The ski trail intersects Upper Dedham Rd. 0.3 mi. before (north of) the firetower trail at the parking area.

Bald Mountain

Distance from parking area
   to Bald Mountain firetower: 0.5 mi. (0.8 km.), 30 min.

RIDER BLUFF (813 ft./248 m.)

This bluff in Holden is in the first line of hills east of the Penobscot River plain. It makes a good outlook for viewing the Bangor-Brewer area and the mountains from Katahdin to Bigelow, Sugarloaf, and Abraham. Most people generally hike up the service road for the WLBZ-TV tower on the summit. (During dry weather, cars can usually make it up this road, too.) Refer to the USGS Brewer Lake quadrangle, 7.5-minute series.

From US 1A, turn southwest on a paved west road 8 mi. from Bangor and 1.4 mi. northwest of East Holden. The turn is just southeast of the Holden Town Hall. In 1.3 mi. the blacktop road makes a sharp left turn. Go straight ahead on the private access road. It descends slightly, crosses a small brook, and then turns right (west), and climbs toward the col between Rider Bluff and Hog Hill. About 0.7 mi. from the blacktop road, it turns and climbs more steeply to the summit.

Rider Bluff

Distance from blacktop road
   to Rider summit: *est.* 1 mi. (1.6 km.), 40 min.

BLACKCAP MOUNTAIN (1022 ft./312 m.)

Five radio and TV masts top Blackcap Mountain, which is in Eddington. Vegetation blocks views, except to the east. Refer to the USGS Orono and Orland quadrangles, 15-minute series, and Chemo Pond quadrangle, 7.5-minute series.

To reach the summit by car, take ME 46 northeast from US 1A at East Holden. Drive 4 mi. and turn right (sign reading Katahdin Area Council Boy Scout Camp). The road to the scout camp goes left from the summit road 0.4 mi. from ME 46. Stay right at that and all other junctions. Continue 1.9 mi. to the end of the road.

Roberts Trail

Hikers can pick up the Roberts Trail either at the summit of Blackcap (near the radio mast with the small green instrument house) or on the scout camp road at the outlet of Fitts Pond, which is opposite a gravel bank near the entrance of the camp 1.5 mi. from the summit road. Other trails also diverge from this point and lead to Burnt Pond and Little Burnt Pond. Blue and white paint blazes and directional arrows mark the Roberts

Trail, which crosses the pond outlet on a tripod bridge and climbs steeply to the cluster of radio and TV masts. It continues along the summit ridge over open ledges and through patches of trees to the southern end of the ridge. Then it drops steeply east and northeast to the southern end of Fitts Pond. It crosses a swampy patch to the eastern shore of the pond and runs along the shore. At first it stays close to the shore. Then it goes up on the bluff and returns to the entrance of the boy scout camp. At the southern end of the pond, be careful not to take a wrong turn onto a jeep road that diverges east.

Roberts Trail

Distances from scout camp entrance

    to radio and TV masts: 0.6 mi., 45 min.

    to southern end of Blackcap summit ridge: 1.4 mi., 1 hr. 10 min.

    to southern end of Fitts Pond: 2.3 mi., 2 hr.

    to scout camp entrance: 3.8 mi. (6.1 km.), 3 hr.

EAGLE BLUFF (790 ft./241 m.)

With one of the more exposed and scenic views in eastern Maine, this sheer cliff overlooks Mountainy Pond and almost unbroken wilderness. A tote road rises gradually to within 0.8 mi. of the summit, which is bare. The sheer southern side is good for rappelling, friction climbing, and rock climbing. The granite is stable, but not many climbers take advantage of it. Refer to the USGS Orono and Orland quadrangles, 15-minute series, and Green Lake quadrangle, 7.5-minute series.

    The trail begins at the Katahdin Scout Camp. (See the preceding section for approach routes.) Park in the lot at the reservation.

    From behind the mess hall (the largest building), the trail follows the road, which rises quickly at first. At about 2.8 mi. turn sharply right into a hunting camp. To the left of the camp, an orange-blazed trail climbs steeply, levels off, and then pitches quickly to the summit.

Eagle Bluff

Distance from scout camp
   to Eagle Bluff summit: 3 mi. (4.8 km.), 2 hr.

WOODCHUCK HILL (SNOWSHOE MOUNTAIN) (834 ft./254 m.)

A very easy hike in the area northeast of Blackcap Mountain, this mountain offers good campsites at both its summit and its base. Refer to the USGS Orono quadrangle, 15-minute series, and Chemo Pond quadrangle, 7.5-minute series.

The approach by road is the same as for Blackcap Mountain. Park in the lot at the scout camp. From a small log cabin immediately behind the parking lot on the left, follow the unmarked road, which soon turns into a poorly marked (polka-dot markers) but obvious trail. The trail passes through a campsite beyond Snowshoe Pond and climbs to a Bangor Water District road (paved) at 0.8 mi. On the road, walk 75 ft. to the right to utility pole 66. Then follow irregular blazes or bushwhack for less than 0.5 mi. to the open summit.

Woodchuck Hill

Distance from scout camp
   to Woodchuck summit: *est.* 1.3 mi. (2.1 km.), 45 min.

PEAKED (1160 ft./354 m.) AND LITTLE PEAKED MOUNTAINS

These two summits make a particularly rewarding snowshoeing trip in winter. It is easy to complete the circuit in an afternoon from many points in the surrounding area.

Peaked Mountain

Peaked Mountain, commonly called Chick Hill, strad-
dles the Clifton/Amherst line. A well-marked and popular MFS trail leads to the summit. Refer to the USGS
Great Pond quadrangle, 15-minute series, and the Hop-
kins Pond quadrangle, 7.5-minute series.

About 18 mi. from Bangor and 3.5 mi. east of the
junction of ME 9 and ME 180, leave ME 9 on the north
(left) side on a gravel road. This turn is roughly opposite
a Maine Highway Department picnic area. In about 0.7
mi., after passing a small group of houses, park. Follow
an old discontinued "Airline" road to the firewarden's
campsite (0.2 mi.). There is a dependable *spring* behind
the campsite. Continue on the old road, and at about 0.6
mi., as the road levels off, turn right onto a clearly
blazed trail. At about 0.9 mi. the trail rises more steeply
and on the lower ledge, you can see nearby Little
Peaked Mountain to the west. Occasional cairns mark
the way to the summit, which offers vistas in all directions and is particularly colorful in fall. The view
includes five lakes, the Penobscot River, the Mount
Desert mountains to the southeast, and Mount Katahdin
to the northwest.

Peaked Mountain

Distance from parking area
   to Peaked Mountain summit: 1.3 mi. (2.1 km.), 50 min.

Little Peaked Mountain

The views from Little Peaked Mountain (Little Chick
Hill) are also good, except to the north. To reach Little
Peaked Mountain, take the trail to the right at the park-
ing area.

Another easy route is to take the trail up Peaked
Mountain. Just before beginning the climb up the steeper part of the peak, turn right, descend briefly to the col,
and bushwhack to Little Peaked Mountain.

For a third route, start up Peaked Mountain Trail. At 0.4 mi., go right on a cairned road closed with a cable for 0.2 mi. Turn right at the cairn and climb directly to the summit.

LEAD MOUNTAIN (HUMPBACK) (1475 ft./450 m.)

Lead Mountain is in T 28 M D in Hancock County, just west of the Washington County line. The trail appears on the USGS Lead Mountain quadrangle, 7.5-minute series.

Take the newly bulldozed road left at the rear of the yard of the MFS station (283 ft.) in Beddington. The station is 0.1 mi. west of the ME 9 bridge over the Narraguagus River and 1.1 mi. east of the ME 9 and 193 junction. Park at the turnaround 1.7 mi. from the station. The trail follows the gated road for ten minutes, then turns right up into the woods just before the University of Maine acid-rain project structures and heads for the summit (blue blazed). At 1.3 mi. a side path leads 200 yd. left to Bear Pond. At 1.5 mi. the trail divides. The left fork goes close to a reliable *spring* 100 ft. to the left of the main trail (sign). Then it rejoins the main trail. At 2.5 mi. you will reach the warden's cabin in a col below the summit. The trail continues straight on past the cabin and then bears left (west) to the site of the firetower, which is on a flat summit several acres in area. The ledges 200 yd. southwest of the summit are a good lookout.

Descending, remember that where the trail divides, the right fork leads past the *spring.*

Lead Mountain

Distances from MFS station
 to side trail to Bear Pond: 1.3 mi., 40 min.
 to warden's cabin: 2.5 mi., 1 hr. 45 min.
 to Lead Mountain summit: 3 mi. (4.8 km.), 2 hr.

PEAKED MOUNTAIN (938 ft./286 m.)

Peaked Mountain is in T 30 in Washington County, north of ME 9 and less than 30 mi. east of the mountain near Clifton with the same name. Refer to the USGS Tug Mountain quadrangle, 15-minute series, and the Peaked Mountain quadrangle, 7.5-minute series.

A good MFS trail leaves the north side of ME 9 at a sign about 9.8 mi. east of the Narraguagus River and about 14.8 mi. west of Wesley. Park about 100 ft. in on the tote road. Follow the tote road to the firewarden's cabin. Then take the trail, which rises gently and follows a telephone line to an open ledge. The MFS abandoned the firetower in 1970. Extensive wilderness spreads out below in all directions.

Peaked Mountain

Distance from parking area on tote road

   to Peaked Mountain firetower (via trail from warden's cabin): 1.3 mi. (2.1 km.), 45 min.

WASHINGTON BALD MOUNTAIN (983 ft./300 m.)

This mountain's MFS firetower was abandoned in 1970. The mountain is in T 42 M D. Refer to the USGS Wabassus Lake and the Fletcher Peak quadrangles, 7.5-minute series.

The St. Regis Paper Co. maintains a gravel road that leaves the northern side of ME 9, 14 mi. east of the Narraguagus River in Beddington and 10.5 mi. west of Wesley. (The approach road to Sabao diverges left 75 yd. from ME 9.) Take the St. Regis road north to its end (13.1 mi.), where there is room to park four or five cars. From this point, logging operations have obscured the trail. A map and compass bushwhack is recommended. Climb the last steep pitch to a tower, which was erected in 1935. There is a well sunk in the granite near the warden's cabin.

Trails lead to the third, fourth, and fifth Machias Lakes from the summit but are not recommended. You can see the first, second, third, and fourth Machias Lakes and many mountains from the 65-ft. tower.

Washington Bald Mountain

Distance from end of St. Regis Co. road

to Washington Bald Mountain firetower (via right fork): 2.2 mi. (3.5 km.), 1 hr. 30 min.

PASSADUMKEAG MOUNTAIN (1465 ft./446 m.)

Passadumkeag Mountain is southeast of Enfield. It runs in a gradual east-west arc for some 5 mi. and rises well above the surrounding countryside, which is particularly flat to the west and southwest. Until 1970 the MFS staffed the firetower on the highest summit and maintained a good logging road to it. Refer to the USGS Saponac quadrangle, 15-minute series, and Burlington and Saponac quadrangles, 7.5-minute series.

Leave West Enfield on ME 155, east from its junction with US 2. After 2.5 mi. go right on ME 188 and follow it to Saponac four corners (green buildings), about 19 mi. from US 2. Turn sharp right onto a gravel road and cross the Passadumkeag River. At 0.4 mi. turn right at the head of a gravel pit. Pass the blue house (a former ranger station) and continue on the increasingly rough road. From this road where logging has obliterated the trail, the climb becomes a bushwhack to the 30-ft. firetower. The tower can also be reached by following the Greenfield Road from the south, starting from US 2 in Costigan. This becomes a rough jeep trail. From the tower, you can see Brandy Pond to the southeast in T 39 M D, Saponac Lake to the north, West Lakes and Nicatous Lake to the east, and many mountains, including Katahdin.

Passadumkeag Mountain

Distances from parking area

   to private cabin: 4.0 mi., 2 hr.

   to Passadumkeag firetower: 4.5 mi. (7.2 km.), 2 hr.
      30 min.

POCOMOONSHINE MOUNTAIN (605 ft./184 m.)

Located in Princeton, this mountain rises nearly 500 ft.
above Pocomoonshine Lake. Before abandoning it in
1970, the MFS built a road on the back side of the
mountain to the tower. Hikers can use this road or the
trail described below. Refer to the USGS Big Lake
quadrangle, 15-minute series, and Princeton quadrangle,
7.5-minute series.

   From US 1 2.3 mi. south of Princeton, turn southwest on a paved road. At 0.9 mi. turn right on a gravel
road. The trail leaves right at 3.8 mi. and ascends to the
summit and tower foundation. There are no views.

Pocomoonshine Mountain

Distance from parking area

   to Pocomoonshine summit: 0.5 mi. (0.8 km.), 30 min.

SECTION 5
Camden Hills

The Camden Hills, a compact and attractive group of mountains, rise above the western shore of Penobscot Bay in the towns of Camden, Lincolnville, and Rockport. They share many characteristics with the Mount Desert mountains 40 mi. to the east—fine softwood forests, bold cliffs and ledges, and wide vistas of water and mountains. Mount Megunticook (1380 ft.) is the highest of the group and, with the exception of Cadillac Mountain, is the highest point along the Atlantic seaboard in the United States. A chain of lower summits continues northeast for several miles; Bald Rock Mountain (1100 ft.) is the most conspicuous. Cameron Mountain (811 ft.) is west of Bald Rock and northeast of Maiden Cliff. The summit is private property, a commercial blueberry field. Mount Battie (800 ft.) lies to the south of Megunticook and is only 0.5 mi. by trail from Megunticook St. in Camden. The Megunticook River and Lake separate the main peaks of the group from the hills running to the southwest, which are, from northeast to southwest, Bald Mountain (1272 ft.), Ragged Mountain (1300 ft.), Spruce Mountain (960 ft.), Pleasant Mountain (1064 ft.), and Meadow Mountain (660 ft.). Refer to the USGS Camden, Lincolnville and West Rockport quadrangles, 7.5-minute series, as well as the map included with this guide.

Camden Hills State Park (5500 acres) embraces much of the Mount Megunticook range, plus a large area to the north and northeast and a short stretch on Penobscot Bay north of Camden on US 1. Park facilities include picnic and camping areas. An automobile road (toll) runs to the summit of Mount Battie from the park headquarters. *The water supply is not reliable* in many parts of the park, so carry water if you hike there. Most trails are blazed with white paint.

Not in the Camden Hills, but included in this section of the guide, are several outlying mountains to the west of the Penobscot River, south of US 2, and east of the Kennebec River. This section also covers the offshore island of Monhegan.

MOUNT BATTIE (800 ft./243 m.)

This mountain lies to the south of Mount Megunticook. For climbing, it is the most popular of the Camden Hills because its open ledges offer outstanding views and it is close to Camden. For several years after 1897, there was a hotel on the summit. The stone viewing tower there now was erected as a war memorial in 1921.

A toll road for cars runs to the summit. Starting at the Camden Hills State Park Headquarters on US 1, it climbs gradually to the Battie-Megunticook col, turns southwest, and finally curves southeast to the top (1.4 mi.).

Mount Battie Trail

This trail, marked with white blazes and cairns, rises steeply over the rocky nose of Mount Battie. Take ME 52 (Mountain St.) from its junction with US 1 in Camden. Then take the fourth right, and then the first left onto Megunticook St. Continue to the end of the street, where there is a small parking area. The trail first climbs northwest and then rises more steeply north through thinning woods. It soon emerges on the open ledges and runs to the summit tower.

Mount Battie Trail

Distance from parking area on Megunticook St.

   to Mount Battie Summit: 0.5 mi. (0.8 km.), 30 min.

Carriage Road Trail

This trail climbs along the more gradual west and north-west slopes of Mount Battie, via the route of the old carriage road up the mountain, and leaves the right (north-eastern) side of ME 52 about 1.3 mi. from the US 1/ME 52 junction. The road runs north 0.3 mi. to where the Carriage Road Trail forks right, while the Carriage Trail, leading to the Tableland Trail, continues.

The Carriage Road Trail rises gently on the old carriage road, which is washed out in many places. The trail joins the toll road near the summit parking area.

Carriage Road Trail

Distance from ME 52

   to Mount Battie summit: 1.1 mi. (1.8 km.), 35 min.

Carriage Trail

In conjunction with the Tableland Trail, this trail provides a route up Mount Megunticook from the southwest. To approach the trail, see Carriage Road Trail above.

The trail climbs very gradually. It reaches the Tableland Trail near the Battie-Megunticook col. To reach Ocean Lookout and, beyond that, the true summit of Mount Megunticook, go left on the Tableland Trail. (To the right, the Tableland Trail leads to the Mount Battie summit.)

Carriage Trail

Distances from ME 52

   to Tableland Trail junction: 1.0 mi., 30 min.

   to Ocean Lookout (via Tableland Trail): 1.7 mi., 1 hr. 20 min.

   to Megunticook summit (via Tableland and Ridge trails): 2.2 mi. (3.5 km.), 1 hr. 35 min.

Nature Trail

This white-blazed trail adds another approach to Mount Battie (besides the toll road for cars) from the east. It leaves the right side of the Mount Battie toll road 200 ft. from the gate house and runs north of the road. It joins the Tableland Trail about 0.7 mi. from that trail's start. Turn left on the Tableland Trail and, crossing the toll road at 0.2 mi., continue to Mount Battie. (To the right, the Tableland Trail reaches Ocean Lookout in about 1 mi.)

Nature Trail

Distances from bottom of toll road

to Tableland Trail junction: 1 mi., 40 min.

to Mount Battie summit (via Tableland Trail): 1.7 mi. (2.7 km.), 50 min.

to Ocean Lookout (via Tableland Trail): 1.8 mi. (2.9 km.), 1 hr. 30 min.

MOUNT MEGUNTICOOK (1380 ft./420 m.)

Mount Megunticook is the highest of the Camden Hills. A ridge forms the mountain and runs northwest-southeast for approximately 3 mi. The true summit has no view, but Ocean Lookout, 0.5 mi. to the southeast, takes in the expanse of Penobscot Bay. Several outlooks on the Ridge Trail offer views to the northwest over Megunticook Lake. Maiden Cliff is a prominent bluff near the northwestern end of the mountain.

Mount Megunticook Trail

This trail climbs the eastern slope of the mountain from the Camden Hills State Park Headquarters to Ocean Lookout. The park headquarters, where there is parking, is on the northwest side of US 1, 1.8 mi. northeast of the junction of US 1 and ME 52 in Camden, and 3.8 mi. south of Lincolnville Beach. The trail starts from the park camping area and climbs first gradually and then steeply. At 1.4 mi. it reaches Ocean Lookout, where the Tableland Trail from Mount Battie comes up from the left (south). From Ocean Lookout, follow the Ridge Trail northwest about 0.4 mi. to the Mount Megunticook summit.

A 2-mi. snowmobile trail has been cut along the eastern side of Mount Megunticook. It leaves the right side of Mount Megunticook Trail just beyond the camping area (sign). It runs around the eastern side of Mount Megunticook and joins the Ski Shelter Trail (see below). Hikers can complete a 5.4-mi. loop trip over Mount Megunticook via the Mount Megunticook Trail, the Ridge Trail, the Slope Trail, and the snowmobile trail.

Mount Megunticook Trail

Distances from park camping area

   to Ocean Lookout: 1.4 mi., 1 hr.

   to Megunticook summit and Slope Trail junction (via Ridge Trail): 1.9 mi. (3 km.), 1 hr. 20 min.

   to Ski Lodge Trail (via Slope Trail): 3.4 mi., 2 hr. 10 min.

   to park camping area (via Slope Trail and snowmobile trail): 5.4 mi. (8.6 km.), 3 hr. 20 min.

Tableland Trail

This trail starts from the summit of Mount Battie. It crosses the parking area and runs to the northeast and gradually descends, crossing the toll road at 0.5 mi., to the Battie-Megunticook col. At 0.7 mi. pass the Nature Trail on the right, and at 0.8 mi. pass the Carriage Trail on the left. Starting the ascent of the Mount Megunticook mass, the Tableland Trail keeps to the right (east) of two lines of cliffs and, again swinging to the northwest, climbs steeply to Ocean Lookout. The true summit is another 0.5 mi. to the northwest along the Ridge Trail.

Tableland Trail

Distances from Mount Battie summit
    to Ocean Lookout: 1.5 mi. (2.4 km.), 1 hr.

Maiden Cliff Trail

Maiden Cliff (800 ft./243 m.) rises abruptly above Megunticook Lake. A wooden cross stands near the spot where Elenora French, a young girl, fell to her death in 1864. The trail starts from the northeastern side of ME 52 (at a parking area about 2.9 mi. north of the junction of ME 52 and US 1 in Camden), where the highway approaches a cove of Megunticook Lake. The trail climbs north, at first following a washed-out logging road. At about 0.4 mi. the Ridge Trail to Mount Megunticook diverges right. The Maiden Cliff Trail then climbs more steeply to open ledges and the wooden cross. For a rewarding alternate route to Maiden Cliff, go right on the Ridge Trail. Then in about 0.3 mi. go left (north) on the Scenic Trail. The Scenic Trail reaches Maiden Cliff in another 0.5 mi. after crossing several open ledges with fine views of the lake.

Maiden Cliff Trail

Distances from ME 52
    to Ridge Trail junction: *est.* 0.5 mi., 30 min.
    to Maiden Cliff: 0.9 mi., 50 min.
    to Maiden Cliff (via Ridge and Scenic trails): 1.2 mi. (1.9 km.), 1 hr. 10 min.

Scenic Trail

This trail forks left (east) from the Maiden Cliff Trail near Maiden Cliff. It climbs over very open ledge with many views, then descends slightly to a junction with the Ridge Trail 0.7 mi. from ME 52.

Scenic Trail

Distance from Maiden Cliff
    to Ridge Trail junction: 0.5 mi. (0.8 km.), 30 min.

Ridge Trail

This trail leaves the Maiden Cliff Trail 0.4 mi. from ME 52 and runs along the main ridge of Mount Megunticook, over the true summit, and on to Ocean Lookout. From the Maiden Cliff Trail junction, hike up to the right. In about 0.3 mi. the Scenic Trail to Maiden Cliff diverges left. The Ridge Trail continues to climb, after a brief descent, with occasional lookouts over Megunticook Lake. About 0.9 mi. from the junction with the Scenic Trail, Zeke's Trail comes in from the left (sign). In another 0.2 mi., the Ridge Trail crosses over a subsidiary summit (1290 ft.), descends slightly, and then climbs gradually to the true summit, which is wooded. Just beyond the summit, the Slope Trail diverges left (north). In another 0.2 mi., the Ridge Trail descends to end at Ocean Lookout.

Ridge Trail

Distances from ME 52
    to start (via Maiden Cliff Trail): 0.4 mi., 30 min.
    to Scenic Trail junction: 0.7 mi., 40 min.
    to Zeke's Trail junction: 1.6 mi., 1 hr. 5 min.
    to Megunticook summit and Slope Trail junction: 2.6 mi., 1 hr. 45 min.
    to Ocean Lookout: 3.1 mi. (5 km.), 2 hr.

Distances from ME 52 via Maiden Cliff and Scenic trails
    to Ridge Trail: 1.4 mi., 1 hr. 15 min.
    to Zeke's Trail junction: 2.3 mi., 1 hr. 40 min.
    to Megunticook summit and Slope Trail junction: 3.3 mi., 2 hr. 15 min.
    to Ocean Lookout: 3.8 mi. (6.1 km.), 2 hr. 30 min.

Megunticook Traverse

This traverse is probably the nicest walk in the Camden Hills area. It offers a series of marvelous views and a lot of ridge walking. Climb the Mount Battie Trail from Camden. Then follow the Tableland Trail to Ocean Lookout. Continue over Mount Megunticook on the Ridge Trail to the Scenic Trail, which leads to Maiden Cliff. Then descend the Maiden Cliff Trail to ME 52. This route is equally good in the opposite direction.

Megunticook Traverse

Distance from parking area on Megunticook St. (Mount Battie trailhead)

>   *to* ME 52 (Maiden Cliff trailhead): 5.8 mi. (9.3 km.), 3 hr. 30 min.

MOUNT MEGUNTICOOK FROM THE NORTH

Hikers can approach Mount Megunticook and its subsidiary summits from the north via a network of trails that for the most part branch from the Ski Shelter Trail. These trails are not as heavily used as those on the southern and western slopes of the mountain, and the woods have suffered logging and extensive blowdowns in the past. So be particularly careful not to wander off the routes described. Since *water* supplies in the northern hills are not always dependable, always carry a canteen.

Ski Shelter Trail

This trail is a state-park fire road. It serves as the chief approach to the trails up Mount Megunticook from the north. It also is the approach from the north for Bald Rock Mountain and for other trails leading to US 1. The road is in poor condition in places.

   To reach Ski Shelter Trail, take ME 173 from Lincolnville Beach. After 2.3 mi. turn left onto Youngtown Rd., and within less than 100 yd. turn left onto the Ski

Shelter Trail (which may be closed or impassable). At
1.3 mi. the Bald Rock Trail goes left and leads to the
summit of Bald Rock Mountain. About 100 yd. farther
along the trail, the Cameron Mountain Trail diverges
right, and in another 0.3 mi., the Sky Blue Trail also
diverges right. At 2.5 mi. along the trail, Zeke's Trail
diverges right and climbs to the Ridge Trail. At 3 mi.
the trail ends at the junction with the Slope Trail, the
snowmobile trail, and the Spring Brook Crossing. The
Slope Trail climbs up to the Ridge Trail near the true
summit of Mount Megunticook.

Ski Shelter Trail

Distances from Youngtown Road

> *to* Bald Rock Mountain Trail and Cameron Mountain
> Trail: 1.3 mi., 50 min.
>
> *to* Sky Blue Trail junction: 1.8 mi., 1 hr.
>
> *to* Zeke's Trail junction: 2.5 mi., 1 hr. 30 min.
>
> *to* junction with Slope and snowmobile trails: 3 mi.
> (4.8 km.), 1 hr. 45 min.

BALD ROCK MOUNTAIN (1100 ft./335 m.)

About 2.5 mi. northeast of Mount Megunticook, this
mountain offers fine views from its ledgy summit. The
Bald Rock Mountain Trail traverses the mountain from
US 1 to the Ski Shelter Trail. There is *no dependable
water* on the upper part of this route.

From the Ski Shelter Trail, the Bald Rock Mountain
Trail diverges left (east) 1.3 mi. from Youngtown Road.
The trail, a well-worn path, climbs to the summit. From
there, it descends southeast quite steeply at first and then
more gradually. It reaches the west side of US 1 at telephone pole 106, about 4 mi. north of Camden, just north
of the Knox-Waldo County line and just south of the
Red Barn Shop.

Bald Rock Mountain Trail

Distances from Ski Shelter Trail

   to Bald Rock Mountain summit: 0.8 mi. (1.3 km.), 30 min.

   to US 1: 2.7 mi. (4.3 km.), 1 hr. 35 min.

Cameron Mountain Trail

This interesting trail diverges right (west) from the Ski Shelter Trail about 100 yd. beyond the Bald Rock Mountain Trail. At about 0.1 mi. it turns left (avoid the first left), following an old town road. It crosses Black Brook and rises gradually past abandoned farmland, old cellar holes, and apple trees. The trail then follows the boundary of Camden Hills State Park and passes about 0.1 mi. to the south of the summit of Cameron Mountain. Then it descends and in about 300 yd. comes to a junction. The north (right) fork descends and ends at the Youngtown Road in about 0.5 mi. (no sign at road, Central Maine Power pole number 91). The Cameron Mountain Trail turns left (south) and starts to climb. In about 0.8 mi. the Sky Blue Trail diverges left. In another 200 ft. the Cameron Mountain Trail ends at Zeke's Trail.

Cameron Mountain Trail

Distances from Ski Shelter Trail (100 yd. beyond Bald Rock Mountain Trail)

   to Cameron Mountain, south of summit: *est.* 1.0 mi., 35 min.

   to junction with trail to Youngtown Road: 1.1 mi., *est.* 40 min.

   to Sky Blue Trail and Zeke's Trail junctions: 1.9 mi., 1 hr. 25 min.

   to Megunticook summit (via Zeke's and Ridge trails): 3.7 mi. (5.9 km.), 2 hr. 25 min.

Sky Blue Trail

This trail has been cleared and its cairns rebuilt. Although it offers few long views, it makes a very pretty walk in the woods. The Sky Blue Trail leaves Ski Shelter Trail about 0.3 mi. southwest of the start of the Cameron Mountain Trail. It follows a course west parallel to the Cameron Mountain Trail and Zeke's Trail, about halfway between the two. At about 1.5 mi. it reaches the Cameron Mountain Trail. At this junction, go left to reach Zeke's Trail or right to reach Cameron Mountain.

Sky Blue Trail

Distances from Ski Shelter Trail

    to start (via Ski Shelter Trail): 0.5 mi., 15 min.

    to Cameron Mountain Trail junction: 2.0 mi. (3.2 km.), 1 hr. 30 min.

Zeke's Trail

This trail diverges right (west) from the Ski Shelter Trail about 2.5 mi. from the start of the trail. The Cameron Mountain Trail diverges right (north) at 0.8 mi. and leads to a junction with the Sky Blue Trail, to Cameron Mountain, and to Youngtown Rd. At 1.3 mi. a trail (sign) leads right to Zeke's Lookout which, after a short, steep climb, offers good views of Bald Rock Mountain and Upper Penobscot Bay. Zeke's Trail ends at its junction with the Ridge Trail, about 1 mi. northwest of the summit of Mount Megunticook.

Zeke's Trail

Distances from Ski Shelter Trail

    to start (via Ski Shelter Trail): 1.2 mi., 40 min.

    to Cameron Mountain Trail junction: 2. mi., 1 hr. 10 min.

    to Zeke's Lookout Trail: 1.3 mi., 1 hr. 20 min.

    to Ridge Trail junction: 1.6 mi. (2.6 km.), 1 hr. 30 min.

Slope Trail

This trail goes from the Ski Shelter Trail east across the bridge over Spring Brook to the summit of Mount Megunticook. The trail climbs steeply and reaches the Ridge Trail close to the true summit of Mount Megunticook.

Slope Trail

Distance from ski lodge
   to Megunticook summit: 1.5 mi. (2.4 km.), 1 hr. 15 min.

Camden Hills North Circuit

This is an interesting and scenic circuit hike. Starting at Youngstown Road, take Bald Rock Trail to Bald Rock Mountain and climb. Return to take Sky Blue Trail to Zeke's Trail and Zeke's Lookout. Return to the Cameron Mountain Trail and climb the mountain. Continue back by the Cameron Mountain Trail to the Ski Shelter Trail and Youngstown Road. This could cover 9 or 10 miles in all.

RAGGED MOUNTAIN (1300 ft./396 m.)

This mountain, 4 mi. west of Camden, is the highest of the hills to the southwest of Megunticook River and Lake. Its summit offers views comparable to those on the main Megunticook Range. There is a radio tower on the summit.

   To approach from Camden, follow US 1 south to John St. on the right (sign reading Snow Bowl). Follow signs to the Snow Bowl.

   Park at the Snow Bowl and follow the longest (T-bar) ski lift as far as it goes. Then enter the woods continuing in the same direction on a trail generally following a power line, climbing to the summit.

Ragged Mountain

Distance from Snow Bowl

    to Ragged Mountain summit: *est.* 1.1 mi. (1.8 km.), 1
    hr. 10 min.

BALD MOUNTAIN (1272 ft./388 m.)

Bald Mountain lies between Ragged Mountain and
Megunticook Lake. The approach is via Howe Hill Rd.
(Camden), which skirts the northeastern slope of the
mountain. Park at a dirt road 0.2 mi. southeast of the
Howe Farm (near height-of-land), near power pole 18.

    This jeep road climbs steadily, at first southwest;
then it swings northwest, leveling off, and becomes a
snowmobile trail. It enters the edge of overgrown fields
at 0.4 mi. At 0.5 mi. reenter the woods and in 100 yd.
turn left off the old road to the trail and climb gradually
through many switchbacks to the summit.

Bald Mountain

Distance from Howe Hill Rd.

    to field area: 0.4 mi.

    to summit: 1.4 mi. (2.2 km.), 1 hr.

FRYE MOUNTAIN (1139 ft./347 m.)

Frye Mountain is in Montville. There is a MFS firetower
on its summit. Refer to the USGS Morrill quadrangle,
7.5-minute series.

    A dirt road that is good enough for cars passes with-
in 0.3 mi. of the top. From the south and west, take ME
220 north from ME 3 near Liberty for 6 mi. (You will
pass the road to Center Montville at about 5 mi.) Turn
right (east) onto a dirt road at the sign reading Frye
Mountain, Game Management Area, State of Maine. At
0.6 mi. turn right (south). At 0.4 mi. cross a stream.
After another 0.5 mi. turn left (east). Drive 1.1 mi. (total

2.6 mi.) to the start of the short trail (right) to the summit (sign reading Firetower and Scenic View). An alternate route to the mountain is by going about 5 mi. south of Fosters Corner (in Knox) on ME 220.

The trail climbs southeast to the summit. The firetower views are excellent.

Frye Mountain

Distance from dirt road

to Frye summit: 0.3 mi. (0.5 km.), 15 min.

MOUNT HARRIS (1233 ft./376 m.)

The highest of the cluster of hills in Dixmont, Mount Harris has a firetower (locked) on its heavily wooded summit. This trail offers a pleasant woods-road walk, but no views in summer. The mountain is nearly halfway between Waterville and Bangor. Refer to the USGS Brooks quadrangle, 15-minute series.

The trail, unmarked, begins on the left side of ME 7, 1.6 mi. south of Dixmont Corner at CMP pole 43. Park by the side of the road.

The lower portion of the trail is a well-graded jeep road rising gently in an almost straight line to the east. The road turns to the left above the first building it reaches, a hunting camp, but returns to the straight line. After it reaches a brown lean-to (enclosed and locked), the road rises more sharply to an intersection at the crest of the col. The trail to the tower leaves to the left. It rises steeply at first, and then more gently to the large, wooden tower on the summit. The warden's cabin and another outbuilding (locked) are nearby.

There is *water* at a public spring at the side of ME 7, 0.1 mi. south of Dixmont Corner.

Mount Harris

Distance from ME 7
  to firetower: 1.3 mi., (2.1 km.), 1 hr.

MOUNT WALDO (1064 ft./324 m.)

This attractive mountain, with its many open ledges, is
in Frankfort. It is best known for the granite quarries on
its eastern side. Refer to the USGS Bucksport quadrangle, 15-minute series.

The trail approach is via US 1A in Frankfort. Turn
west on a blacktop road 0.15 mi. south of the Frankfort
Town Office Building. Go under a railroad overpass and
up the hill. At 0.2 mi., turn right on a blacktop road and
go to a fork, taking the unpaved left branch (rough but
passable by car) for 1.6 mi. Leave the car there and walk
up the cart road that heads off to the left across open
fields and ledges to the top with its microwave tower.
Long views to the west are visible all the way up the
trail, and on top the view takes in an area from the
Penobscot River Valley to Penobscot Bay.

Mount Waldo

Distance from parking place
  to Waldo summit: 1 mi. (1.6 km.), 45 min.

MONHEGAN ISLAND

This rugged island, with its spectacular sea cliffs and
pleasant hiking trails, is 12 mi. off the coast of Maine.
In summer, visitors can get to the island either by excursion boat from Boothbay Harbor or by mail boat from
Port Clyde. The village of Monhegan clusters around
the harbor, while the rest of the island is still in its natural state. The area of the island is about three quarters of
a mile by one and a half miles.

A hiking trail goes around the shore of the island, and many trails connect this shore path with the village. The southwestern section of the shore path gets more use and is easier to follow than the northeastern part. The most popular connecting trail goes from the end of the road in back of the lighthouse to Whitehead, the highest sea cliff on the island. Another popular trail goes through Cathedral Woods, a lovely stand of tall spruce.

Camping is *not* allowed on the island. There are several small hotels and guest houses, and visitors can buy maps of hiking trails at stores on the island.

SECTION 6
Southwestern Maine

This section includes the mountains of York and Cumberland counties and those of Oxford County south of and near US 302. The mountains and hills of southwestern Maine are low, and woods cover many of them all the way to the top. The summits that are open provide fine views of the surrounding country northwest toward the White Mountains and east and southeast to the coast. Because they are close to summer camps and population centers, many of the mountains in this section are popular hiking areas. Pleasant Mountain (2006 ft.) is the highest. Most of the others are around 1000 ft. or lower.

Camping facilities are available at Bradbury Mountain and Sebago Lake state parks, as well as at many privately operated camping areas.

BRADBURY MOUNTAIN (484 ft./147 m.)

This summit in Pownal is only partly wooded and offers good views of the countryside. Refer to the USGS Freeport quadrangle, 15-minute series, and the North Pownal quadrangle, 7.5-minute series.

To reach Bradbury Mountain, drive west from I-95 on ME 136 in Freeport and immediately turn left on Pownal Rd. Drive 4 mi. to Pownal center and turn right, northeast, on ME 9. Drive 0.8 mi. to Bradbury Mountain State Park, which has parking, picnic tables, playgrounds, and camping areas. A trail leads 0.3 mi. from the northwest corner of the picnic area to the ledgy south summit of Bradbury. Near the top another trail leads right to an outlook toward the north. From the summit a series of short, well-marked trails interconnect to cover the whole park area. Get information and a map from the ranger.

Bradbury Mountain

Distance from state park picnic area

   to Bradbury Mountain, south summit: 0.3 mi. (.5 km.), 15 min.

RATTLESNAKE MOUNTAIN (1035 ft./315 m.)

This summit in the southwestern part of Casco is a favorite climb for camp groups in the vicinity. Refer to the USGS Gray quadrangle, 15-minute series, or Raymond quadrangle, 7.5-minute series.

Approaching from the south on US 302, turn right on ME 85 about 0.5 mi. south of Raymond and drive 5.4 mi. to the intersection just north of the outlet of Crescent Lake. (From the north, turn south off ME 11 at Crescent Lake. The intersection is 2.6 mi. from ME 11.) Turn left (west) and follow Plains Rd. west for 0.6 mi. to Nubble Pond Brook (culvert). Park on the right near the brook.

The trail, blazed blue in 1986 (no sign), leads north along the western side of the brook and crosses under a power line. At 0.2 mi. it turns sharply right to cross the dam at the foot of Nubble Pond (an alternate trail follows the west shore). Then it skirts the rough eastern shore of the pond. Climb the hill and follow the top of the ledges to avoid the jumble of boulders at their feet. The ledges offer good views of the pond and Rattlesnake Mountain. The trail reaches an abandoned campsite on the lake shore at 0.5 mi., and it passes the head of the pond at 0.6 mi., joining the west shore trail. The trail runs north through abandoned pasture land. Continue on the main trail and watch for a left turn to the northwest. At that point the main trail begins to follow an old logging road. (The road to the right leads 0.6 mi. to ME 85, 0.1 mi. south of Camp Kokatosi.) It passes a *spring* and climbs more steeply to a saddle between the main summit to the north and a subsidiary peak to the south. At the saddle, the trail forks right, climbs gently to the foot of some ledges, and then turns sharp left and climbs to an open (south) ledge near the main summit. This south ledge offers good views to the south and west.

The trail continues past the actual summit 0.6 mi. to the north ledge (views). At 0.1 mi. beyond this is the junction, where the Sheep Pasture Trail starts down steeply to a woods road and ME 85, and the northern approach trail comes up from Webb's Mills. *Note:* In 1992, flagrant incidents of public misuse of the area caused the Friends of Nubble Pond to shut off this southern access, we hope temporarily. The mountain can still be enjoyed from the alternate approaches below.

For the northern approach to the mountain, go 0.3 mi. west of ME 85 on ME 11. Turn left on a dirt road, bear left past side roads for the 0.3 mi., and park. Take the woods road on the right which parallels a pair of stone walls. Follow the road and trail, which turn up left, for 1.2 mi. to reach the Sheep Pasture Trail junction above.

Rattlesnake Mountain

Distances from Plains Rd.

> *to* right turn over Nubble Pond dam: 0.2 mi., 5 min.
>
> *to* north shore of Nubble Pond: 0.6 mi., 20 min.
>
> *to* saddle: 1.4 mi., 50 min.
>
> *to* ledge near summit: 1.6 mi., 1 hr.
>
> *to* Rattlesnake main summit: 1.8 mi. (2.9 km.), 1 hr. 10 min.

MOUNT AGAMENTICUS (691 ft./210 m.)

This 691-ft. monadnock rises above the coastal plain of southern York County. Because it was so conspicuous, it was an important landmark for the early European explorers who sailed along the New England coast.

According to legend, it was also the burial place of either St. Aspinquid or Passaconaway. There is a firetower at the top, which was the site of a radar observation post during World War II. There is an unused ski development on the north slope of the mountain. Refer to the USGS York Harbor quadrangle, 7.5-minute series.

The best approach route from the south is the Maine Turnpike. Take the York exit right just before the toll gate; turn left across the turnpike and take the second right on Chase Pond Rd. (Go past Chase Pond on the left.) Turn left on Mountain Rd. and bear left at a small village. From this point it is 1.6 mi. to the Big A summit road. From the north, follow US 1 through Ogunquit. Turn right on Clay Hill Rd. Cross I-95 at 2.4 mi. from US 1, and at 4.1 mi. turn right on Mountain Rd. At 5.7 mi. reach the summit road.

The blacktop entrance road turns right and goes uphill 0.7 mi. to the summit. The dirt road straight ahead leads around the mountain 1.1 mi. to a road on the right, which leads 0.3 mi. to the parking area at the base of the ski lifts.

The road to the summit, which has two hairpin turns, should be driven with care. At the summit is a parking area and a closed ski lodge. Because of vandalism the road may be closed except when the firewarden is on duty.

The trail (now a jeep road) from the base starts from the northeast corner of the clearing and climbs, steeply at times, around the north and east of the mountain, joining the blacktop road near the top. A path diverges right from the trail near the top and leads through woods to the open summit.

Mount Agamenticus

Distance from ski-area base

  to Agamenticus summit: 0.5 mi. (0.8 km.), 30 min.

OSSIPEE HILL (1058 ft./322 m.)

Ossipee Hill (also called Ossipee Mountain) is located in Waterboro. There are several radio towers, buildings, and a MFS firetower on its summit. The views are especially good to the east over the flat Saco River Valley and on to Portland Harbor and Casco Bay. A forest fire in 1947 burned off much of the mountain. Refer to the USGS Buxton quadrangle, 15-minute series, or the Waterboro quadrangle, 7.5-minute series.

From ME 5 at Waterboro Center, take the crossroad southwest and immediately turn sharp right onto a paved road beyond the fire station. This road is good enough for all kinds of cars for 1 mi. The road rises gradually west-northwest about 1.8 mi. to a saddle. Then it turns south. A heavily gated road leads right to the summit.

Ossipee Hill

Distances from ME 5
   to saddle: 1.8 mi.
   to Ossipee summit: 2.6 mi. (4.2 km.), 1 hr. 40 min.

DOUGLAS MOUNTAIN (1416 ft./430 m.)

This small mountain in Douglas Hill, west of Sebago Lake, offers excellent views of the Presidentials, Pleasant Mountain, and the Atlantic Ocean. It is the highest of the Saddleback Hills. Refer to the USGS Sebago Lake quadrangle, 15-minute series.

Turn west from ME 107 onto Douglas Mountain Rd. There is no sign, but the intersection is 0.5 mi. north of the junction of ME 107 and Macks Hill Rd., and 1 mi. south of Sebago. After 0.9 mi. take a sharp left turn at the top of a hill and go 0.5 mi. farther to a loop-shaped parking area with a Nature Conservancy sign. The path starts between two stone pillars and is easy to follow to the top, where there is a stone observation tower and a large rock inscribed *Non sibi sed omnibus* (Not just for myself, but for all). An orange-blazed nature trail makes a .75-mi. loop from the summit.

Douglas Mountain

Distance from parking area

   to Douglas summit: 0.3 mi. (0.5 km.), 15 min.

MOUNT CUTLER (1232 ft./375 m.)

The open ledges of this summit in Hiram offer good views of the White Mountains to the northwest. Refer to the USGS Cornish and Hiram quadrangles, 7.5-minute series.

    At the junction of ME 5 and ME 117 in Hiram, cross the cement bridge to the west bank of the Saco River. Drive to the left of Hiram Village Store and continue west on Mountain View Rd. to the site of a former railroad station, where there is ample parking. The red-blazed trail starts across the tracks. In 100 yd. it turns right into a picnic area. (The trail to the left leads to an old gold mine.) The trail up the mountain continues straight ahead from the upper left end of the picnic area. It climbs the first ledge, and soon it turns sharply left. At this turn a faint trail to the right leads 60 yd. to an overlook above the ledges facing the bridge. The main trail soon reaches the long, open ridge of Mount Cutler, where south-facing ledges look down on the Saco River. The trail turns right (west) to the east summit, descends to a side road, then climbs to the main summit.

Mount Cutler

Distances from railroad station site

   to overlook: 0.4 mi., 20 min.

   to Mount Cutler, east summit: 0.7 mi., 40 min.

   to Mount Cutler, main summit: 1.3 mi. (2.1 km.), 1 hr. 5 min.

PLEASANT MOUNTAIN (2006 ft./610 m.)

This mountain on the Denmark-Bridgton town line rises abruptly from the comparatively flat surrounding countryside. It is an isolated mountain mass that stretches about 4 mi. on a north-south line. The ledgy, open main summit, where there is a MFS firetower, was once known as House Peak because there was a hotel there from 1873–1907. At least six other summits along the ridge also have names. The mountain was burned over in about 1860, and the forest and ledges are open enough for many views. The views from the main summit and from Big Bald Peak are outstanding. The southeastern face of Mount Washington, 29 mi. to the northwest, is particularly noticeable. The Shawnee Peak ski area is on the northern slope of the north peak. Refer to the USGS Pleasant Mountain quadrangle, 7.5-minute series.

Firewarden's Trail (Old Carriage Road)

Although not the most scenic route up Pleasant Mountain, this trail is the most popular one. It climbs to the main summit from the west. From US 302 turn south on the road opposite Cabins in the Pines Motel. This turn is 2.6 mi. west of the access road to the ski area and 7 mi. east of Fryeburg. On the side road, stay right at all road junctions. There is a farmhouse on the left 1.2 mi. from US 302 with free parking and trail signs.

For its first half, the trail is actually a truck road (sometimes open to private cars). It crosses a brook and climbs easily along its north bank. It recrosses the brook at the warden's cabin, where there is a *spring* and an approved campsite with a shelter. The trail narrows to a rough jeep road (not open to private cars) and swings right (southeast) and climbs steadily to the summit ridge. In the final 0.2 mi., the Bald Peak Trail (blue blazed) comes in on the left (sign) and there is a storm shelter to the right.

Firewarden's Trail

Distances from parking area at farmhouse

    to warden's cabin, spring, and campsite: 1.3 mi., 50 min.

    to Bald Peak Trail junction: 2.3 mi., 1 hr. 50 min.

    to Pleasant Mountain summit: 2.5 mi. (4 km.), 2 hr.

MacKay Pasture Trail (Southwest Ridge Trail)

This attractive scenic trail, which was once popular but has not been maintained for many years, is now again being used by hikers and local camp groups and for snowmobiling.

The trail leaves the northeast side of Lake Road (gravel) 3.5 mi. from the Moose Pond dam on ME 160 in Denmark and 2.9 mi. from US 302 in East Fryeburg. It begins at a logging yard (1987) opposite a gravel driveway leading to Long Pond, and follows a woods road marked by cairns, generally northeast through mixed hardwoods, then becoming steeper through pine forest. At approximately 0.4 mi. the trail turns sharply right (southeast), slabs across the hill, turns left, and reaches the open ledges at 0.6 mi. The trail ascends the mostly open ridge, northeasterly, marked by cairns to the southwest summit (1900 ft.) at 1.6 mi., with almost constant views over Moose Pond and Beaver Pond, as well as back to Long Pond. The trail, keeping to the ridge, descends over a short saddle and ascends to the open middle summit (1904 ft.) at 2.0 mi., drops into a saddle and passes a very small pond, swings east at approximately 2.4 mi., climbs to the ridge, and ends at the Ledges Trail (blue blazed) at 2.7 mi.

MacKay Pasture Trail

Distances from Lake Road

    to southwest summit: 1.6 mi.

    to middle summit: 2.0 mi.

    to Ledges Trail: 2.7 mi.

> *to* Pleasant Mountain summit: 2.9 mi. (4.7 km.), 2 hr.
> 15 min.

Ledges Trail (formerly called Moose Trail)

The trail leaves the western side of the paved road along
the western side of Moose Pond 3.3 mi. south of US
302, 1.5 mi. south of the Bald Peak Trail, and 0.6 mi.
north of the Walker's (narrows) Bridge separating the
two sections of Moose Pond. Park beside the road.

The trail, blue blazed, begins on a logging road
(sign) and gradually climbs through overgrown hardwoods. At 0.5 mi. cross two often dry stream beds.
Climb steeply for 0.3 mi. to open ledges with views
south and southeast.

The trail follows the ledges with the southwest sum-
mit visible ahead on the left. At 1.6 mi. the MacKay
Pasture Trail comes in on the left. It climbs through oak
scrub and blueberry bushes to the main summit tower.
Views to the west, including Fryeburg and the Saco
River basin and ponds, are outstanding.

Descending, the trail enters the woods on a south-
easterly bearing from the tower.

Ledges Trail

Distances from paved road

> *to* fork: *est.* 0.5 mi., 25 min.
> *to* lower end of ledges: 1 mi., 1 hr.
> *to* Southwest Ridge Trail junction: 1.6 mi., 1 hr. 30
> min.
> *to* Pleasant Mountain summit: 1.8 mi. (2.9 km.), 1 hr.
> 40 min.

Bald Peak Trail

This trail climbs the eastern side of Pleasant Mountain
to Big Bald Peak, and then runs south along the ridge to
join the Firewarden's Trail just below the main summit.

When combined with the Ledges Trail and a 1.5-mi. walk on the road, the Bald Peak Trail forms an enjoyable circuit. The ski trail described below also allows a circuit. There is *no sure water* on this trail during dry periods.

To reach the trail follow the paved road along the western shore of Moose Pond to a point about 1.8 mi. south of the road's junction with US 302, and about 1.3 mi. south of the Shawnee Peak ski area. Just south of Shawnee Peak East and 0.1 mi. south of the entrance to East Pinnacle Condominiums, a logging road on the right (between poles 30 and 31) leads into a yarding area (sign). Park there. The trail (blue blazed) starts west from the back right corner of the clearing, crosses a brook, and climbs steeply. At 0.2 mi. turn left and follow the north bank of the brook. At 0.4 mi. a short spur trail (sign) leads left to the Needle's Eye, a brook cascading through a cleft in the ledge. At 0.7 mi., just before the second of two small brooks, turn left (the North Link Trail turns right). Climb steeply through a stand of hemlocks, then come out of some scrub onto the ledges (cairn) and, turning left 100 yd., reach Big Bald Peak (1940 ft.) at 1.1 mi. There are excellent views in all directions.

At the cairn (and sign), the red-blazed North Ridge Trail comes in on the right from the top of the ski area via the north peak. *Descending,* note that the trail to the ski area continues straight ahead (north); the Bald Peak Trail bears right (east-northeast).

From Big Bald Peak, the Bald Peak Trail follows the crest of the ridge, first south and then southwest over two humps toward the main summit. At 2.2 mi. from the start, the trail joins the Firewarden's Trail, which leads left (south) past the storm shelter to Pleasant Mountain summit and the firetower.

Descending, the Bald Peak Trail diverges right from the Firewarden's Trail (sign) about 0.2 mi. north of the tower.

Bald Peak Trail

Distances from road

   to Needle's Eye Trail: 0.4 mi., 35 min.
   to brook crossing and North Link Trail junction: 0.7 mi., 50 min.
   to Big Bald Peak summit: 1.1 mi., 1 hr. 20 min.
   to Firewarden's Trail junction: 2.2 mi., 1 hr. 50 min.
   to Pleasant Mountain main summit (via Firewarden's Trail): 2.4 mi. (3.9 km.), 1 hr. 55 min.

Sue's Way *(formerly North Link Trail)*

This new trail (blue blazed) named in memory of Sue W. Blood, runs from a point 0.7 mi. up the Bald Peak Trail to the North Ridge Trail near North Peak. It allows an interesting loop hike over these two peaks.

Sue's Way

Distance from Bald Peak Trail
   to North Ridge Trail: *est.* 0.5 mi. (0.8 km.), 25 min.

North Ridge Trail

This trail begins at the base of the Shawnee Peak ski area. From the base lodge (which is open all year), the trail (red blazed) follows the chairlift directly up the mountain for 1 mi. to the warming hut at North Peak. The views are extensive. The North Ridge Trail leads south from the warming hut past the chairlift from Shawnee Peak East. Descend 100 yd. on the upper edge of the southernmost ski trail. At the first turn enter the woods on the right. Sue's Way (blue blazed) enters from the gully on the left. The trail turns due west, stays level for a bit, and then goes slightly downhill. At 1.2 mi. it turns left and slabs around the west side of North Peak through open pitch pine to a low peak about 0.5 mi. from the warming hut. The trail bears right to cross an open ledge with a view of Big Bald Peak and the Main Peak, then drops steeply into a col before heading up to Big Bald Peak. Just before the final climb up the cone, the Bald Peak Trail comes in from the left.

North Ridge Trail

Distances from Pleasant Mountain ski-area base lodge

    to warming hut: 1 mi., 1 hr.

    to North Link Trail junction: 1.1 mi., 1 hr. 5 min.

    to Big Bald Peak summit (via Bald Peak Trail): 2 mi. (3.2 km.), 1 hr. 45 min.

BURNT MEADOW MOUNTAIN (north peak 1575 ft./479 m.)

Located in Brownfield, this mass consists of three summits of nearly equal height. Deep cols separate the middle peak, Stone Mountain (1624 ft.), from the northern and southern peaks (1575 ft. and 1592 ft., respectively). Fire swept the entire mountain in 1947, and the trails that existed then disappeared. Trail development by snowmobilers and the construction of a ski area, now abandoned, have opened up new routes. Refer to the USGS Kezar Falls quadrangle, 15-minute series, and the Brownfield quadrangle, 7.5-minute series.

One approach is the eastern spur of the northern peak. This trail was reopened in 1984. From the junction of ME 113/5 and ME 160 in East Brownfield, drive west and south on ME 160 through Brownfield and past Burnt Meadow Pond. Park where the prominent eastern spur of the northern peak comes down to the highway. This point is 3 mi. from the junction with ME 113 and 0.4 mi. south of Burnt Meadow Pond. The cairned, blue-blazed trail heads west up the slope, staying on the southern edge of the ridge. At 0.4 mi. it passes over a small hump and drops slightly into a shallow col.

Beyond the col, continue west up the crest of the spur, which becomes steeper and more open, with a sharp drop off on the left, as it rises to the summit. There is *no water* on the trail.

Another approach to the summit leads up the slopes of the Burnt Meadow Mountain ski area, which is visible from ME 113. The ski area is south of the ME 113/60 junction on ME 160 and west of Burnt Meadow Pond. Follow the ski trail to the ridge, turn left, and travel along the ridge (snowmobile trail) for about 0.6 mi. to the summit.

Burnt Meadow Mountain

Distance from ME 160 (via eastern spur)

 to northern peak summit: 1.2 mi. (1.9 km.), 1 hr. 30 min.

PEARY MOUNTAIN (958 ft./292 m.)

The open ledges of this little mountain in Brownfield afford good views of the White Mountains and the mountains of western Maine. Refer to the USGS Brownfield quadrangle, 7.5-minute series.

At the junction of ME 160 and ME 113 in East Brownfield proceed north on ME 113 for 2.2 mi. to Farnsworth Rd. (5 mi. south of the US 302/ME 113 junction in Fryeburg). Turn west on Farnsworth Rd. 1.4 mi. to the bridge crossing the Little Saco River. The trail (snowmobile trail), not marked, begins at the east side of the stream and heads south on the level and then at a gradual grade to a col in a small clearing at 0.8 mi., with a fireplace on the right. Turn left (southeast) off the trail at this point through open woods and ledges 0.2 mi. to the south summit. There are good views in all directions. The main summit is 0.4 mi. northeast across open ledges and scrub without a trail. Views are to the east and north.

Peary Mountain
Distances from trailhead
> *to* col: 0.8 mi., 35 min.
> *to* south summit: 1 mi. 45 min.
> *to* main summit: 1.4 mi. (2.3 km.), 1 hr.

STARKS MOUNTAIN (1037 ft./315 m.)

This interesting, low mountain southwest of Fryeburg may be climbed by either of two routes. Refer to USGS Fryeburg quadrangle, 15-minute and 7.5-minute series.

Turn southeast from US 302 on a blacktop road 1.0 mi. southwest of ME 113. Cross the railroad tracks and follow a dirt road left 0.4 mi., near where the road and RR tracks turn east. To the right a well-worn jeep road leads 0.5 mi. to the summit.

For an alternate route, continue east on the dirt road to an open area on the right. This was the base for a long-abandoned ski area. Climb this slope to the top of the lift line, then join the jeep road to the summit ledges.

Starks Mountain
Distance from dirt road
> *to* Starks summit (either route): 0.5 mi. (0.8 km.), 25 min.

JOCKEY CAP (600 ft./182 m.)

This ledge near Fryeburg ME rises perpendicularly about 200 ft. above the valley, and offers an excellent view in all directions. At the top, there is a bronze profile of the surrounding summits, a monument to Robert E. Peary. Refer to the USGS Fryeburg quadrangle, 7.5-minute series.

A trail leaves the north side of US 302, 1 mi. east of Fryeburg, through a gateway between a store and the Jockey Cap Cabins. It soon reaches Molly Lockett's cave, named for the last of the Pequawket Indians, who is said to have used it for a shelter. The trail then divides. The left branch continues ahead, circling to the west; the right branch turns abruptly right and climbs steeply, hugging the east side of the ledge. Be alert descending, since there are many side paths that do not lead back to the cabins. (Round trip by either route: 25 min.)

Jockey Cap

Distance from US 302
    to summit: 0.2 mi. (3 km.), 15 min.

SECTION 7
Oxford Hills

This section describes the part of Oxford County that lies between US 302 on the south and the Androscoggin River on the north. The summits in the eastern part of the Oxford Hills are scattered. They include, among others, Streaked Mountain (1770 ft.) near South Paris; Speckled Mountain (2207 ft.) in the secluded Shagg Pond area; Mount Zircon (2240 ft.) south of Rumford; Mount Abram (1960 ft.), with its ski slope, near Locke Mills; and Mount Tire'm (1104 ft.), a good viewpoint in Waterford.

Farther west the hills build up into the continuous mountainous areas of the Evans Notch–Chatham region, which is along the Maine–New Hampshire border. Most of these mountains lie within the White Mountain National Forest, where the network of trails is more complete and signs and maintenance are usually better. This guide describes those summits that lie in Maine, plus West Royce, just over the line in New Hampshire. For a description of the other New Hampshire summits, see the *AMC White Mountain Guide*. Most of the western Oxford Hills appear on the Carter-Mahoosuc map in this guide.

The minerals of the Oxford Hills are interesting, especially the Mount Mica Mine near Paris Hill and the Bumpus Mine between Bethel and Lynchville.

There are four small White Mountain National Forest campgrounds in the region covered here. One is Crocker Pond, which you can reach from US 2 at West Bethel or from ME 5 south of Bethel. Hastings Campground is on the Evans Notch Rd. just south of its junction with the Wild River Rd. The Cold River and Basin campgrounds are 0.3 mi. west of the Maine–New Hampshire border and just south of Evans Notch.

STREAKED MOUNTAIN (1770 ft./539 m.)

Streaked Mountain, in Hebron and Buckfield, is a conspicuous, rounded summit with open ledges commanding fine views in all directions. It is easy to reach, and there is a MFS firetower on the summit as well as several antenna arrays. Refer to the USGS West Sumner quadrangle, 7.5-minute series.

Turn southeast from ME 117 on paved Streaked Mountain Road about 5.3 mi. northeast of ME 26 in South Paris and 5.3 mi. southwest of Buckfield. Drive 0.5 mi. past the power line, which leads straight up the mountain. The path starts to the right of the brook, soon enters the woods, and climbs steeply onto the ledges. After that it is an open climb to the top, as the trail slabs along the ledges to the left and joins the power line. *Descending,* leave the power line at the second pole, and slab left down the ledges. Be careful not to go too far south and miss the point where the trail enters the woods.

From the Buckfield side, the climb to the summit is longer but more gradual. Turn south off ME 117 on Sodom Rd., about a mile west of the center of Buckfield and 3.5 mi. east of the Buckfield/Paris line. Keep straight on paved and gravel road 2.3 mi. Park out of the way of logging operations where Times Square is painted in yellow on a small hemlock tree with a geodetic marker at its foot. The trail begins on a woods road to the right, crossing Bicknell Brook several times. Go right of the triangular piece where the road from Kings Hill comes in from the left. (See the snowmobile signs to Streaked Mountain.) The road widens through logging operations, then reenters woods. Bear left up into small hemlocks at the next fork, then through hard-woods. Turn left at the intersection with Whitman School Rd. (unmarked here). After passing a house on the left, the road swings around right, passes a cabin, and goes west and southwest up ledges to the summit.

Streaked Mountain

Distance from road on South Paris side
    to Streaked Mountain summit: 0.5 mi. (0.8 km.), 30 min.

Distance from Times Square sign on Buckfield side
    to Streaked Mountain summit: 4 mi. (6.4 km.), 2 hr.

SINGEPOLE RIDGE (1420 ft./433 m.)

Across the valley southwest of Streaked Mountain, this open ridge offers a broad view to the west and south-west. Brett Hill Rd. climbs south off ME 117, 3.1 mi. west of the Buckfield/Paris line for 0.4 mi. and turns west. The trail begins straight ahead (south) on a gravel road. Take the left fork at 0.4 mi. where the trail levels out. At 1.1 mi. take the right fork up the ledge or bear right at the next fork soon thereafter. The open ledge summit at 1.3 mi. continues to an outlook at 1.4 mi. Back down 0.1 mi. a road leads north by a quarry and down to rejoin the trail.

Singepole Ridge

Distance from Brett Hill Rd. turn
    to summit: 1.3 mi. (2.1 km.), 40 min.

CROCKER HILL (1374 ft./419 km.)

Crocker Hill, locally called Brown Mountain, in Paris, site of George L. Vose's 1868 panorama of the White Mountains, also offers views of the surrounding coun-tryside and other mountains. Refer to the USGS West Sumner quadrangle, 7.5-minute series.

Leave Paris Hill between two houses on a rise at the east end of Lincoln St. and continue east (Mt. Mica Rd.) for 0.8 mi. Take the dirt road left 0.8 mi. to a left turn and park. The Old Crocker Hill carriage road leaves straight ahead. The first road left leads to the old stamping mill. The main trail is a little farther on. Take the left fork where the old carriage road divides. The trail ascends gradually, then veers sharply right just above the mill. A few yards after the switchback, on the left, is the old mine shaft. Farther on, after a switchback left, the trail leaves the road and proceeds right up over ledges.

At the first summit clearing continue east to another clearing for an overlook of other hills and villages. An alternate return trail leads right (south) from the path between the two clearings. This trail proceeds down through the woods and comes out at the fork in the carriage road.

Details about local climbs and mineral dumps can be obtained at either the white or the red house on the dirt road (AMC members).

Crocker Hill

Distance from parking place
  to Crocker Summit: 0.5 mi. (0.8 km.), 30 min.

BEAR MOUNTAIN (1208 ft./367 m.)

Access to Bear Mountain in Hartford is via the Old County Rd. This road used to serve a firetower (now dismantled) and logging operations. It is no longer good enough for passenger cars. Refer to the USGS Buckfield quadrangle, 7.5-minute series.

From ME 4 at North Turner, turn west on ME 219. At 0.4 mi. turn right across the outlet of Bear Pond. Then take an immediate (0.1 mi.) left along the northern shore of the pond. Follow the blacktop road 2.3 mi. to a crossroad, turn right, and drive 0.1 mi. to the last house on the left. Ask the owner for permission to park in the farmyard. Follow the road past a brook immediately beyond the farm and, still following the road, gradually climb the ridge. As the road levels out, a trail to the right leads to the western summit of Bear Mountain. (Stay to the right at all intersecting logging roads.) There is a good view to the southwest.

The main road continues straight ahead toward the height-of-land. After passing a road on the left, it swings around to the right, south. Note the view to the south across Bear Pond. Trucks and jeeps can usually handle the road to the summit.

Bear Mountain

Distances from farmyard

>   *to* side trail to western summit: *est.* 0.8 mi., 35 min.
>   *to* main summit: 2 mi. (3.2 km.), 1 hr. 25 min.

BLACK MOUNTAIN (2133 ft./650 m.)

A broad, flat mass, this mountain lies in Sumner and Peru, east of adjacent Speckled Mountain. There are about five more or less definite summits, running roughly east and west. A trail with no signs climbs to the easternmost summit (2080 ft.) from the Sumner side. Refer to the USGS Worthley Pond quadrangle, 7.5-minute series.

Turn north off ME 219, 3.3 mi. west of Hartford/ Sumner Elementary School. Go left on Labrador Pond Rd. at 1.4 mi. At 2.4 mi. take the right fork onto Black Mountain Rd. (Redding Rd., the left fork, reaches Shagg Pond in 5 mi.) Drive another 1.5 mi. to the last house, bear left 0.4 mi. on a very rough dirt road, and park near a wood road on the right. Just before a logging yard, fork left across a brook on a stone culvert and take the right trail up the mountain (approximately 20° mag.). The road levels out in 0.5 mi. and crosses the brook.

Beyond the brook, pass the cairn in sight and soon bear left (northeast) onto the trail at the next cairn. The trail, partly eroded but well cleared in 1986, climbs steadily northeast to ledges and the eastern summit. The view to the east and south is only partly open. Woods cover the main summit, 0.5 mi. to the west-northwest, and there is no trail.

Black Mountain

Distance from parking place

    to Black Mountain, eastern summit: 1.3 mi. (2.1 km.), 1 hr. 20 min.

BALD MOUNTAIN (1692 ft./516 m.)

This mountain is in the northeastern corner of Woodstock near Shagg Pond. Together with neighboring Speckled Mountain, just to the east, it offers interesting hiking in a little-known, secluded area. It is easiest to reach by approaching Shagg Pond through Sumner from ME 219. Refer to the USGS Mount Zircon quadrangle, 7.5-minute series.

From the public landing at Shagg Pond, continue along the road for 0.5 mi. to a parking area at the top of the hill. (You can also reach the parking area by driving southeast from Abbotts Mill.) Park and take the road on the right leading to Little Concord Pond, which comes in sight in 0.4 mi. The trail up Bald Mountain leads right just before the road reaches the pond. The trail starts at the top of a 20-ft. ledge (cairn). To reach it, climb the crack of the ledge to the right. At the top, locate the cairn and from there hike up the ridge to the summit. From the ledges south of the summit is a fine view of the Shagg Pond area. The next item describes how to reach Speckled Mountain from the Bald Mountain ledges.

Bald Mountain

Distances from parking area
>   *to* Little Concord Pond: 0.4 mi.
>   *to* Bald Mountain summit: 1 mi. (1.6 km.), 1 hr.

SPECKLED MOUNTAIN (2183 ft./665 m.)

Speckled Mountain is to the east of Bald Mountain in Peru. The route to it from the summit of Bald Mountain drops into a col and follows the ridge to the Speckled summit. This mountain's outstanding feature is its rugged southern face—a line of nearly sheer cliffs. The views from the summit are extensive in all directions. Refer to the USGS Mount Zircon quadrangle, 7.5-minute series.

Route from Bald Mountain

From the ledge viewpoint on Bald Mountain follow the open ledge southeast to find a red-blazed trail north to the col, cross a snowmobile trail, then climb generally east to the ridge and summit of Speckled Mountain. The trail is obscure in some areas.

Route from Bald Mountain

Distance from Bald Mountain ledges
>   *to* Speckled Mountain summit: 1.3 mi. (2.1 km.), 1 hr. 10 min.

Speckled Mountain Pasture Trail

The Speckled Mountain Pasture Trail offers a direct approach to the mountain in addition to the traverse from Bald Mountain. Views are open to the north.

From ME 108 in West Peru, drive southwest past a school for about 4.8 mi. The trail starts as a very rough jeep road to the left (south) at the top of a rise.

From the main road, go 1 mi. to an old wood yard and a fork in the road. Take the right fork (the left fork is a snowmobile trail, which crosses the brook) and follow the road, passing an old camp on the right, for another mile to a large and obvious stone wall. Turn left and follow the line of the wall. After the wall ends in about 0.3 mi., just after crossing a wide logged area, its line becomes a yellow/red-blazed property line of the Oxford Paper Company and leads directly toward the ridge of Speckled Mountain. About 200 ft. from the ridge, the blazed property line turns west. From this point, you can follow the blazes, cairns, and yellow flagging to the summit.

Speckled Mountain Pasture Trail

Distance from paved road

> *to* Speckled Mountain summit (via ridge): 3 mi. (4.8 km.), 2 hr.

MOUNT ZIRCON (2240 ft./683 m.)

This mountain is in the towns of Milton and Peru. The view is well worth the climb. To reach Mount Zircon, take the highway between Rumford and Abbotts Mill on the south bank of the Androscoggin. Refer to the USGS Mount Zircon quadrangle, 7.5-minute series.

A rebuilt private road with a gate (which may be locked) leaves the highway just west of the former Mount Zircon Spring Water Company bottling plant. Take the left fork at 1.0 mi. Parking is possible at a clearing 1.6 mi. from the highway, after passing the spring house on the left at 1.5 mi. The trail, marked with orange arrows and blazes, leaves the eastern side of the path about 2 mi. south of the highway. It climbs steadily to the rocky summit. Hikers can get *water* just south of the foot of the trail near the site of the former warden's cabin.

Mount Zircon

Distances from main highway

> *to* start of trail (via truck road): 2 mi., 1 hr. 10 min.
> *to* Zircon summit: 2.8 mi. (4.5 km.), 1 hr. 55 min.

MOUNT ABRAM (1960 ft./597 m.)

Mount Abram, in Greenwood, offers interesting views to the north and west from high pastures and ledges. There is a ski area on the northeastern slope of the mountain, but it does not affect the route described here. A chairlift runs to the summit, however. Refer to the USGS Bryant Pond and Greenwood quadrangles, 7.5-minute series.

Take a paved road that goes east from ME 35 about 3 mi. south of Bethel and about 0.3 mi. north of the Albany-Greenwood town line. About 1 mi. from the turn take the left fork to B.L. Harrington's farm high on the western slope of the mountain. A dirt road bears right just before the farm and continues for 0.4 mi. up to the renovated old Harrington homestead. From the northern end of this building walk north, then to the right across an open field. The trail starts up the slope in about 0.1 mi., crossing a small brook at the edge of the woods. At 0.3 mi. take the right fork uphill in an easterly direction. (The left fork is a gently undulating snowmobile trail, through woods, around the mountain. It crosses a field to a large red house, reaching Howe Hill Rd. 0.6 mi. from the junction.) Continue up the trail, cross the clearing and then up steeply, reaching a hedgerow with snowmaking pipes at 0.7 mi. Clamber across, noting the location for return, and turn right up a wide ski trail to the summit and Ski Patrol hut. The best views are to the west, reached by an open path to a field a bit below the summit. The ski trail can be rejoined from the field's lower right corner.

Alternatively, you can leave ME 26 on a road leading south in Greenwood. At about 1.4 mi. the road bears left (west), and soon after that a road leads left to the base of the ski area. From there, you can follow ski trails to the summit.

Mount Abram

Distance from old Harrington homestead
*   to* Abram summit: 1.1 mi. (1.8 km.), 1 hr.

MOUNT TIRE'M (1104 ft./336 m.)

Mount Tire'm in the town of Waterford yields a good view, with little effort, of the Long Lake region. Refer to the USGS Norway quadrangle, 15-minute series.

Daniel Brown Trail (Old Squire Brown Trail)

The trail starts 100 yd. beyond and across the road from the Wilkins Community House. Park there or at the trailhead. A 1979 plaque on the left, reading Daniel Brown Trail, marks the start. Visitors are requested to stay on the trail, because it is on private property. After passing two stone walls, the trail curves left and crosses a gully. About 75 yd. beyond, the path forks. Follow the right fork. Then the trail emerges from the woods with widening views of the hills and lakes of Waterford and Norway. Along with views, the summit has woods and boulders to explore.

Daniel Brown Trail (Old Squire Brown Trail)

Distance from Waterford Center Community Building
*   to* Tire'm summit: 0.7 mi. (1.1 km.), 40 min.

SABATTUS MOUNTAIN (1253 ft./382 m.)

The chief feature of this summit in Center Lovell is the immense, nearly vertical cliff that forms its southwestern face. From the top of the cliff impressive views of the countryside spread from Pleasant Mountain to the Baldfaces. Refer to the USGS Center Lovell quadrangle, 7.5-minute series.

You can reach the trail by following ME 5 north from Lovell to Center Lovell. Turn right, (east) 0.7 mi. past the Center Lovell General Store and continue to a fork 1.8 mi. from ME 5. Bear right on Sabattus Mountain Road at the fork and drive 0.3 mi. on the dirt road, past a house, to a small parking area on the left. The trail starts opposite the parking area. It runs along the left side of a stone wall and through a logged area. It then climbs easily past an old firetower site to the open summit ledges. A faint trail to the east leads in 0.3 mi. to a large boulder.

Sabattus Mountain

Distance from parking area
   to Sabattus summit: 0.8 mi. (1.3 km.), 30 min.

EVANS NOTCH–CHATHAM REGION

The Cold River runs south from Evans Notch and flows into an extensive valley 3 mi. to the south. The valley floor is not over 600 ft. above sea level. It is divided between Stow ME, and Chatham NH; the line runs almost directly up the valley. The principal summits in Maine are East Royce (3116 ft.), Ames (2686 ft.), Speckled (2906 ft.), and, to the north of Evans Notch, Caribou (2828 ft.).

The AMC Cold River Camp is in North Chatham. Two WMNF campgrounds, Basin and Cold River, are at the north end of the valley, on the west side of NH/ME 113 about 0.3 mi. west of the ME/NH border. The WMNF Hastings Campground entrance is 0.2 mi. south of the junction of NH/ME 113 and Wild River Rd. Wild River Campground (WMNF) is reached by Wild River Rd. It is about 5.7 mi. southwest of the junction of Wild

River Rd. and NH/ME 113. The Kimball Ponds, South Chatham, and Fryeburg offer opportunities for fishing.

To obtain more current information about the condition of trails in the Evans Notch–North Chatham area, contact the WMNF Evans Notch Ranger District, Bridge St., Bethel ME 04217 (207-824-2134).

The 7.5-minute USGS maps are a very valuable addition to the map that comes with this guide. Trails are named on the 7.5-minute quadrangles. See especially those for Wild River in New Hampshire, and for Speckled Mountain, East Stoneham, Bethel, Center Lovell, and Gilead, in Maine. In the older 15-minute series, see the Bethel and Fryeburg quadrangles for Maine, and the Gorham and North Conway quadrangles for New Hampshire.

The Chatham Trails Association, Inc. (CTA), has published an all-new 1992 map of the Cold River Valley and Evans Notch. Copies may be obtained from 161 Summer Street, Danvers MA 01923-1136, or in season at Cold River Camp, AMC. The price is $5.00/map.

Evans Notch Rd. (NH/ME 113)

This scenic auto road, NH/ME 113, continues the Valley Rd. of North Chatham northward past the Brickett Place, under the impressive cliffs of East Royce, and through Evans Notch to Hastings. It crosses Evans Brook twice and ends 3.4 mi. farther at US 2, just east of the bridge over Wild River in Gilead.

Evans Notch Rd. (NH/ME 113)

Distances from the Brickett Place

> *to* Royce Trail (west): 75 ft.
>
> *to* service road to Speckled Mountain (east): 0.3 mi.
>
> *to* Laughing Lion trailhead: 2.1 mi.
>
> to East Royce (west) and Spruce Hill (east) trailheads: 3.1 mi.
>
> *to* Haystack Notch (east) trailhead: 4.6 mi.

to Mud Brook (east) trailhead: 5.6 mi.

to Caribou (east) trailhead: 6.3 mi.

to Wheeler Brook Trail (Little Lary Brook Rd.) (east): 7 mi.

to Hastings (west) trailhead: 7.5 mi.

to Roost (east) trailheads: *est.* 7.1 mi. and 7.8 mi.

to US 2/Gilead: 10.9 mi. (17.4 km.)

THE ROOST (1374 ft./419 m.)

This small hill, near Hastings, has fine views of the Wild River Valley, the Evans Brook Valley, and many mountains.

Roost Trail (WMNF)

This trail ascends to the Roost from two trailheads about 0.7 mi. apart on the east side of ME 113. The north trailhead is located just north of a bridge over Evans Brook, 0.1 mi. north of the junction of ME 113 with Wild River Road at Hastings ME; the south trailhead is located just south of another bridge over Evans Brook.

Leaving the south trailhead, the trail ascends a steep bank for 30 yds., then bears right (east) and ascends gradually along a wooded ridge. It crosses a small brook at 0.3 mi., then rises somewhat more steeply to emerge on a small rock ledge at the summit at 0.5 mi. Here a side trail descends 0.1 mi. west through woods to spacious open ledges where the views are excellent. The main trail descends generally southeast at a moderate grade and crosses a small brook, then turns right (west) on an old road (no sign) and follows it past a cellar hole and an old clearing back to ME 113.

Roost Trail

Distances from ME 113, north trailhead

    to the Roost: 0.5 mi., 30 min.

    to ME 11, south trailhead: 1.2 mi. (2.0 km.), 50 min.

Wheeler Brook Trail (WMNF)

The trailheads for this trail are located on the south side of US 2, 2.3 mi. east of the junction of US 2 and ME 113; and on the Little Lary Brook Rd. (FR 8) 1.6 mi. from its junction with ME 113, which is 9.2 mi. north of the road to Cold River Campground and 3.7 mi. south of the junction of US 2 and ME 113.

From US 2, the Wheeler Brook Trail follows the west side of Wheeler Brook, crosses the brook four times, and rises about 1400 ft., generally following an old logging road, to its highest point on the northwest slope of Peabody Mountain at 2.1 mi. (There is no trail to the wooded summit of Peabody Mtn.) The trail then descends generally southwest, swings left onto an old logging road, and reaches Little Lary Brook Rd. Turn left on Little Lary Brook Road, then left at the junction with FR 185, and continue to a locked gate near the bridge over Little Lary Brook, 1.6 mi. from ME 113.

In the reverse direction, proceed along Little Lary Brook Rd. about 100 yd. from the locked gate, then turn right at the junction where FR 185 continues straight ahead. The trail leaves the road on the right in another 0.3 mi. It is very sparsely marked at this end, so exercise care in following it.

Wheeler Brook Trail

Distance from US 2

   to gate on Little Lary Brook Road: 3.5 mi. (5.6 km), 2 hr. 30 min.

MOUNT CARIBOU (2828 ft./862 m.)

This mountain, called Calabo in the 1853 Walling map of Oxford County, is in the town of Mason ME. The bare, ledgy summit affords excellent views. The Caribou and Mud Brook trails make a pleasant loop.

Caribou Trail (WMNF)

This trail gives access to the attractive ledges of Caribou Mtn. Its west trailhead, which it now shares with the Mud Brook Trail, lies on the east side of ME 113 about 6 mi. north of the road to WMNF Cold River Campground. The east trailhead is on Bog Rd. (FR 6), which leaves the south side of US 2 1.3 mi. west of the West Bethel Post Office (there is currently a sign for Pooh Corner Farm at this junction, but no road sign) and leads 2.8 mi. to the trailhead, where a gate ends public travel on the road.

From ME 113, the trail runs north, crosses Morrison Brook on a footbridge at 0.3 mi. and follows the brook, crossing it several more times. The third crossing, at 1.9 mi., is located at the head of Kees Falls, a 25-ft. waterfall. The trail levels off at the height-of-land as it crosses the col between Gammon Mtn. and Mt. Caribou at 2.9 mi. Soon the Mud Brook Trail leaves right to return to ME 113 via the summit of Mt. Caribou, passing Caribou Shelter and Caribou Spring (unreliable) in 0.3 mi. The Caribou Trail continues ahead at the junction, descends more rapidly, turns northeast toward the valley of Bog Brook, which lies east of Peabody Mountain, and follows a succession of logging roads. At 4.8 mi. it bears left in a clearing, then bears left again on the extension of Bog Rd. (FR 6) and continues to the gate.

Caribou Trail

Distances from ME 113

> *to* Mud Brook Trail: 2.9 mi., 2 hr. 10 min.
>
> *to* Caribou Mtn. summit (via Mud Brook Trail): 3.5 mi., 2 hr. 40 min.
>
> *to* Bog Rd.: 5.4 mi. (8.7 km.), 3 hr. 25 min.

Mud Brook Trail (WMNF)

This trail begins on ME 113 at the same point as the Caribou Trail, about 6 mi. north of the road to WMNF Cold River Campground, then passes over the summit of Mt. Caribou and ends at the Caribou Trail in the pass between Caribou Mtn. and Gammon Mtn. Despite its ominous name, the footing on the trail is good.

From ME 113 the trail runs generally south, then turns east along the north side of Mud Brook, rising gradually, then crosses the headwaters of Mud Brook at 2.4 mi. and swings left (north) uphill, climbing more steeply. The trail crosses several smaller brooks and at 3.3 mi. comes out on a small, bare knob with excellent views east. It turns left into the woods and makes a short descent into a small ravine, then emerges above timberline and crosses ledges to the summit of Mt. Caribou at 1.8 mi. It then descends north, passes Caribou Spring *(unreliable water source)* left at 4.1 mi. and Caribou Shelter right 70 yd. farther, and meets the Caribou Trail in the pass.

Mud Brook Trail

Distances from ME 113

> *to* Mount Caribou summit: 3.8 mi., 2 hr. 55 min.
> *to* Caribou Trail junction: 4.4 mi. (7.1 km.), 3 hr. 10 min.

Haystack Notch Trail (WMNF)

This trail, with good footing and easy grades but some potentially difficult brook crossings, runs through Haystack Notch. Its west trailhead lies on the east side of ME 113, 4.8 mi. north of the road to WMNF Cold River Campground. The east trailhead is located on the Miles Notch Trail 0.2 mi. from the trail's north terminus, which is reached by following the road that leads south from US 2 opposite the West Bethel Post Office to a crossroads at 3.1 mi., then taking the road that runs right (west), continuing straight ahead at a junction just beyond a small cemetery. The road becomes rather rough after about 1 mi. from the crossroads, and it may not be possible for some cars to drive all the way to the trailhead, which is about 2.5 mi. from the crossroads.

Leaving ME 113, the trail runs generally east along the east branch of Evans Brook, crossing it several times. The first crossing in particular may be difficult at high water. At 2.1 mi. it crosses through Haystack Notch and descends the valley of the West Branch of the Pleasant River, making several crossings of that brook, some of which may be difficult at high water. Eventually it merges into an old logging road and meets the Miles Notch Trail, where it ends.

Haystack Notch Trail

Distances from ME 113

   to Haystack Notch: 2.1 mi., 1 hr. 30 min.

   to Miles Notch Trail: 5.4 mi. (8.7 km.), 3 hr. 5 min.

ALBANY MOUNTAIN (1910 ft./582 m.)

Views from the open summit ledges are excellent in all directions. The area is just off the east side of the Carter-Mahoosuc map. Refer to the USGS Bethel quadrangle, 15-minute series, and the East Stoneham quadrangle, 7.5-minute series.

Albany Notch Trail (WMNF)

This trail passes through the notch west of Albany Mtn. Parts of its northern section still suffer from invasion by berry bushes as a result of the loss of mature forest in the windstorm of 1980, and the southern section, which is located mostly on old, overgrown logging roads, is poorly marked and requires much care to follow. Most hikers use the north section, which makes possible a loop hike over Albany Mtn. in combination with the

Albany Mountain Trail and the branch trail that runs from the height-of-land in Albany Notch to the base of the ledges on the Albany Mountain Trail. To reach the north trailhead, follow the road that leads south from US 2 opposite the West Bethel Post Office, which becomes FR 7 when it enters the WMNF at 4.5 mi. At 5.8 mi., turn right on FR 18, following signs for Crocker Pond Campground. The trailhead is located on the right in another 0.6 mi., just past the end of an extensive beaver swamp; the sign is hard to see from the road because it is located at the back of a small clearing and is blocked by a large tree. To reach the south trailhead, leave ME 5 at the west end of Keewaydin Lake, 2.4 mi. west of the East Stoneham Post Office and 0.7 mi. east of the Lovell-Stoneham town line, and follow Bartlettboro Rd. north. Bear right on Birch Ave. at 0.4 mi. from ME 5. Park carefully to avoid blocking any roads; the road that the trail follows is passable for at least another 0.2 mi., but parking is extremely limited.

Leaving the clearing on FR 18, the trail follows an old logging road that becomes well defined after the first few yards. At 0.6 mi. the Albany Notch Trail bears right at the junction where the Albany Mountain Trail diverges left (south). At 1.2 mi. it enters the region damaged by blowdown, where berry bushes are a nuisance, though the trail becomes markedly drier underfoot. Returning to mature woods at 1.4 mi., it climbs at a moderate grade to the left of a small brook, and at 1.7 mi. it reaches the junction where the branch trail leads left (east) 0.4 mi. to the Albany Mountain Trail at the base of the ledges.

The trail now descends moderately with a few steeper patches just below the pass, and crosses a small brook several times. It then runs mostly on a very old road until it reaches a much newer logging road at 2.4 mi. and turns left on this road (when ascending, turn sharp right). The

road, which is fairly easy to follow but rather wet and
overgrown, with little evident footway, passes junctions
with a snowmobile trail on the left at 2.8 mi. and 3.1 mi.;
at the second junction the road bears right and improves
greatly, then crosses Meadow Brook on a snowmobile
bridge at 3.6 mi. and continues to the trailhead.

Albany Notch Trail

Distances from FR 18

> *to* Albany Mountain Trail: 0.6 mi., 25 min.
> *to* branch trail junction in Albany Notch: 1.7 mi., 1
> hr. 15 min.
> *to* trailhead on Birch Ave.: 4.2 mi. (6.7 km), 2 hr. 30
> min.

Albany Mountain Trail (WMNF)

This trail ascends the north slope of Albany Mtn. to an
open ledge near its summit that affords a good view east
and north. It begins on the Albany Notch Trail 0.6 mi.
from FR 18.

Leaving the Albany Notch Trail, it soon turns left
onto a skidder road that it follows for 20 yd., then bears
right off it and continues to ascend moderately through
woods where there has been some light to moderate
wind damage. At 0.6 mi. the trail turns right at the foot
of a small, mossy rock face, and climbs to the junction
at 0.9 mi. where the branch trail leads right (west) 0.4
mi. to the Albany Notch Trail at the height-of-land in
Albany Notch. Soon the trail passes a ledge with a good
view of the Baldfaces and Mt. Washington and continues to the northeast outlook, where regular marking
ends. The true summit, wooded and not reached by any
well-defined trail, is located about 100 yd. south. The
summit area has other viewpoints not reached by the
trail that repay efforts devoted to cautious exploration
by experienced hikers. The best viewpoint on the moun-

tain lies about 0.1 mi. southwest of the true summit; a
sketchy and incomplete line of cairns leads to it.

Albany Mountain Trail

Distance from Albany Notch Trail

  to Albany Mtn. upper outlook: 1.3 mi. (2.1 km.), 1
    hr. 5 min.

Albany Brook Trail (WMNF)

This short, easy trail follows the shore of Crocker Pond
and then leads to attractive, secluded Round Pond. It
begins at the turnaround at the end of the main road at
Crocker Pond Campground (do not enter the actual
camping area), reached by following the road that runs
south from US 2 opposite the West Bethel Post Office,
which becomes FR 7 when it enters the WMNF at 4.5
mi. At 5.8 mi., turn right on FR 18, following signs 1.5
mi. to the campground entrance.

Leaving the turnaround, the trail descends to a small
brook and follows the west shore of Crocker Pond for
0.2 mi., then joins and follows Albany Brook with gentle ups and downs. At 0.9 mi. it goes straight through a
logging-road intersection with a clearing visible on the
right, and soon reaches the north end of Round Pond.

Albany Brook Trail

Distance from Crocker Pond Campground

  to Round Pond: 1.0 mi. (1.6 km.), 30 min.

SPECKLED MOUNTAIN (2906 ft./886 m.)

This mountain lies east of Evans Notch, in Batchelder's
Grant and Stoneham ME. It is one of at least three
mountains in Maine that have been known by this name.
The summit's open ledges have excellent views in all
directions. There is a *spring* about 0.1 mi. northeast of
the summit, off the Red Rock Trail.

Miles Notch Trail (WMNF)

This trail runs through Miles Notch, giving access to the east end of the ledgy ridge that culminates in Speckled Mtn. To reach its south terminus, near which the Great Brook Trail also begins, leave ME 5 in North Lovell ME on a road with signs for Evergreen Valley Ski Area; follow that road northwest for 1.8 mi., then turn right onto Hut Rd. just before the bridge over Great Brook and continue 1.5 mi. to the trailhead. To reach the north terminus, follow the road that leads south from US 2 opposite the West Bethel Post Office to a crossroads at 3.1 mi., then take the road that runs right (west), continuing straight ahead at a junction just beyond a small cemetery. The road becomes rather rough after about 1 mi. from the crossroads, and it may not be possible for some cars to drive all the way to the trailhead, which is about 2.5 mi. from the crossroads.

From the south terminus, the trail follows an old logging road generally north and at 0.3 mi. bears left off the road (arrow). It climbs over a small ridge and at 1.2 mi. enters another old logging road and follows it to the left for 0.2 mi., after which it leaves the old road on the right and soon crosses a branch of Beaver Brook. At 2.3 mi. it crosses Beaver Brook, passes over a steeper section, runs in the gully of a small brook, and reaches Miles Notch at 2.9 mi. The trail now descends gradually, and at 3.2 mi. the Red Rock Trail leaves on the left for the summit of Speckled Mtn. The Miles Notch Trail then descends moderately, crossing Miles Brook repeatedly. At 5.4 mi. the Haystack Notch Trail enters on the left and the Miles Notch Trail soon reaches its northern end.

Miles Notch Trail

Distances from south terminus

   to Red Rock Trail: 3.2 mi., 2 hr. 15 min.
   to north terminus: 5.6 mi. (9.0 km.), 3 hr. 30 min.

Red Rock Trail (WMNF)

This trail ascends Speckled Mtn. from the Miles Notch Trail 0.3 mi. north of Miles Notch, 3.2 mi. from its southern trailhead and 2.4 mi. from its northern trailhead. It traverses the long eastern ridge of the Speckled Mtn. range, affording fine views of the surrounding mountains.

It leaves the Miles Notch Trail, descends to cross Miles Brook in its ravine, then angles up the north slope of Miles Knob and gains the ridgecrest northwest of that summit. It descends to a col, then ascends to the summit of Red Rock Mtn. at 1.2 mi. and follows the ridge, with several ups and downs, over Butters Mtn. at 2.5 mi. and then on to the next col to the west. Here, at 3.4 mi., the Great Brook Trail diverges left (east) and descends southeast to its trailhead, very close to the southern trailhead of the Miles Notch Trail. The Red Rock Trail swings south, crosses the summit of Durgin Mtn. at 4.4 mi., then runs generally southwest to the junction with the Cold Brook Trail and Bickford Brook Trail 30 yd. east of the summit of Speckled Mtn. There is a *spring* near the trail about 0.1 mi. east of the summit.

Red Rock Trail

Distances from Miles Notch Trail

 to Great Brook Trail: 3.4 mi., 2 hr. 15 min.
 to Speckled Mtn. summit: 5.6 mi. (9.0 km.), 3 hr. 50 min.

Great Brook Trail (WMNF)

This trail ascends to the Red Rock Trail east of Speckled Mtn. To reach its trailhead, leave ME 5 in North Lovell ME on a road with signs for Evergreeen Valley Ski Area; follow that road northwest for 1.8 mi, then turn right onto Hut Rd. just before the bridge over Great Brook and continue 1.5 mi. to the trailhead, which is located about 100 yd. past the southern trailhead for the Miles Notch Trail.

The trail continues up the gravel road and bears right onto FR 4 at 0.8 mi. just after crossing Great Brook on a bridge with a gate. At 1.8 mi. it turns left onto a grassy, older road and follows Great Brook. At 3.0 mi. it crosses a branch of Great Brook, then bears left (arrow), becomes steeper, and continues along Great Brook to the ridgecrest, where it joins the Red Rock Trail in the col between Butters Mtn. and Durgin Mtn.

Great Brook Trail

Distances from trailhead
> *to* Red Rock trail: 3.7 mi. (5.9 km.), 2 hr. 35 min.
> *to* Speckled Mtn. summit (via Red Rock Trail): 5.8 mi. (9.3 km), 4 hr. 20 min.

Cold Brook Trail (WMNF)

This trail ascends Speckled Mtn. from a trailhead reached from ME 5 in North Lovell ME. Follow the road with signs for Evergreen Valley Ski Area for 1.9 mi. and take the first right (with an Evergreen Valley sign) just after the bridge over Great Brook, then continue to a gravel road on the right 2.2 mi. from ME 5. The WMNF sign is on the paved road, but it may be possible to drive 0.5 mi. on the rough gravel road to a parking area.

Beyond here the road becomes rougher, and in 0.7 mi. from the paved road it bears left past a gate. The next 1.0 mi. is on a muddy road that circles on contour to a cabin, the Duncan McIntosh House. Continuing ahead on the road, take the left fork, then the right. The trail descends to Cold Brook and crosses it at 1.9 mi., just above a fork. It then climbs and circles along the farther branch, passes west of Sugarloaf Mtn., and ascends the south side of Speckled Mtn., passing a junction left at 2.7 mi. with the Link Trail from the Evergreen Valley Ski Area. It emerges on semiopen ledges at 1.5 mi., passes two excellent south outlooks, and bears right to reenter the woods at 4.4 mi. At 4.9 mi. it

emerges on semiopen ledges again and soon reaches the
junction with the Red Rock Trail right and the Bickford
Brook Trail left, where it follows the latter trail left 30
yd. to the summit of Speckled Mtn.

Cold Brook Trail

Distance from paved road
> *to* Speckled Mtn. summit: 4.9 mi. (7.9 km.), 3 hr. 45
> min.

Link Trail (WMNF)

Park in the large lot below the "Inn" at Evergreen Valley resort in East Stoneham ME.

Follow the paved road uphill past the Inn and the
condominiums on the left. Continue climbing steeply
straight ahead on a dirt road. At 0.5 mi. turn right to the
Chalet, then turn left and pass the small structure on the
right (sign). This part of the trail, blazed blue, 1986,
leads generally north to meet the Cold Brook Trail at an
elevation of about 1200 ft.

Link Trail

Distances from Inn at Evergreen Valley
> *to* right turn to Chalet: 0.5 mi.
> *to* Cold Brook Trail junction: 1.4 mi., 1 hr.
> *to* Speckled Mtn. summit: 3.6 mi. (5.8 km.), 3 hr.

BLUEBERRY MOUNTAIN (1820 ft./555 m.)

This mountain is a long, flat, outlying spur running
southwest from Speckled Mountain. The top is mostly
one big ledge, with sparse and stunted trees. There are
numerous open spaces with excellent views, especially
the southwest ledges on the summit. There is *water* in
many places at the top except in dry seasons.

Stone House Trail (CTA)

This trail ascends to the scenic ledges of Blueberry Mtn. from Shell Pond Rd. To reach the trailhead, leave NH 113 on the east side 0.7 mi. north of AMC Cold River Camp and follow Shell Pond Rd. 1.1 mi. to a padlocked steel gate that makes it necessary to park cars at that point.

The trail leaves left (north) 0.5 mi. beyond the gate, east of an open shed. It follows a logging road, and approaches Rattlesnake Brook. At 0.2 mi. it merges with a private road (descending, bear right at arrow) and immediately reaches the junction with a spur path that leads right 30 yd. to a bridge overlooking Rattlesnake Flume, a small, attractive gorge. The main trail soon swings right (arrow) and at 0.5 mi. another spur leads right 0.1 mi. to Rattlesnake Pool, which lies at the foot of a small cascade. The main trail soon enters the WMNF and at 1.2 mi. begins to climb rather steeply straight up the slope, running generally northwest to the top of the ridge, where it ends at the Blueberry Ridge Trail only a few steps from the top of Blueberry Mtn. To reach Speckled Mtn., turn right on the Blueberry Ridge Trail.

Stone House Trail

Distance from Shell Pond Rd.

to Blueberry Mtn. summit: 1.5 mi. (2.4 km.), 1 hr. 20 min.

White Cairn Trail (CTA)

This trail provides access to the open ledges on Blueberry Mtn. and, with the Stone House Trail, makes an easy half-day circuit. It begins on Shell Pond Rd., which leaves NH 113 on the east side 0.7 mi. north of AMC Cold River Camp and runs 1.1 mi. to a padlocked steel gate that makes it necessary to park cars at that point. The trail leaves Shell Pond Rd. at a clearing 0.3 mi.

beyond the gate. It follows old logging roads north and west to an upland meadow, passing into the WMNF at 0.3 mi., then at 0.8 mi. begins to climb steeply up the right (east) margin of the cliffs visible from the road, then turns sharp left and begins to climb on ledges. The grade moderates as the trail runs northwest along the crest of the cliffs to the west, with views to the south. At 1.2 mi. it passes a *spring,* then swings right (north) and passes another *spring* before ending at the junction with the Blueberry Ledge Trail, 0.2 mi. west of the upper terminus of the Stone House Trail. A loop trail near its junction with this trail provides a scenic alternate route to the Stone House Trail.

White Cairn Trail

Distance from Shell Pond Road
    to Blueberry Ridge Trail: 1.4 mi. (2.3 km.), 1 hr. 20 min.

Blueberry Ridge Trail (CTA)

This trail begins and ends on the Bickford Brook Trail, leaving at a sign 0.6 mi. from its trailhead at the Brickett Place on ME 113, and rejoining 0.5 mi. below the summit of Speckled Mtn. (The upper part of the Blueberry Ridge Trail may also be reached from Shell Pond Rd. via the Stone House or White Cairn trails.) It descends toward Bickford Brook, and at 0.1 mi., just before the main trail crosses Bickford Brook, it crosses the Bickford Slides Loop.

    Bickford Slides Loop. This loop path, 0.5 mi. long, leaves the Blueberry Ridge Trail 0.1 mi. from its lower junction with the Bickford Brook Trail. At this junction, a spur path descends along Bickford Brook 50 yd. to the Lower Slides, while the main path crosses Bickford Brook and climbs along it 0.3 mi. to another junction near the base of the Upper Slides. Here the main path recrosses the brook at the base of the Upper Slides and joins the Bickford Brook Trail 0.9 mi. from NH 113, while a spur path 0.3 mi. long continues up along the brook and the Upper Slides, then crosses the brook above the slides and joins the Bickford Brook Trail 1.1 mi. from ME 113.

From the junction with Bickford Slides Loop the Blueberry Ridge Trail crosses the brook (may be difficult in high water) and ascends southeast to an open area just over the crest of Blueberry Ridge, where the White Cairn Trail enters right at 0.7 mi. An overlook loop 0.5 mi. long, with excellent views to the south, leaves the Blueberry Ridge Trail shortly after this junction and rejoins it shortly before the Stone House Trail enters on the right at 0.9 mi., a few steps past the high point of the trail on Blueberry Mtn. From this junction with the Stone House Trail, marked by signs and a large cairn, the Blueberry Ridge Trail bears left and descends to a spring *(unreliable water source)* a short distance from the trail on the left (north). Here it turns sharp right and continues over ledges marked by cairns, through occasional patches of woods, passing over several humps. The trail ends at the Bickford Brook Trail in the shallow pass at the head of the Rattlesnake Brook Ravine, about 0.5 mi. below the summit of Speckled Mtn.

Blueberry Ridge Trail

Distances from Bickford Brook Trail, lower junction

to Stone House Trail: 0.9 mi., 55 min.

to Bickford Brook Trail, upper junction: 3.1 mi. (5.0 km.), 2 hr 25 min.

Bickford Brook Trail (WMNF)

This trail ascends Speckled Mtn. from the Brickett Place on ME 113, 0.2 mi. north of the road to WMNF Cold River Campground. The trail enters the woods near the garage, then turns right onto an old WMNF service road to Speckled Mtn. at 0.3 mi., and the two coincide for the next 2.5 mi. At 0.7 mi. the Blueberry Ridge Trail leaves right (east) for the lower end of the Bickford Slides and Blueberry Mtn.; it rejoins the Bickford Brook Trail 0.5 mi. below the summit of Speckled Mtn., affording the opportunity for a loop hike. At 0.9 mi. the Bickford Slides Loop enters on the right from the lower end of the Upper Slides, and at 1.1 mi. the spur path along the Upper Slides enters on the right. The Bickford Brook Trail soon swings away from the brook and winds up a southwest spur to the crest of the main west ridge of the Speckled Mtn. range, where the Spruce Hill Trail enters left at 3.1 mi. The Bickford Brook Trail then passes west and north of the summit of Ames Mtn. into the col between Ames Mtn. and Speckled Mtn., where the Blueberry Ridge Trail rejoins right at 3.8 mi. The Bickford Brook Trail then continues upward to the summit.

Bickford Brook Trail

Distances from ME 113

> *to* Blueberry Ridge Trail, lower junction: 0.7 mi., 35 min.
>
> *to* Spruce Hill Trail: 3.1 mi., 2 hr. 30 min.
>
> *to* Blueberry Ridge Trail, upper junction: 3.8 mi., 2 hr. 55 min.
>
> *to* Speckled Mtn. summit: 4.3 mi. (6.9 km.), 3 hr. 20 min.

Spruce Hill Trail (WMNF)

This trail begins on the east side of ME 113 3.0 mi. north of the road to the WMNF Cold River Campground, opposite the start of the East Royce Trail, and ascends to the Bickford Brook Trail, with which it forms the shortest route (though not a particularly scenic one) to the summit of Spruce Hill at 1.5 mi. It then descends into a sag and climbs to meet the Bickford Brook Trail on the ridgecrest west of Ames Mtn.

Spruce Hill Trail

Distances from ME 113

> *to* Bickford Brook Trail: 1.9 mi., 1 hr. 30 min.
>
> *to* Speckled Mtn. summit (via Bickford Brook Trail): 3.1 mi. (5.0 km.), 2 hr. 20 min.

MOUNT ROYCE (east summit 3116 ft./950 m. and west summit 3202 ft./976 m.)

This mountain north of North Chatham has two distinct summits. While the summit of West Royce is in New Hampshire, this section includes the trail description from the junction of the trails to the two summits. For descriptions of other trails to New Hampshire summits from the Evans Notch–Chatham region, see Section 10 of the 1992 edition of the *AMC White Mountain Guide*.

East Royce Trail (AMC)

This trail, blazed in blue, leaves the west side of NH/ME 113 (off-road parking) just north of the height-of-land and 3.1 mi. north of the Brickett Place. It immediately crosses Evans Brook and rises steeply, crossing several other brooks in the first half mile. At a final brook crossing at 1 mi. (*last water*) the Royce Connector Trail to West Royce enters from the left. The East Royce Trail emerges on open ledges at about 1.1 mi., reaches an open subsidiary summit at 1.3 mi., and the true summit, also bare, 0.1 mi. farther. A spur trail can be followed over several more ledges to a large, open ledge with a beautiful outlook to the north and west.

East Royce Trail

Distance from NH/ME 113 (Evans Notch Road)

> *to* East Royce summit: 1.4 mi. (2.3 km.), 1 hr. 50 min.

Royce Trail (AMC)

This trail starts on the western side of NH/ME 113 about 75 ft. above the entrance to the Brickett Place (about 0.3 mi. north of the entrance to the WMNF Cold River Campground). Follow the narrow logging road for about 0.3 mi. Cross Cold River and bear right on the trail, which is blazed in blue. At 1.4 mi., the trail crosses and recrosses the river; then, crossing the southern branch of Mad River, it rises more steeply and soon passes Mad River Falls. A side trail leads left 70 ft. to a viewpoint. About 0.8 mi. above the falls, the logging road becomes a trail—rather rough with large boulders—and rises steeply below the imposing ledges for which this mountain is famous. At 1 mi. beyond the falls, the Laughing Lion Trail enters on the right. At a height-of-land, 0.2 mi. farther, after a very steep climb, a connecting trail to the East Royce Trail leads right 150 ft. to open ledges that offer excellent views of the Chatham Valley. The connecting trail continues 200 yd. to join the East Royce Trail.

From there, the Royce Trail levels off, turns left (west), descends slightly, and in 0.1 mi. crosses a brook. After that it descends, then climbs to the height-of-land between the peaks, where the Burnt Mill Brook Trail to Wild River Rd. (see the *AMC White Mountain Guide*) bears slightly right, while the Royce Trail turns abruptly left (west) and climbs the steep wall of the col. It then continues by easy grades over ledges and through stunted spruce to the summit, where it meets the Basin Rim Trail (see the *AMC White Mountain Guide*).

Royce Trail

Distances from NH/ME 113 (Evans Notch Road)

   to Mad River Falls: 1.6 mi., 1 hr.

   to Laughing Lion Trail junction: 2.6 mi., 2 hr.

   to Royce Connector Trail junction: 2.8 mi., 2 hr. 20 min.

   to West Royce summit: 4.0 mi. (6.4 km.), 3 hr. 30 min.

Laughing Lion Trail (CTA)

This trail leaves the west side of NH/ME 113 just north of a roadside picnic area, about 2.1 mi. north of the Brickett Place. It descends in a northerly direction to Cold River, then climbs steeply, mostly southwest and west, with occasional fine views down the valley. The trail continues north, generally steep, leveling off just before it ends at the Royce Trail, south of the col between East and West Royce.

Laughing Lion Trail (CTA)

Distances from NH/ME 113 (Evans Notch Road)
  to Royce Trail junction: 1 mi., 1 hr.
  to East Royce summit (via Royce Trail): 1.8 mi. (2.9 km.), 2 hr.

Royce Connector Trail (AMC)

This short trail connects the Royce Trail and the East Royce Trail. (Distance from Royce Trail junction to East Royce Trail junction: 0.2 mi.)

Leach Link Trail (CTA)

This trail gives access to Little Deer Hill and Big Deer Hill from Shell Pond Rd., which leaves NH 113 on the east side 0.7 mi. north of AMC Cold River Camp. The trail leaves Shell Pond Rd. just east of the bridge over Cold River and at 0.4 mi. crosses Shell Pond Brook (may be difficult at high water). On the far bank the Shell Pond Brook Trail enters on the left; this is an alternate route from Shell Pond Rd., 0.5 mi. long, that makes the Shell Pond Brook crossing on a snowmobile bridge (useful at high water). At 1.1 mi. a spur path leads right to the Little Deer–Big Deer trail, which is crossed in another 50 yd.; to the left the Little Deer–Big Deer Trail ascends Little Deer Hill, and to the right it leads to the dam at the AMC Cold River Camp. From here the

Leach Link Trail continues along the river, ending at the Ledges Trail.

Leach Link Trail
Distance from Shell Pond Rd.
   to Ledges Trail: 1.5 mi. (2.4 km.), 45 min.

Ledges Trail (CTA)

The Ledges Trail passes interesting ledges and a cave, but is very steep and rough, dangerous in icy conditions, and not recommended for descent. It leaves the south end of the Leach Link Trail and climbs steeply with numerous outlooks. At 0.2 mi. the connecting path that leads in 0.8 mi. to the Little Deer-Big Deer Trail south of Big Deer diverges right, affording an alternate route to the summit of Little Deer via the spur path (0.2 mi. long) that leaves it 0.2 mi. from the Ledges Trail. At 0.4 mi. the Ledges Trail divides; the right branch, which is slightly longer, rejoins in about 100 yd. Just above the point where these branches rejoin, the spur path from the connecting path mentioned above enters on the right, and soon the trail reaches the summit of Little Deer Hill.

Ledges Trail
Distance from Leach Link Trail
   to Little Deer Hill summit: 0.5 mi. (0.8 km.), 35 min.

Little Deer–Big Deer Trail (CTA)

This trail ascends Little Deer Hill and Big Deer Hill, running from the AMC Cold River Camp to Deer Hill Rd. (FR 9). It leaves Cold River Camp on a gravel road that runs east, passing the Conant Path on the right, the Tea House Path on the left, and then a spur left to the Leach Link Trail just after crossing Cold River on the dam. It crosses the Leach Link Trail at 0.3 mi. and climbs moderately past an outlook west, then bears left onto ledges and reaches the summit of Little Deer Hill at 0.9 mi. Here the Ledges Trail enters on the right. The main trail descends into a sag, then climbs to the summit of Big Deer Hill at 1.6 mi. It then descends the south ridge with several fine outlooks, turning left at 2.1 mi. where a connecting path to the Ledges Trail and Little Deer Hill leaves on the right. (This connecting path descends to a spur path at 0.6 mi., which leads right 0.2 mi. to the summit of Deer Hill, and then continues from the spur junction to end at the Ledges Trail at 0.8 mi.) Soon the main trail turns left again, then turns right onto an old logging road at 2.3 mi. Here a spur path follows the logging road left for a few steps, then descends in 0.2 mi. to Deer Hill Spring (Bubbling Spring), an interesting shallow *pool* with air bubbles rising through a small area of light-colored sand. The main trail descends from the junction to Deer Hill Rd.

Little Deer–Big Deer Trail
Distances from Cold River Camp

to Little Deer Hill summit: 0.9 mi., 45 min.

to Big Deer Hill Summit: 1.6 mi., 1 hr. 20 min.

to Deer Hill Rd.: 2.9 mi. (4.7 km.), 2 hr.

Conant Trail (CTA)
This loop path to Pine Hill and Lord Hill is frequently referred to (and may be signed as) the Pine-Lord-Harndon Trail, though it does not go particularly close to the summit of Harndon Hill; it should not be confused with the Conant Path, a short trail near AMC Cold River Camp. It is an interesting and fairly easy walk with a number of good outlooks, but since it passes through areas where the windstorm of 1980 destroyed the forest canopy, following parts of it may require care. It is reached by following Deer Hill Rd. (FR 9) and making a right turn 1.5 mi. from NH 113, then turning left almost immediately and parking near a dike.

The trail runs straight ahead along the dike across Colton Brook—Colton Dam is located several hundred yards to the right from here—and continues to the loop junction at 0.4 mi., where the path divides. From here the path is described in a counterclockwise direction. The south branch turns right and follows a logging road (Hemp Hill Rd.) to a level spot at 1.0 mi. near the old Johnson cellar hole, then turns left on a logging road, then left again in a few steps. The trail turns left again at 1.2 mi. and ascends Pine Hill, rather steeply at times, passing a ledge with a fine view to the west at 1.4 mi. It reaches the west end of the summit ridge and continues to the most easterly knob, which has a good view north, at 0.2 mi. The trail zigzags down past logged areas, crosses Bradley Brook at 2.3 mi. and then climbs, crossing the logging road that provides access to the mine on Lord Hill and passing an outlook over Horseshoe Pond. It reaches ledges near the summit of Lord Hill at 3.0 mi. where the Mine Loop leaves on the left.

Mine Loop. This path is 1.0 mi. long, 0.1 mi. shorter than the section of Conant Trail it bypasses. Except for one critical turn mentioned below, it is fairly easy to follow. From the junction with the Conant Trail near the summit of Lord Hill, it climbs briefly to the ledge at the top of the old mica mine and then descends on a woods road, and at 0.1 mi. it passes a spur path leading right 30 yd. to the mine. At 0.3 mi. it turns sharp left on a logging road, then at 0.5 mi. it reaches a fork and turns sharp right back on the other branch of the road, which shows less evidence of use. This turn is easily missed because it is difficult to mark adequately and the correct road is less obvious than the main road. (The main road, continuing straight at this fork, crosses the Conant Trail between Pine Hill and Lord Hill and continues south toward Kezar Lake.) At a clearing the Mine Loop leaves the road on the right and descends 50 yd. to rejoin the Conant Trail 1.1 mi. from its trailhead.

From Lord Hill the Conant Trail descends to the junction with the Horseshoe Pond Trail on the right at 3.2 mi., where it turns left, then soon turns left again and runs at a fairly level grade along the south side of Harndon Hill. It passes a cellar hole, and the Mine Loop rejoins on the left at 4.1 mi. At 4.5 mi. the road passes a gate, becomes wider, reaches the loop junction, and continues straight ahead across the dike to the trailhead.

Conant Trail
Distance from trailhead off Deer Hill Rd.
  for complete loop: 5.2 mi. (8.3 km.), 3 hr. 10 min.

Horseshoe Pond Trail (CTA)
This trail, blazed with bright yellow paint, starts from Deer Hill Rd. (FR 9), 4.7 mi. from NH 113, at a parking area at a curve in the road, where the pond is visible; it ends on the Conant Trail. It descends moderately past the Styles grave, enclosed by a stone wall, then enters a recent logging road and turns right on it. In a few steps, the Horseshoe Pond Loop, 0.4 mi. long, leaves left for the northwest shore of Horseshoe Pond. The main trail continues on the logging road at 0.3 mi., and the Horseshoe Pond Loop rejoins on the left at an incipient apple orchard in 100 yd. The trail ascends through the clear-cut resulting from timber salvage operations after the 1980 windstorm, following cairns and overgrown skid roads back into the woods to the old trail, which continues to the Conant Trail between Lord Hill and Harndon Hill.

Horseshoe Pond Trail
Distance from Deer Hill Rd.
  to Conant Trail: 1.1 mi. (1.8 km.), 50 min.

SECTION 8
Grafton Notch and
Mahoosuc Range Areas

This section covers the area bounded on the south and west by the Androscoggin River; on the north by Umbagog, Richardson, and Mooselookmeguntic lakes of the Rangeley Lakes chain; and on the east by ME 17. Grafton Notch, in the heart of this area, lies between Old Speck (4180 ft.) on the west and Baldpate Mountain (3812 ft.) on the east. It is traversed by ME 26.

The Mahoosuc Range, which appears on the Carter-Mahoosuc map that comes with this guide, extends southwest from Old Speck across the Maine–New Hampshire line to Mount Hayes near Gorham NH. As the crow flies the range is about 17 mi. long, but it is nearly 30 mi. long by trail. Mount Goose Eye (3870 ft.) and Mahoosuc Notch are among the many interesting features of the Mahoosuc Range. Both lie on the Maine side of the border, but the usual access is via the Mahoosuc Trail, which involves overnight camping, or via trails from the Success Pond Rd., which leads east from Berlin NH, to ME 26 north of Grafton Notch.

Rumford Whitecap (2197 ft.) is the most popular of the low range of mountains lying between Andover and Rumford.

To provide detailed descriptions of alternative approaches from the west to the trails in the Mahoosuc Range, this guide incorporates relevant trail descriptions from the Mahoosuc Range Area from the 1992 edition of the *AMC White Mountain Guide*. In addition to the map in this guide, refer to the USGS Old Speck and Gorham NH/ME quadrangles, 15-minute series; Old

Speck Mtn., Puzzle Mtn., Shelburne, and Success Pond quadrangles, 7.5-minute series, or map 7 in the MATC *Guide to the Appalachian Trail in Maine.*

GRAFTON NOTCH STATE PARK

Grafton Notch State Park contains 3132 acres extending on both sides of ME 26, west and north, from the Newry-Grafton town line to about 1.5 mi. north of the Appalachian Trail crossing. It includes the summit and northeastern slopes of Old Speck and the lowest western and southwestern slopes of Baldpate, including Table Rock.

The area is now a major hiking center. In addition to the mountain trails, short, graded trails and paths lead from some parking areas to points of interest nearby.

Scenic Areas and Short Walks
Step Falls
At the lower (southern) end of Grafton Notch, a short trail from the east side of the road leads 0.5 mi. to Step Falls, a series of cascades, with a total drop of 200 ft. The falls are on Wight Brook, which drains the southeastern slope of Baldpate Mountain. The area is a Nature Conservancy reservation and there is parking on the east side of ME 26 where the trail (sign) starts.

Screw Auger Falls and the Jail
Farther north, in the Pools, a parking area and picnic tables overlook Screw Auger Falls. The Jail, a large pothole, is just above the picnic area (about 0.4 mi. west of the falls). It is not visible from the road, and nothing marks its location; but you can find it easily by entering the woods to the south (left) of the highway about 100 yd. east of the first highway bridge above Screw Auger Falls. To reach the Jail from below, enter the woods about 150-200 yd. farther east of the bridge and go south to the brook. Follow the brook upstream to a falls. The Jail is on the right (north) bank.

Mother Walker Falls and Moose Cave

Mother Walker Falls are 1.2 mi. north of Screw Auger Falls. There is a parking area on the north side of ME 26. Moose Cave, a narrow and deep flume, is about 0.2 mi. farther north and 0.6 mi. south of the Old Speck Trail (Appalachian Trail). It is about 0.1 mi. from the parking area via a series of trails, walks, and steps. There is a grand view of Table Rock from the highway at this point.

Grafton Notch Parking Area

Near the height-of-land, 2.7 mi. northwest of Screw Auger Falls, there is a Maine Department of Parks and Recreation parking area (sign reading Hiking Trails) on the left (west) side of ME 26. All trails on Old Speck and Baldpate Mountain leave from this point. The Appalachian Trail crosses ME 26 at this point.

Spruce Meadow Picnic Area

The Spruce Meadow Picnic Area is approximately 0.6 mi. farther on ME 26 and offers outstanding views down the Notch. It also provides excellent facilities for picnicking.

OLD SPECK (4180 ft./1274 m.)

Old Speck, so named to distinguish it from the Speckled Mountains in Stoneham and Peru, dominates the western side of Grafton Notch. Long thought to be the second-highest peak in the state after Hamlin Peak on Katahdin, Old Speck has now yielded that honor to Sugarloaf Mountain and ranks third. There is an open observation tower on the wooded summit. Refer to the Carter-Mahoosuc map with this guide; the USGS Old Speck quadrangle, 15-minute series, or the Old Speck Mountain quadrangle, 7.5-minute series.

Old Speck Trail

This trail, part of the Appalachian Trail and blazed in white, ascends Old Speck Mtn. from a well-signed parking area on ME 26 at the height-of-land in Grafton Notch. From the north side of the parking lot follow the left trail; the right trail goes to Baldpate Mtn. In 0.1 mi., the Eyebrow Trail leaves right to circle over the top of an 800-ft. cliff shaped like an eyebrow. The Old Speck Trail crosses a brook and soon begins to climb, following a series of switchbacks to approach the falls on Cascade Brook. Above the falls the trail, now heading more north, crosses the brook for the last time (*last available water*), and at 1.1 mi. passes the upper terminus of the Eyebrow Trail on the right. The main trail bears left, ascends gradually to the north ridge, where it bears more left and follows the ridge, which has occasional views southwest. High up, the trail turns southeast toward the summit, and at 3.1 mi. the Link Trail (no sign) diverges left. The Old Speck Trail turns more south and ascends to the Mahoosuc Trail, where it ends. The flat, wooded summit of Old Speck, where an observation tower affords fine views, is 0.3 mi. left (east); Speck Pond Shelter is located 1.1 mi. to the right.

Old Speck Trail

Distances from ME 26

    to Eyebrow Trail, upper junction: 1.1 mi., 1 hr. 5 min.

    to Link Trail: 3.1 mi., 2 hr. 40 min.

    to Mahoosuc Trail: 3.5 mi., 3 hr. 10 min.

    to Old Speck Mtn. summit (via Mahoosuc Trail): 3.8 mi. (6.0 km.), 3 hr. 20 min.

Eyebrow Trail

The Eyebrow Trail provides an alternative route to the lower part of the Old Speck Trail, passing along the edge of the cliff called the Eyebrow that overlooks Grafton Notch. The trail leaves the Old Speck Trail on the right 0.1 mi. from the parking area off ME 26. It turns right at the base of a rock face, crosses a rock slide (potentially dangerous if icy), then turns sharp left and ascends steadily, bearing right where a side path leaves straight ahead for an outlook. Soon the trail runs at a moderate grade along the top of the cliff, with good views, then descends to an outlook and runs mostly level until it ends at the Old Speck Trail.

Eyebrow Trail
Distance from Old Speck Trail, lower junction
> *to* Old Speck Trail, upper junction: 1.2 mi. (1.9 km.), 1 hr. 10 min.

Link Trail
The Link Trail descends very steeply from the Old Speck Trail, 3.1 mi. from ME 26, to the site of the former firewarden's cabin, giving access to the East Spur Trail, which provides an attractive but much more difficult loop to the summit. It is blazed in blue and fairly well beaten, but may not have signs at either end.

Link Trail
Distance from Old Speck Trail
> *to* East Spur Trail: 0.3 mi. (0.5 km.), 15 min.

East Spur Trail
This trail ascends the east spur of Old Speck; it is much steeper and rougher than the Old Speck Trail, and can be fairly hard to follow, but it has much better views. *Caution:* This trail is not recommended for inexperienced hikers or in bad weather. It begins at the site of the old firewarden's cabin, reached from the Old Speck Trail via the Link Trail. Both trails are marked here only by blue blazes on rocks, and you must avoid the abandoned firewarden's trail, which was once the Appalachian Trail and can still be seen quite clearly running up and down the ravine. The East Spur Trail crosses the

brook and ascends steeply, then angles upward around the nose of the ridge, passing through an extensive area of open ledge with good views. It then swings left and climbs through scrub that still permits views, and ends at the north terminus of the Mahoosuc Trail in a small clearing 30 yd. north of the summit of Old Speck Mtn.

East Spur Trail
Distance from Link Trail
   to Old Speck summit: 1.0 mi. (1.6 km.), 1 hr.

Speck Pond Trail (AMC)
This trail ascends to Speck Pond from Success Pond Rd.; take the right fork of the road 11.4 mi. from Hutchins St. and continue 0.8 mi. to the trailhead. The trail leaves the road, enters the woods, and follows the north side of a small brook for 1.4 mi. It then swings left away from the brook, climbing steeply at times, passes a relatively level section, then climbs steeply to the junction at 3.1 mi. with the May Cutoff, which diverges right and leads over the true summit of Mahoosuc Arm to the Mahoosuc Trail. The Speck Pond Trail passes an excellent outlook over the pond and up to Old Speck, then descends steeply to the pond and reaches the campsite and the Mahoosuc Trail.

Speck Pond Trail
Distance from branch of Success Pond Rd.
   to Speck Pond Campsite: 3.6 mi. (5.8 km.), 3 hr.

May Cutoff (AMC)
This short trail runs from the Speck Pond Trail to the Mahoosuc Trail, across the true summit of Mahoosuc Arm, with only minor ups and downs.

May Cutoff
Distance from Speck Pond Trail
   to Mahoosuc Trail: 0.3 mi. (0.5 km.), 10 min.

MOUNT GOOSE EYE (3860 ft./1177 m.)

Mount Goose Eye in Riley ME shares a common trail-head with Mount Carlo (see below) and makes possible a very interesting loop hike.

Notch Trail (AMC)

This trail ascends to the southwest end of Mahoosuc Notch, providing the easiest access to this wild and beautiful place. It begins on a spur road that leaves Success Pond Rd. 10.9 mi. from Hutchins St. and runs 0.3 mi. to a small parking area. The trail continues on the spur road across two bridges, then turns left (sign) onto an old logging road at 0.3 mi. It ascends easily along a slow running brook with many signs of beaver activity, following logging roads much of the way with bypasses at some of the wetter spots. At the height-of-land it meets the Mahoosuc Trail. Turn left for the notch; very soon after entering the Mahoosuc Trail, the valley, which has been ordinary, changes sharply to a chamber formation, and the high cliffs of the notch, not visible earlier on the Notch Trail, come into sight.

Notch Trail

Distance from spur road off Success Pond Rd.
    to Mahoosuc Trail: 2.2 mi. (3.5 km.), 1 hr. 30 min.

Wright Trail

This new Maine Bureau of Public Lands trail, rated strenuous or difficult, climbs the east side of Goose Eye Mtn. from the Sunday River Road in Ketcham. For a loop, it splits near the upper end into a north-fork ascent through old-growth forest and a south-fork descent affording particularly scenic valley views from the ridge.

From Bethel take ME 2 and 26 north for 3 mi. Turn left onto the Sunday River Road and follow it past Artist Covered Bridge for about 7 mi. The road turns left at a junction with Twin Bridges (steel). Cross the bridges and immediately turn right. Follow this dirt road for another 1.5 mi. until it crosses Goose Eye Brook on the only bridge. The trailhead and parking lot are on the left 200 yds. up the road.

The Wright Trail, with blue blazes, leaves the south side of this parking lot and heads toward Goose Eye Brook. It follows along the north side of the brook for 0.5 mi. past several large pools and a 30-ft. gorge before turning left onto an old logging road. It follows this road for 0.3 mi., again turns left, and descends 0.1 mi. to the confluence of Goose Eye Brook and an unnamed feeder stream. Stay on the north side of this stream for 150 yds., turn sharply left, and cross it. For the next 1.3 mi., the trail more or less follows the north bank of Goose Eye Brook, then splits into two sections of a loop.

The north fork continues along Goose Eye Brook for 0.2 mi., crossing it twice before veering right and climbing moderately from the valley floor. The trail then passes beneath several large rock slabs, and comes out on one (0.3 mi.). From here the whole of a cirque formation can be seen. The trail descends off the lower slabs, crosses the valley and begins a steep climb to the ridge (0.5 mi.). It lightens to a moderate climb and turns sharply right to cross the last year-round *stream* at about 3100 ft. Continuing at a moderate to steep climb for 0.3 mi., it meets the AT. Turn left and climb the steep slabs of East Peak, 0.1 mi. to the summit. Continue south on the AT for another 0.1 mi. to the junction with the south fork of the Wright Trail.

Descending off the Mahoosuc Ridge down a subsidiary ridge line for 1.7 mi., the Wright Trail crosses over two peaks and one exposed slab before descending steeply into a saddle, 0.2 mi. It weaves its way through to the north side of the saddle and descends moderately for

0.6 mi. to Goose Eye Brook. Cross the brook obliquely to the right and down to the junction of the forks.

Wright Trail

Distance from parking area

   to Goose Eye summit: *est.* 4 mi., 3 hr. 30 min.

   loop trip: 8 mi. (12.8 km.), 7 hr.

Goose Eye Trail (AMC)

This trail ascends Goose Eye Mtn. from Success Pond Rd., starting with the Carlo Col Trail 8.1 mi. from Hutchins St., and reaches the Mahoosuc Trail 0.1 mi. beyond the summit. This is a generally easy trail to a very scenic summit, but there is one fairly difficult scramble up a ledge just below the summit. From the road the two trails follow a broad logging road, and in 100 yd. the Goose Eye Trail diverges sharply left down an embankment. It then turns sharply right onto another logging road, while the Carlo Col Trail continues straight ahead on the first road. The Goose Eye Trail follows the logging road, crosses two brooks, and enters a more recent gravel road that comes in from the right (*descending,* bear right). In 100 yd. it diverges right (watch carefully for sign) from the gravel road, passes through a clear-cut area, crosses a wet section, and at 1.4 mi. reaches the yellow-blazed Maine–New Hampshire state line. The trail angles up the south side of a ridge at a moderate grade through hardwoods, climbs more steeply uphill, then becomes gradual at the crest of the ridge; at 2.6 mi. there is a glimpse of the peak of Goose Eye ahead. The trail ascends moderately along the north side of the ridge, then steeply, scrambling up a difficult ledge that may be dangerous if wet or icy, then comes out on the open ledges below the summit. From the summit, which has magnificent views, the trail continues 0.1 mi. to the Mahoosuc Trail, which turns right (southbound) and runs straight ahead (northbound).

Goose Eye Trail
Distances from Success Pond Rd.
   to Goose Eye Mtn. summit: 3.1 mi., 2 hr. 40 min.
   to Mahoosuc Trail: 3.2 mi. (5.2 km.), 2 hr. 45 min.

MOUNT CARLO (3562 ft./1086 m.)

Mount Carlo, in Riley ME, may be climbed from a common trailhead with the Goose Eye Trail on Success Pond Rd., 8.5 mi. from Berlin and 11.5 mi. from ME 26.

Carlo Col Trail (AMC)

This trail ascends to the Mahoosuc Trail at the small box ravine called Carlo Col; it leaves Success Pond Rd. in common with the Goose Eye Trail 8.1 mi. from Hutchins St. From the road the two trails follow a broad logging road, and in 100 yd. the Goose Eye Trail diverges sharply left down an embankment, while the Carlo Col Trail continues straight ahead on the road, which it follows east for 0.8 mi. with little gain in elevation. Turning left off the road at a log yard, the trail immediately crosses the main brook (may be difficult at high water), continues near it for about 0.3 mi., then turns away from the brook, and bends east up the rather steep south bank of the south branch. Avoiding several false crossings of the brook, it climbs to Carlo Col Shelter at 2.4 mi. (*last water*, perhaps for several miles). The trail continues up the dry ravine and ends at the Mahoosuc Trail at Carlo Col. There is a fine outlook ledge a short distance to the right (west) on the Mahoosuc Trail.

Carlo Col Trail
Distance from Success Pond Rd.
   to Mahoosuc Trail: 2.6 mi. (4.1 km.), 2 hr. 5 min.

MOUNT SUCCESS (3565 ft./1087 m.)

Mount Success, in Success NH, (reached also from Shelburne on the south via the Austin Brook and Mahoosuc trails), is accessible from Success Pond Rd. 5.5 mi. from Berlin and 14.5 mi. from ME 26.

Success Trail (AMC)

This trail ascends to the Mahoosuc Trail 0.6 mi. north of Mt. Success from Success Pond Rd. 5.4 mi. from Hutchins St. Note that the trail sign is easy to miss. The trail follows a logging road, bears right at a fork at 0.1 mi., and passes straight through a clearing, entering the woods at a sign in 0.4 mi. Soon the trail starts to climb steadily on the road, and at 1.4 mi. reaches the upper edge of an area of small second-growth trees, swings right, and ascends more steeply. At 1.6 mi. a loop path 0.3 mi. long diverges right to a spectacular ledge outlook with fine views of the Presidentials and the mountains of the North Country. In a little over 100 yd. the upper end of the loop path rejoins, and the main trail ascends to a ridgecrest, from which it descends very gradually to a brook *(unreliable water source)* at an old logging campsite. The trail now makes an easy climb up a shallow ravine, part of the way in the bed of a small, unreliable brook (follow paint blazes carefully), and soon reaches the Mahoosuc Trail at the main ridgecrest.

Success Trail

Distances from Success Pond Rd.
   to Mahoosuc Trail: 2.4 mi., 2 hr.
   to Mt. Success summit (via Mahoosuc Trail): 3.0 mi. (4.8 mi.), 2 hr. 30 min.

Austin Brook Trail (AMC)

This trail ascends to the Mahoosuc Trail at Gentian Pond from North Rd., 0.6 mi. west of Meadow Rd. (which crosses the Androscoggin at Shelburne village). There is limited parking on the south side of the road. The trail passes through a turnstile on private land and follows the west side of Austin Brook, crossing the Yellow Trail at 0.4 mi. The trail follows logging roads along the brook, then crosses it and reaches the gravel Mill Brook Rd., which is normally gated at North Rd., at 1.1 mi. (Austin Stream). Turn left on the logging road, and continue past a brook crossing to the junction left with the Dryad Fall Trail at 1.9 mi. At 2.1 mi. the trail turns left onto an old logging road. At 3.1 mi. the trail crosses the brook that drains Gentian Pond and climbs steeply to the Mahoosuc Trail at Gentian Pond Shelter.

Austin Brook Trail

Distance from North Rd.
  to Gentian Pond: 3.5 mi. (5.7 km.), 2 hr. 30 min.

Lary Flume

This is a wild chasm in the south slope of the Mahoosuc Range that resembles the Ice Gulch and Devils Hopyard, with many boulder caves and one fissure cave.

There is no trail, but experienced climbers have followed up the brook, which may be reached by going east where the Austin Brook Trail begins its last 0.5 mi. of ascent to Gentian Pond.

Dryad Fall Trail (AMC)

This trail runs from the Austin Brook Trail to the Peabody Brook Trail near Dream Lake, passing Dryad Fall, one of the highest cascades in the mountains—particularly interesting for a few days after a rainstorm, since its several cascades fall at least 300 ft. over steep ledges. The trail is blazed in yellow.

The trail leaves the Austin Brook Trail on the left 1.9 mi. from North Rd., just past the third brook crossing. It gradually ascends old logging roads, then drops down (right) to Dryad Brook, which it follows nearly to the base of the falls at 0.5 mi. *Caution:* Rocks in the vicinity of the falls are very slippery and hazardous. From here the trail climbs steeply northeast of the falls. It then turns left on another road and crosses Dryad Brook at 0.9 mi., then climbs at mostly moderate grades to the Peabody Brook Trail near Dream Lake 0.1 mi. east of the Mahoosuc Trail. (*Descending,* watch carefully for the junction where the trail turns down steeply to the right of the logging road above the falls.)

Dryad Fall Trail
to Dryad Fall: 0.5 mi., 30 min.
to Peabody Brook Trail: 1.8 mi. (2.9 km.), 1 hr. 40 min.

Peabody Brook Trail (AMC)
This trail ascends to the Mahoosuc Trail at Dream Lake from North Rd., 1.3 mi. east of US 2. Overnight parking is not permitted at the base of this trail.

The trail follows a logging road between two houses and turns right onto an old logging road at 0.5 mi. It continues north along the brook and bears right at a fork at 0.8 mi., soon becomes a trail, and begins to ascend moderately. At 1.2 mi. a path leaves left and leads in 0.3 mi. to Giant Falls. The main trail rises more steeply, and at 1.5 mi. is a glimpse of Mt. Washington and Mt. Adams through open trees. The trail climbs a short ladder just beyond here. At 2.1 mi. it crosses the east branch of the brook, then recrosses it at 2.4 mi. From here the trail climbs easily to Dream Lake and the junction on the right with the Dryad Fall Trail at 3.0 mi., and continues to the Mahoosuc Trail.

Peabody Brook Trail
Distance from North Rd.
to Mahoosuc Trail: 3.1 mi. (5.0 km.), 2 hr. 20 min.

Centennial Trail (AMC)

This trail, part of the Appalachian Trail, begins on Hogan Rd.; this dirt road turns west from North Rd. north of where it crosses the Androscoggin River, just before it swings abruptly to the east. There is a small parking area 0.2 mi. from North Rd., and parking is also permitted at the junction of North Rd. and Hogan Rd.; in any case do not block the road. The Centennial Trail was constructed by the AMC in 1976, its centennial year.

From the parking area on Hogan Rd., the trail runs generally northwest. After 50 yd. on an old road, it bears left up a steep bank into the woods, levels off, and reaches the first of many stone steps in 0.1 mi. The trail ascends rather steeply, then more gradually, with a limited view of the Androscoggin River. It turns left onto a woods road and crosses a brook at 0.7 mi. (*last available water*). The trail then crosses a logging road and climbs past several restricted viewpoints, then descends to a sag in a birch grove at 1.6 mi. Climbing again, it soon turns sharply left and continues upward past ledges that provide increasingly open views. At 2.8 mi., the trail reaches an easterly summit of Mt. Hayes, where there is an excellent view of the Carter–Moriah Range and Northern Presidentials from open ledges. The trail descends slightly, then ascends across a series of open ledges to end at the Mahoosuc Trail at 3.1 mi. The summit of Mt. Hayes, with fine views, is 0.2 mi. left; the Appalachian Trail turns right (north) on the Mahoosuc Trail.

Centennial Trail

Distance from Hogan Rd.

to Mahoosuc Trail: 3.1 mi. (5.0 km.), 2 hr. 30 min.

MAHOOSUC RANGE AREA

This section includes the region along the Maine–New Hampshire border from Lake Umbagog southward to the big loop of the Androscoggin River from Gorham to Bethel. The area is drained principally by this river and its branches.

The Mahoosuc Trail extends the entire length of the Mahoosuc Range from Gorham to Old Speck, and there are many side trails. All of the trails in this section are east of NH 16, north of US 2, and west of ME 26.

Grafton Notch State Park includes the highway corridor of ME 26 and the summit of Old Speck. The remainder of the ridgecrest, followed by the Appalachian Trail from the NH/ME boundary to Dunn Notch, passes through Public Reserved Land.

In 1976 the State of Maine negotiated an exchange of land with the Brown Paper Company, now the James River Corp., which had owned most of the Mahoosuc Range summits. The state gave up rights in public lots and lands in various townships along the Mahoosuc Range extending west and south from the boundary of Grafton Notch State Park.

State laws restrict wood and charcoal fires to designated sites (shelters and Trident Col).

ACCESS ROADS

Success Pond Rd. runs from the east side of the Androscoggin River in Berlin to Success Pond in about 14 mi., and continues to ME 26 north of Grafton Notch. Over the years this has been perhaps the most difficult road in the White Mtns. for a person unfamiliar with the area to find; important landmarks disappeared or changed and the first part of the road itself was moved with astounding but unpredictable regularity. However, it now appears that the situation may have become somewhat stable. Leave NH 16 just south of Berlin, 4.5 mi. north of the eastern junction of US 2 and NH 16 in Gorham, and cross the Androscoggin on the Cleveland Bridge. At the east end of the bridge, the road (Unity St.) swings left and passes straight through traffic lights in 0.7 mi. from NH 16. At 0.8 mi. the road bears right across railroad tracks and becomes Hutchins St. It turns sharply left at 1.6 mi., at Frank's Village Store, and continues past the James River millyard. At 1.9 mi. from NH 16, where there has usually been a large sign reading OHRV PARKING 1 MILE, the Success Pond Rd. begins on the right (east). It no longer winds among the huge wood piles of the millyard, but you should still watch for large trucks, especially those entering from the right. The first part of the road has been difficult to distinguish from branch roads, but once past this area it is well defined. The road is not generally open to public vehicular use in winter. Trailheads are marked only with small AMC standard trail signs, often at old diverging logging roads with no well-defined parking area, so you must look for them carefully. The lower parts of the trails originating on this road have been disrupted frequently in the past by construction of new logging roads; great care is necessary to follow the proper roads, ascending or descending.

Success Pond Rd. leaves ME 26 southwesterly about 2.8 mi. north of the Old Speck trailhead in Grafton Notch.

Approximate distance from ME 26:

Speck Pond Trail, marked by a blue blaze and sign on low post, leaves left at about 7 mi.;

Notch Trail spur road (sign), about 8.5 mi.;

Carlo Col/Goose Eye trailhead, about 11.5 mi. (signs);

Success Trail (unmarked) about 14 mi.;

Hutchins Road, Berlin NH, about 20 mi.

North Road provides access to the trails on the south side of the Mahoosuc Range. This road leaves US 2 about 2.8 mi. east of its easterly junction with NH 16 in Gorham, and crosses the Androscoggin River on the Lead Mine Bridge; the Appalachian Trail follows this part of the road. North Rd. then swings east and runs along the north side of the river to rejoin US 2 just north of Bethel ME. Bridges connect North Rd. with US 2 at the villages of Shelburne NH and Gilead ME.

MAHOOSUC TRAIL (AMC)

The trail, here described from southwest to northeast, extends along the entire length of the Mahoosuc Range from Gorham NH to the summit of Old Speck. Beyond its junction with the Centennial Trail, the Mahoosuc Trail is a link in the Appalachian Trail. To protect fragile soils and vegetation, camping is limited to the tentsites at Trident Col and to the four shelters: Gentian Pond (with tentsites), Carlo Col, Full Goose, and Speck Pond (which also has tent platforms). The sites may have a caretaker, in which case a fee is charged. *Water is scarce,* particularly in dry weather, and its purity is always in question. This is a rugged trail, particularly for those with heavy packs—with numerous minor humps and cols, and many ledges, some of them quite steep, that are likely to be slippery when wet. ***Caution:*** Mahoosuc Notch is regarded by many who have hiked the entire length of the Appalachian Trail as the most difficult mile; it can be hazardous in wet or icy conditions and can remain impassable due to unmelted snowdrifts through the end of May and perhaps even longer. Do not be deceived by the relatively low elevations; this trail is among the most rugged of its kind in the White Mtns.

Part 1. Gorham to Centennial Trail

To reach the trail, cross the Androscoggin River by the footbridge under the Boston & Maine Railroad bridge, 1.3 mi. north of the Gorham Post Office on NH 16. On the east bank, follow the road to the right (southeast) along the river for 0.4 mi., then cross the canal through the open upper level of the powerhouse (left of entrance). Beyond, keep straight ahead about 100 yd. to the woods at the east end of the dam, where the trail sign will be found. The trail is sparsely blazed in blue. Turn left and follow an old road north along the side of the canal for 0.1 mi., then turn right uphill on an old logging road. At 0.8 mi. from NH 16 the trail crosses a power-line clearing, then bears right and reaches but does not cross a brook, and follows it closely for 100 yd. It ascends at only a slight grade to a side path at 1.1 mi. that leads right 0.2 mi. to Mascot Pond, just below the cliffs seen prominently from Gorham. Mahoosuc Trail crosses a woods road, then ascends a brook valley, which it crosses several times. At 2.5 mi. it passes a short spur (sign) that leads left to Popsy Spring, climbs steeply, and emerges on the southwest side of the flat, ledgy summit of Mt. Hayes. An unmarked footway leads a few yards right to the best viewpoint south over the valley. A cairn marks the true summit of Mt. Hayes at 3.1 mi. The trail descends on open ledges with good views north to the junction on the right with the Centennial Trail at 3.2 mi.

Part II. Centennial Trail to Gentian Pond

From here north the Mahoosuc Trail is part of the Appalachian Trail, marked with white blazes. It descends north to the col between Mt. Hayes and Cascade Mtn. at 4.1 mi., where there is sometimes *water*. The trail then ascends Cascade Mtn. by a southwest ridge, over ledges and large fallen rocks, emerging on the bare summit ledge at 5.1 mi. It turns back sharply into the woods, descending gradually with occasional upgrades to the east end of the mountain, then enters a fine forest and descends rapidly beside cliffs and ledges to Trident Col at 6.3 mi., where a side path leads left 0.2 mi. to Trident Col Tentsite, which has space for four tents. *Water* is available about 50 yd. below (west of) the site. The bare ledges of the rocky cone to the east of Trident Col repay the effort required to scramble to its top; a route ascends between two large cairns near the tentsite side path.

The trail descends rather steeply to the southeast, and runs along the side of the ridge at the base of the Trident, which is made up of the previously mentioned cone, the ledgy peak just west of Page Pond, and a somewhat less prominent peak between them. The trail crosses several small brooks, at least one of which usually has *water*. It follows a logging road for 0.1 mi., then turns left off the road at a sign and ascends to Page Pond at 7.3 mi. The trail passes the south end of the pond, crosses a beaver dam, and climbs gradually, then more steeply to a short spur path at 7.9 mi. that leads left to a fine outlook from ledges near the summit of Wocket Ledge, a shoulder of Bald Cap. The main trail crosses the height-of-land and descends east, crosses the upper (west) branch of Peabody Brook, then climbs around the nose of a small ridge and descends gradually to the head of Dream Lake. The trail bears left here, then right around the north end of the lake and crosses the inlet brook at 9.0 mi. Just beyond, the Peabody Brook Trail leaves on the right.

From this junction, the Mahoosuc Trail follows a lumber road left for 100 yd. It soon recrosses the inlet brook, passes over a slight divide into the watershed of Austin Brook, ascends through some swampy places, and descends to Moss Pond at 10.5 mi. It continues past the north shore of the pond and follows an old logging road down the outlet brook, then crosses the brook, turns abruptly right downhill from the logging road, and descends to Gentian Pond. It skirts the southwest shore of the pond, then drops to cross the outlet brook. A few yards beyond, at 11.2 mi., is Gentian Pond Campsite (shelter and tentsites), and here the Austin Brook Trail diverges right for North Rd. in Shelburne.

Part III. Gentian Pond to Carlo Col

From Gentian Pond Shelter the trail climbs to the top of the steep-sided hump whose ledges overlook the pond from the east, then descends moderately to a sag. It then starts up the west end of Mt. Success, climbing steeply at first to the lumpy ridge, and passes a small stream at 12.6 mi. in the col that lies under the main mass of Mt. Success. The trail now climbs rather steeply and roughly for about 0.5 mi. to the relatively flat upper part of the mountain, then ascends over open ledges with an outlook to the southwest, passes through a belt of high scrub, crosses an alpine meadow, and finally comes out on the summit of Mt. Success at 14.0 mi.

The trail turns sharp left here and descends through scrub, then forest, to the sag between Mt. Success and a northern subpeak, where the Success Trail enters left at 14.6 mi. The main trail climbs slightly, then descends moderately to the main col between Mt. Success and Mt. Carlo at 15.3 mi. The trail then rises over a low hump and descends to a lesser col, where it turns right, then left, passes the Maine–New Hampshire border signs, and ascends moderately again. At 16.4 mi. it drops sharply past a fine outlook ledge into the little box ravine called Carlo Col. The Carlo Col Trail from Success Pond Rd. enters left here; Carlo Col Shelter is located 0.3 mi. down the Carlo Col Trail, at the head of a small brook.

Part IV. Carlo Col to Mahoosuc Notch

From Carlo Col the trail climbs steadily to the bare south-west summit of Mt. Carlo at 6.8 mi., where there is an excellent view. It then passes a lower knob to the north-east, and descends through a mountain meadow, where there is a fine view of Goose Eye ahead, to the col at 17.4 mi. The trail turns north and climbs steeply to a ledgy knoll below Goose Eye, then passes through a sag and climbs steeply again to the narrow ridge of the main peak of Goose Eye Mtn. at 18.2 mi. Use care on the ledges. Here, at the ridge top, the Goose Eye Trail branches sharply left, passes the south branch of the Wright Trail leaving right, and reaches the open summit of the East Peak of Goose Eye Mtn. Here it turns sharp left (north) down the open ledges of the ridge, and enters the scrub at the east side of the open part. The north branch of the Wright Trail enters on the right. Beyond the col the trail runs in the open nearly to the foot of the North Peak, except for two interesting box ravines, where there is often *water*. At the summit of the North Peak, at 19.8 mi., the trail turns sharp right (east) along the ridgecrest, then swings northeast down the steep slope, winding through several patches of scrub. At the foot of the steep slope it enters the woods and angles down the west face of the ridge to the col at 20.8 mi. Full Goose Shelter is located on a ledgy shelf near here; there is a *spring* 80 yd. to the right (east of the shelter). The trail then turns sharp left and ascends, coming into the open about 0.3 mi. below the summit of the South Peak of Fulling Mill Mtn., which is reached at 21.3 mi. Here the trail turns sharp left, runs through a meadow, and descends northwest through woods, first gradually, then steeply, to the head of Mahoosuc Notch at 22.3 mi. Here the Notch Trail to Success Pond Rd. diverges sharp left (southwest).

Part V. Mahoosuc Notch to Old Speck

From the head of Mahoosuc Notch the trail turns sharp right (northeast) and descends the length of the narrow notch along a rough footway, passing through a number of boulder caverns, some with narrow openings where progress will be slow and where ice remains into the summer. The trail is blazed on the rocks with white paint. *Caution:* Use great care when traveling through the notch due to slippery rocks and dangerous holes; the notch may be impassable through early June because of snow, even with snowshoes. Heavy backpacks will impede progress considerably.

At the lower end of the notch, at 23.4 mi., the trail bears left and ascends moderately but roughly under the east end of Mahoosuc Mtn. along the valley that leads to Notch 2, then crosses to the north side of the brook at 23.9 mi. The trail then winds upward among rocks and ledges on the very steep wooded slope of Mahoosuc Arm with a steep, rough footway. A little more than halfway up it passes the head of a little flume, in which there is sometimes *water.* At 25.0 mi., a few yards past the top of the flat ledges near the summit of Mahoosuc Arm, the May Cutoff diverges left and leads 0.3 mi. over the true summit to the Speck Pond Trail. The Mahoosuc Trail swings right and wanders across the semiopen summit plateau from about 0.5 mi., then drops steeply to Speck Pond (3430 ft.), one of the highest ponds in Maine, bordered with thick woods. The trail crosses the outlet brook and continues around the east side of the pond to Speck Pond Campsite at 25.9 mi. (in summer, there is a caretaker and a fee for overnight camping). Here the Speck Pond Trail to Success Pond Rd. leaves on the left.

The trail then climbs to the southeast end of the next hump on the ridge, passes over it, and runs across the east face of a second small hump. In the gully beyond, a few yards east of the trail, is an *unreliable spring.* The trail climbs on the west shoulder of Old Speck, reaching an open area where the footway is well defined on the crest. Near the top of the shoulder the trail bears right, reenters the woods, and follows the wooded crest with blue blazes marking the boundary of Grafton Notch State Park. The Old Speck Trail, which continues the Appalachian Trail north, diverges left to Grafton Notch at 27.0 mi., and the Mahoosuc Trail runs straight ahead to the summit of Old Speck and its observation tower, where the rather poorly marked East Spur Trail enters.

Mahoosuc Trail

Distances from NH 16 in Gorham

   to Mt. Hayes summit: 3.1 mi., 2 hr. 20 min.
   to Centennial Trail: 3.3 mi., 2 hr. 25 min.
   to Cascade Mtn. summit: 5.1 mi., 3 hr. 35 min.
   to Trident Col: 6.3 mi., 4 hr. 20 min.
   to Page Pond: 7.3 mi., 5 hr.
   to Wocket Ledge: 7.9 mi., 5 hr. 50 min.
   to Dream Lake, inlet brook crossing: 9.0 mi., 6 hr. 20 min.
   to Gentian Pond Shelter: 11.2 mi., 8 hr.
   to Mt. Success summit: 14.0 mi., 10 hr. 50 min.
   to Success Trail: 14.6 mi., 11 hr. 20 min.
   to Carlo Col Trail: 16.4 mi., 13 hr. 20 min.
   to Mt. Carlo: 16.8 mi., 13 hr. 50 min.
   to Goose Eye Trail: 18.2 mi., 15 hr. 20 min.
   to Goose Eye Mtn. East Peak: 18.6 mi., 15 hr. 45 min.
   to Full Goose Shelter: 20.8 mi., 16 hr. 35 min.
   to Notch Trail: 22.3 mi., 17 hr. 30 min.
   to foot of Mahoosuc Notch: 23.4 mi., 19 hr. 20 min.
   to Mahoosuc Arm summit: 25.0 mi., 21 hr.
   to Speck Pond Shelter: 25.9 mi., 21 hr. 40 min.
   to Old Speck Trail junction: 27.0 mi., 22 hr. 45 min.
   to Old Speck summit: 27.3 mi. (43.9 km.), 23 hr.

Table Rock Trail

The Table Rock Trail, which climbs 900 ft., offers a short, fairly steep, but spectacular climb to the prominent rock ledge on Baldpate Mountain, which is on the eastern side of Grafton Notch. From this ledge, the trail continues to rejoin the Appalachian Trail. There is an extensive slab-cave system, possibly the largest in the state, on this trail.

The trail leaves the Appalachian Trail to the right (south) 0.1 mi. from the trailhead on ME 26 (described below). For 0.3 mi. from this junction the trail rises gently along the side of a hill above a marsh until it reaches a drop-off. From there it climbs steadily through mature hardwoods and reaches a rocky, caribou-moss–covered area called the boulder patch at 0.6 mi. After several switchbacks along rocky ledges, the trail enters a deep ravine between two rock faces. At the top of the ravine bear right. The trail climbs less steeply to a prominent outlook at 0.8 mi. At 0.9 mi. it reaches the base of the ledges that form Table Rock, where the slab caves begin. *Caution:* Be careful if you explore the caves. Some are quite deep, and a fall could mean serious injury.

On the trail, continue south around the bottom of Table Rock. (On the ledges above, note the weather-formed rock that looks like a shark's fin.) At 1 mi., after swinging behind Table Rock, you will meet a blue-blazed trail. Table Rock is 20 yd. to the left.

To the right, the blue-blazed upper Table Rock Trail continues, with only a slight change in elevation, about 0.5 mi. to the Appalachian Trail. Turn right (east) to reach Baldpate; go left (west) to return to the trailhead on ME 26.

Table Rock Trail

Distances from state parking area, ME 26

to start (via Baldpate Mountain Trail): 0.1 mi.

to Table Rock and junction with upper trail: 1 mi.

to state parking area, ME 26 (via Baldpate Mountain Trail): 2.4 mi. (3.9 km.), 1 hr. 45 min.

BALDPATE MOUNTAIN (East Peak 3812 ft./
1162 m. and West Peak 3680 ft./1122 m.)

Baldpate Mountain, once known as Saddleback and
Bear River Whitecap, rises to the east of Grafton Notch.
There are two main summits: the fine open East Peak
and the West Peak. The Appalachian Trail traverses
both. Refer to the USGS Old Speck Mountain quadrangle, 15-minute series; the Old Speck quadrangle, 7.5-
minute series; or map 7 in the MATC *Guide to the
Appalachian Trail in Maine.*

Baldpate Mountain via the Appalachian Trail
The Appalachian Trail, which traverses the range, is
maintained by the MATC and blazed in white. The following describes approaches from both the west and east.

From Grafton Notch
The trail leaves the north side of the state-park parking
lot on ME 26 (take the trail to the right). It soon crosses
ME 26. Then it runs briefly through woods and beside a
marsh until, at 0.1 mi., it crosses a brook on a log footbridge. Almost immediately after crossing the bridge,
the trail passes the start of the Table Rock Trail, which
leaves right. At 0.4 and 0.6 mi. trails lead left to the
Grafton Notch Shelter (MATC, accommodates six).
After that, the trail rises gradually on an old woods road.
At 0.9 mi. it passes another blue-blazed trail on the right
leading to Table Rock. The main trail climbs steadily
and then more steeply to the western knob of Baldpate,
with good views to the northwest. The trail then slabs
the northern side of the knob to a ridge extending
toward West Peak, soon descending to a brook. Then it
climbs steeply over rough terrain to the West Peak,
which is covered with tiny scrub, but offers vistas in
almost all directions. The trail, turning in a more
northerly direction, drops only about 240 ft. before

climbing to the East Peak nearly a mile beyond. From there it continues to Andover–East B Hill Rd.

From Andover–East B Hill Rd.

The trail leaves the left (south) side of East B Hill Rd. about 8 mi. west of Andover Village. It descends from the road, crosses a small brook, then turns south along the edge of a progressively deeper gorge cut by this brook, which it follows for 0.5 mi. before turning west into the mouth of Dunn Notch. At 0.8 mi. the trail crosses the west branch of the Ellis River (a large stream at this point) at the top of a double waterfall plunging 60 ft. into Dunn Notch. You can reach the bottom of the falls via an old logging road across the stream. (Upstream, there are a small, rocky gorge and the beautiful upper falls.) The Appalachian Trail crosses the old road and climbs steeply up the eastern rim of the notch. It then climbs moderately to the south.

At 1.3 mi. the trail turns left and climbs gradually through open hardwoods along the edge of the north arm of Surplus Mountain. At 3 mi. it slabs right (southwest) around the nose of Surplus and climbs gently along a broad ridge and passes near the summit. In another 1.6 mi. it descends steeply over rough ground to the Frye Notch Lean-to, near the head of Frye Brook. At 1.7 mi. from the lean-to, the trail reaches and climbs the crest of a ridge to the open summit of Baldpate's East Peak. The trail then drops down, climbs West Peak, and descends into Grafton Notch via the trail from the west (described above).

Baldpate Mountain via the Appalachian Trail
Distances from parking area, ME 26

   to lower side trail to Table Rock: 0.1 mi., 5 min.
   to upper side trail to Table Rock: 0.9 mi., 45 min.
   to Baldpate, West Peak: 2.9 mi., 2 hr. 30 min.
   to Baldpate, East Peak: 3.8 mi., 3 hr. 10 min.

to Andover–East B Hill Road: 10.1 mi. (16.3 km.), 6 hr. 40 min.

Distances from Andover–East B Hill Rd.
    to waterfall: 0.8 mi., 55 min.
    to Frye Notch Lean-to: 4.6 mi., 3 hr.
    to Baldpate, East Peak: 6.3 mi., 4 hr. 30 min.
    to Baldpate, West Peak: 7.2 mi., 5 hr. 15 min.
    to state parking area, ME 26: 10.1 mi. (16.3 km.), 7 hr.

PUZZLE MOUNTAIN (3133 ft./955 m.)

Puzzle Mountain in Newry is a flat-topped rocky mass, occupying a large area. The true summit is wooded but the bare peak to the southwest is only a few feet lower. Hikers using the route should have a compass. *Water* may be available to within 0.3 mi. or less of the summit. Refer to the USGS Old Speck Mountain quadrangle, 15-minute series, and Puzzle Mountain quadrangle, 7.5-minute series.

From the junction of ME 26 and US 2 at Newry, turn northwest on ME 26 for 3.6 mi. to a widely cleared logging road on the right, across from a stone wall. This road, the start of the trail, is 0.2 mi. beyond Great Brook. Bearing 115°, the road parallels the brook for 0.3 mi. and then joins the brook. At 0.6 mi. take the right fork into the woods, and at 0.9 mi. cross the brook on a slab-repaired bridge. At 1.0 mi. the road crosses a small feeder brook and reaches a clearing 50 yd. farther. At 1.1 mi. leave the road, turn left, descend to the brook, and cross it on a log bridge into a clearing. From the clearing, begin the climb up on an overgrown logging road bearing 30° and following a stream bed (dry in summer). Beyond this point the trail becomes obscure. Map and compass are recommended. The way is generally 30° gently uphill through underbrush and open hardwoods, and then a steeper climb begins through softwoods and ledges. The ledges are slightly cairned, and there are fine views to the rear of the Mahoosucs. The best views are from open ledges southeast of the summit.

Puzzle Mountain

Distances from ME 26

 to first fork in road: 0.6 mi.

 to Puzzle Mountain summit: 2.5 mi. (4 km.), 3 hr.

RUMFORD WHITECAP (2197 ft./670 m.)

This mountain is a long, bare-topped ridge in the northwest part of Rumford. It runs east and west and yields excellent views with relatively little effort. Refer to the USGS East Andover quadrangle, 7.5-minute series.

 The trail climbs up from the west. From US 2 0.5 mi. west of Rumford Point, go north on ME 5 toward Andover. About 3 mi. from US 2 turn right (east) on the side road that crosses the Ellis River. In 0.3 mi. turn left (north), and then in 1.6 mi. turn right (east) on Farmer's Hill Rd. toward Roxbury Notch. At 0.8 mi. the trail leaves the right side of the road on a logging road (not passable for cars) and climbs steeply. Just after a badly eroded section of the road at about 0.5 mi., turn left onto the trail. It shortly crosses a brook (dry in dry weather) and leads generally east through the woods to open ledges at the western end of the ridge.

 The final 1 mi. is a delightful walk along the open ridge to the summit. From the summit, the antenna on Black Mountain and the Satellite Station at Andover are visible. The trail through the woods and along the ridge is marked by ribbons and cairns with few paint blazes. *Descending,* take great care to find and follow the correct trail west into the woods since there are many cairns and paths leading in different directions. Ribbons mark the critical points.

Rumford Whitecap

Distances from Farmer's Hill Rd.

   to left turn off logging road: 0.5 mi.

   to ledges: 1 mi.

   to Rumford Whitecap summit: 2 mi. (3.2 km.), 1 hr. 40 min.

OLD BLUE MOUNTAIN (3600 ft./1097 m.)

The Appalachian Trail crosses Old Blue Mountain, which is south of Elephant Mountain and east of the road from Andover to the South Arm of Lower Richardson Lake. The summit of Old Blue is covered with dense evergreen trees 2 to 3 ft. high, allowing excellent views in all directions. Refer to the USGS Old Speck Mountain and Rangeley quadrangles, 15-minute series; the East Andover quadrangle, 7.5-minute series, or map 7 in the MATC *Guide to the Appalachian Trail in Maine.*

   To reach the Appalachian Trail, follow the road to the South Arm for 8.5 mi. north of Andover to Black Brook Notch. From the South Arm Rd., the Appalachian Trail climbs very steeply up the east wall of Black Brook Notch. At 0.6 mi. the trail reaches the top of the notch, then it gradually climbs to the base of Old Blue, which it reaches at 2.3 mi. Here the trail begins the final 0.5-mi. ascent to the summit.

   From the summit, the Appalachian Trail descends north 800 ft. into the high valley between Old Blue and Elephant Mountain. In this valley the Appalachian Trail runs through a virgin red spruce forest for more than a mile.

   For detailed information about the Appalachian Trail north of Old Blue, see the 1988 edition of the MATC *Guide to the Appalachian Trail in Maine.*

Old Blue Mountain

Distances from South Arm Rd.

 to top of Black Brook Notch: 0.6 mi.

 to base of Old Blue: 2.3 mi.

 to Old Blue summit: 2.8 mi. (4.5 km.), 2 hr. 40 min.

BEMIS MOUNTAIN (3592 ft./1095 m.)

Bemis Mountain is an open ridge with outstanding views. It rises south of Mooselookmeguntic Lake. The ridge, which runs northeast-southwest, has four peaks descending in elevation to the northeast. The highest peak is wooded. The three lower peaks all have excellent views. The Appalachian Trail crosses the Bemis Ridge and there is a new lean-to near Third Peak. Refer to the USGS Oquossoc and Rangeley quadrangles, 15-minute series; the Houghton and Melallak Mountain quadrangles, 7.5-minute series, or map 7 in the MATC *Guide to the Appalachian Trail in Maine.*

Via the Appalachian Trail

Access is from ME 17 at a turnout 11 miles south of Oquossoc and 26 miles north of Rumford. Park at a clearing 0.6 mi. farther south at the Bemis Stream trailhead.

 The trail descends 0.8 mi. to the ford where Bemis Stream splits. There are two long crossings, difficult at high water. At 1.0 mi. cross the gravel logging road, which was the bed of the old Rumford and Rangeley Lakes Railroad in the 1930s. There is a small *spring* at 1.1 mi. After climbing through woods, emerge to open ledges at 1.5 mi. and cross a series of rocky knobs, the first at 1.7 mi. The ridge trail crosses three peaks: First Peak (2604 ft.), at 2.2 mi.; Second Peak (2923 ft.), 3.1 mi.; lean-to, 4.6 mi.; and Third Peak (3138 ft.), 5.0 mi. At 5.1 mi. the trail begins the ascent to the two wooded knobs of Fourth Peak (3592 ft.), which are reached at 6.2 and 6.3 miles.

For an interesting loop hike, climb Bemis by way of the Appalachian Trail and return via the Bemis Stream Trail, a total of almost 14 miles.

Via Bemis Stream Trail

This trail starts from a cleared parking area off ME 17, 0.6 miles south of the Appalachian Trail crossing mentioned above. Hikers on either trail should park here.

The trail fords a brook at 0.2 mi., winds down to the gravel RR bed road at 1.2 mi., and climbs to reach Bemis Stream. It follows the west bank up to ford the stream at about 2.0 mi., recrossing to the west side at 2.8 mi. Climbing, it crosses again at 4.6 mi. and 5.0 mi. near the site of the former Elephant Mountain Lean-to. Then the trail swings up and west to join the Appalachian Trail at 6.5 mi. (This point is 7.3 mi. along the Appalachian Trail from ME 17.)

For a detailed description of the Appalachian Trail beyond Fourth Peak, see the 1992 edition of the MATC *Guide to the Appalachian Trail in Maine.*

Bemis Mountain
Distances from ME 17 via Appalachian Trail
    to Fourth Peak: 6.3 mi., 4 hr. 30 min.
    to Bemis Mountain Lean-to: 4.6 mi.
    loop distance via Appalachian Trail, Bemis Stream Trail and ME 17: 14 mi. (22.4 km.), 8 hr. 30 min.

SECTION 9
Weld Region

Weld Village lies on the eastern shore of Lake Webb (678 ft.) and is almost encircled by mountains. Tumbledown Mountain (3068 ft.), with its tremendous cliffs, three peaks, and high pond, is the most interesting mountain in the area and one of the state's outstanding summits. Little Jackson (3434 ft.), Jackson (3535 ft.), and Blueberry (2942 ft.) mountains are also in the Tumbledown Range, which forms the northern and northwestern walls of the valley. Mount Blue (3187 ft.) lies to the east. The ledgy summits of Bald Mountain (2386 ft.) and Saddleback Wind Mountain (2572 ft.) close the valley on the southeast. Brush (2430 ft.) and West (2782 ft.) mountains are to the west.

Mount Blue State Park (1273 acres) has two sections. The area along the western shore of Lake Webb offers picnicking, swimming, and camping facilities. The section east of the lake and Weld includes the Center Hill parking overlook and picnic area and Mount Blue itself. Information on accommodations and trail conditions may be obtained at the supervisor's headquarters 1.5 mi. from Weld on the road toward Center Hill and Mount Blue.

TUMBLEDOWN MOUNTAIN (3068 ft./935 m.)

Although not the highest peak of the Tumbledown Range, Tumbledown Mountain, at the southwestern end, is in many ways the most interesting. The enormous cliff on the southern side of the mountain attracts many rock climbers. Of the three summits, 3068-ft. West Peak is slightly higher than the others. Another feature of the mountain is Tumbledown Pond (called Beaver or Crater by some), located on the eastern slope of the mountain and surrounded on three sides by higher elevations. The views from the summit ridges are good, except where higher mountains in the range block them to the north and northeast. There are four trails to the pond. In addition to the map in this guide, you can refer to the USGS Dixfield and Rangeley quadrangles, 15-minute series, and the Roxbury quadrangle, 7.5-minute series.

The Loop Trail

The Loop Trail leaves Byron Notch Rd. 5.8 mi. west of Weld Corner, heading north on the east side of the brook. There is sometimes a sign at the start of the trail, but vandals steal it periodically. There is a clearing diagonally opposite the trail's entrance into the woods. The trail (blue blazes) rises gradually, crossing a brook twice, and at 1.0 mi. passes the huge Tumbledown Boulder. From there it rises steeply, coming out on open ledges (Great Ledges) from which there are splendid views of the 700-ft. cliffs of Tumbledown Mountain. On the ledges, at a large cairn, the Loop Trail to the saddle turns right.

The trail crosses a brook and then climbs steeply in a gully. Near the top of the gully, a side trail leads right to a fissure cave (Fat Man's Misery). Above this is an opening in the boulders with iron rungs. (This section makes the trail unsuitable for dogs.) At 0.6 mi. from the Great Ledges cairn, reach the saddle with a *spring (unreliable in dry weather)*. From here the trails lead east and west.

There are no trails on the North Peak of Tumbledown, but you can reach it by bushwhacking through the valley between the East and North peaks or by going east around Tumbledown Pond and up the upper reaches of Parker's Ridge.

The Loop Trail

Distances from Byron Notch Rd.

 to Tumbledown Boulder: 1 mi.

 to cairn (Great Ledges): 1.3 mi.

 to saddle (Tumbledown Ridge Trail): 1.9 mi. (3.1 km.), 1 hr. 45 min.

Brook Trail

This is a direct route to Tumbledown Pond from Byron Notch Rd. It leaves the road 1.8 mi. west of the start of the Parker's Ridge Trail and 4.4 mi. west of Weld Corner. The trail diverges north just before where the road crosses a large double steel culvert over Tumbledown Brook at prospect "X" 1102. The trail is marked Brook Trail on a rock at the start and is blue blazed throughout its length. For the first mile it is a logging road passable for jeeps. At 1 mi. the trail diverges to the right into a low spot, then climbs steeply, generally following the brook to the pond.

Brook Trail

Distances from Byron Notch Rd.

 to right turn off logging road: 1 mi.

 to Tumbledown Pond: 1.5 mi. (2.4 km.), 1 hr. 30 min.

Parker's Ridge Trail

This is the oldest of the trails up Tumbledown. Take the road to the right (northwest) from Byron Notch Rd. about 2.7 mi. west of Weld Corner and about 0.3 mi. west of a cemetery. Follow the road northwest about 0.9 mi. to a clearing and shelter. Park here. From this area the Little Jackson Trail leaves on a logging road, northwest.

The Parker's Ridge Trail, blazed blue, enters the woods left (west), crosses a brook, and turns northwest, joining a logging road. For 1 mi., the trail rises gently through second growth, then steeply for a short distance over three ledges. After that, the trail rises steadily.

Then it crosses the open ledges of Parker's Ridge with views of Tumbledown's three peaks ahead, and descends west to Tumbledown Pond.

Parker's Ridge Trail

Distances from parking area
    to Parker's Ridge: 1.9 mi., 2 hr.
    to pond (outlet): 2.2 mi. (3.5 km.), 2 hr. 10 min.

Tumbledown Ridge Trail

From the pond outlet junction with the Brook Trail and Parker's Ridge Trail, the Tumbledown Ridge Trail ascends west over mostly open ledge to East Peak and to the junction with the Loop Trail. A short spur extends to the summit of West Peak offering views into the Swift River valley and to Old Blue and Elephant mountains to the west.

Tumbledown Ridge Trail

Distances from pond outlet
    to East Peak: 0.4 mi.
    to Loop Trail junction: 0.6 mi.
    to West Peak: 0.7 mi. (1.1 km.), 45 min.

Pond Link Trail

From the Parker's Ridge Trail 0.1 mi. east of the pond the Pond Link Trail, blazed blue, heads north, skirting the east end of the pond for about 100 yd. It then turns east to ascend to the height-of-land between Parker's Ridge and Little Jackson at 0.3 mi. from the pond. The trail continues generally east to a junction with the Little Jackson Trail. This makes an interesting loop trip.

Pond Link Trail

Distances from the pond
    to start of Pond Link Trail: 0.1 mi.
    to height-of-land: 0.3 mi.
    to Little Jackson Trail: *est.* 1 mi. (1.6 km.), 40 min.

LITTLE JACKSON MOUNTAIN (3434 ft./1047 m.)
JACKSON MOUNTAIN (3535 ft./1077 m.)
(TUMBLEDOWN RANGE)

For the road approach see the Parker's Ridge Trail section. If you want to supplement the map in this guide, refer to the USGS Rangeley quadrangle, 15-minute series, and the Roxbury quadrangle, 7.5-minute series.

The trail leaves the shelter area northwest on a logging road. There are no trail signs along the way, but the trail is well blazed and fairly well worn. There are many intersecting logging roads. Stay close to the edge of the valley that leads toward the Jacksons. About 0.5 mi. from the shelter, the route heads north toward the col between Little Jackson on the west and Jackson on the east. At about 1.5 mi. the trail turns right (northeast), and the blue-blazed Pond Link Trail leads straight ahead (northwest). At about 2.3 mi. the trail crosses a brook and continues onto open ledges 0.3 mi. beyond. At the ledges, the trail turns left and, ascending across open ledges with fine outlooks, climbs to the summit of Little Jackson.

Descending from the open areas on Little Jackson, the trail bears well to the right and is somewhat hard to see, so it is easy to get confused in the puckerbrush.

Few hikers visit the summit of Jackson, a large rambling mountain partially covered with spruce. It is possible to climb up from the col between Jackson and Little Jackson. The distance from the col to the summit is about 1 mi.

Little Jackson Mountain

Distances from parking area

    to Pond Link Trail junction: *est.* 1.5 mi.

    to col: 2.5 mi., 2 hr.

    to Jackson summit (via bushwhack from col): *est.* 3.5 mi.

    to Little Jackson summit (via trail): 3.3 mi. (5.3 km.), 2 hr. 30 min.

BLUEBERRY MOUNTAIN (2942 ft./897 m.)

See the USGS Phillips quadrangle, 15-minute series or
Madrid quadrangle, 7.5-minute series, if you want to
supplement the map in this guide.

The trail leaves ME 142 1.5 mi. from Weld Corner
toward Phillips. Blueberry Mountain Bible Camp maintains a road that runs 1.8 mi. to a clearing above the
buildings. A gate near the base may be locked, blocking
cars, but to date, personnel at the camp have been coop-
erative about letting people use their road. They ask that
you park near the main building, *not* up in the clearing.
From the middle of the north side of the clearing, follow
a logging road to a trail with blue blazes, which soon
splits right. Trail maintenance has been sporadic. It rises
steeply, first through conifers and then over ledges, to
the summit. There are interesting geological formations
at the top, which is bare and offers excellent views in all
directions. There is *no water* on the trail.

Blueberry Mountain Trail

Distances from ME 142

   to clearing (via Bible camp road): 1.8 mi.
   to Blueberry summit: 3.5 mi. (5.6 km.), 2 hr. 30 min.

MOUNT BLUE (3187 ft./971 m.)

From Mount Washington, this peak is one of the most per-
fect cones on the skyline. The former firetower on the
summit has no cab. In addition to the map in this guide,
you can refer to the USGS Dixfield quadrangle, 15-minute
series, and the Mount Blue quadrangle, 7.5-minute series.

In Weld Village, take the road that leads uphill east
from the four corners and bear left at the fork at 0.5 mi.
Take the right fork at a little over 3 mi. and continue to
the parking place at about 6 mi. (signs). The trail crosses
a field northeast of the woods, where it is joined by an
old telephone line. The path is broad and well worn and

passes the old firewarden's cabin, where there is a fine *spring*. From this point the trail becomes somewhat steep until it reaches the summit, where in addition to the tower, there is a board shelter once used by the firewarden, but there is *no water.* The summit is wooded, but views are excellent from ledge outcroppings around it.

Mount Blue

Distances from parking place
   to firewarden's cabin: 0.6 mi.
   to Mount Blue summit: 1.7 mi. (2.7 km.), 1 hr. 40 min.

BALD MOUNTAIN (2386 ft./727 m.)

The trail up Bald Mountain leaves the southern side of ME 156 about 8.5 mi. west of Wilton and about 5.5 mi. east of Weld at a small parking area, where there is a sign on a post marking the start of the trail. In addition to the map in this guide, you can refer to the USGS Dixfield quadrangle, 15-minute series, and the Mount Blue quadrangle, 7.5-minute series.

Cross the brook immediately *(last sure water)* and enter the woods. The trail climbs steadily through the woods, marked by paint blazes. On the open ledges it is marked by paint and cairns to the summit, where there are fine views in every direction. A faint trail may be followed 2 mi. farther to the summit of Saddleback Wind Mountain, which is slightly higher but attracts fewer visitors.

Bald Mountain

Distances from ME 156
   to ledges: 0.9 mi., 45 min.
   to Bald Mountain summit: 1.5 mi. (2.4 km.), 1 hr. 15 min.

SADDLEBACK WIND (2572 ft./784 km.)

The Anderson Brook Trail up Saddleback Wind in Carthage makes an excellent loop when combined with the Bald Mountain Trail. However, the route is bushy and hard to follow, so you should carry a map and compass. If you want to supplement the map in this guide, see the USGS Dixfield quadrangle, 15-minute series, and the Mount Blue quadrangle, 7.5-minute series.

The trail starts on the south side of ME 156 about 6.2 mi. from Wilton (and 7.7 mi. from Weld). There is no mark or sign, but the trail starts by a log bridge over a stream. Park by the bridge, being careful not to block the logging road. After crossing the bridge, turn right (northwest) across a field and follow the logging road about 0.5 mi. to the top of a small rise. The road ends in another 200 ft. Find an overgrown road that leads left up an obvious ridge. The trail is hard to pick out. Follow the ridge for 0.8 mi. to open and steep ledges. After a 200-ft. climb, the trail reaches a beautiful open ridge, which leads for 0.8 mi. through interesting convolutions in the rock, to the summit.

To reach Bald Mountain, drop into the col between Saddleback Wind and a secondary peak, and then drop into the major col between the two mountains. The route is extremely hard to follow and densely wooded; carry a compass. From the bottom of the second col, the climb up Bald Mountain is over open rock.

Anderson Brook Trail

Distance from ME 156

to Saddleback Wind summit: 2.5 mi. (4 km.), 2 hr.

SUGARLOAF MOUNTAIN (1521 ft./464 m.)

Sugarloaf Mountain in Dixfield is conspicuous because of its two prominent summits. It offers fine vistas from its open northern summit. Refer to the USGS Dixfield quadrangle, 7.5- and 15-minute series.

For the shortest route to the summit go north from the corner of Main (US 2) and Weld streets in Dixfield. Take ME 142 for 1.7 mi. The blue-blazed trail starts in back of a brown house across ME 142 from CMP Pole J 17. Climbing steadily, the trail reaches the Bull Rock Trail on the right at 0.4 mi. *Note:* In this area a 1992 logging operation has destroyed part of the Sugarloaf and Link trails. Bearing left and climbing more steeply for 0.2 mi., reach the col between the north and south peaks. By a large boulder a trail to the right has been cut to the south peak. Continue left out of the col and climb to the north summit. Explore north of this summit to find more open ledge viewpoints.

Sugarloaf Mountain
Distance from ME 142
> *to* junction with Link Trail: 0.4 mi.
> *to* col: 0.6 mi.
> *to* North Summit: 0.9 mi. (1.4 km.), 45 min.

BULL ROCK (920 ft./280 m.)

Perched on the side of Sugarloaf Mountain in Dixfield, Bull Rock offers a delightful preview of the views from Sugarloaf. Hang-glider pilots now fly from Bull Rock and land in the field by the road.

Start from Dixfield as for the trail to Sugarloaf and proceed 1.5 mi. north on ME 142 to a driveway on the right just before CMP pole J 10 and a blue house with a swimming pool. Sixty feet from ME 142, turn right on the blue-blazed trail for 50 yds. Turn left, cross a small brook, pass a white house on the right, and climb a steep hogback to the open ledge.

In 1990 a blue-blazed trail was cut to connect Bull Rock with the Sugarloaf Trail. *Note:* A 1992 logging operation has destroyed part of this Link Trail and the Sugarloaf Trail. Reopening is planned.

Bull Rock
Distance from ME 142
> *to* Bull Rock ledges: 0.4 mi. (0.6 km.), 20 min.

SECTION 10
Rangeley and Stratton Area

This section includes the mountains north of Rangeley Lakes; the area westward to Lake Aziscohos and the New Hampshire border; the isolated mountains north toward the Canadian border, reached by a network of private logging roads and ME 27; and the important and outstanding cluster of 4000-ft. mountains, including Saddleback, Abraham, Sugarloaf, Crocker, and Bigelow, reached through the towns of Rangeley, Stratton, Kingfield, and Phillips. This last group includes eight of the state's 4000-ft. peaks. Sugarloaf, at 4237 ft., is Maine's second-highest mountain (aside from the subsidiary summits of Katahdin), although Abraham (4049 ft.), Saddleback (4116 ft.), and especially Bigelow (4150 ft.) are more interesting for hiking.

There are two large ski areas in this region, on Sugarloaf and Saddleback mountains.

Accommodations are ample along ME 16/27 between Rangeley, Stratton, and Kingfield. The Rangeley Lake State Park on the southern shore opened in 1967, with full camping, boating, and swimming facilities. You can drive to the park via ME 17 or 4. There are additional public facilities at Mount Blue State Park in Weld, just south of this section.

The town of Eustis maintains Cathedral Pines camping area and trailer park, with laundry and recreation building, on ME 27, 3 mi. north of the ME 16/27 junction at Stratton and 2.3 mi. south of Eustis.

The MFS maintains the following camping areas (fires permitted): on the northern side of ME 16 about 5 mi. east of Rangeley and near Dallas; on the western shore of

Flagstaff Lake at the end of the Old Flagstaff Rd., 2 mi. east of a junction with ME 27 (near Flagstaff Memorial Church) and 0.8 mi. north of Cathedral Pines campground; on the western side of ME 27 about 3 mi. south of Chain of Ponds; at Upper Farm on the eastern shore of Chain of Ponds just off ME 27; and on the eastern shore of Chain of Ponds at its northern end, off ME 27.

MOUNT AZISCOHOS (3215 ft./980 m.)

South of Lake Aziscohos, this mountain offers excellent views of the Rangeley Lakes region. Fifteen lakes are visible from the summit. The trails lead to the eastern, and slightly lower, of the two peaks, where an abandoned MFS firetower is down. Refer to the USGS Oquossoc and Errol quadrangles, 15-minute series, and Richardson Pond and Wilsons Mills quadrangles, 7.5-minute series.

There are two routes up the mountain. Opinions differ as to what they should be named; therefore, the descriptions are simply "from the northwest" and "from the north."

From the Northwest

Sometimes called the Tower Man's Trail or South Trail, this route begins on the southern side of ME 16, at a small parking area 100 yd. east of the bridge over the Magalloway River at Aziscohos Dam. The trail follows an old dirt logging road, crosses the remains of a bridge at 0.8 mi., and continues gradually uphill. Cross the small stream at 1.1 mi. and take the left (south) fork. At 1.7 mi. the road reaches the clearing at the site of the former MFS firewarden's cabin, where there is an enclosed *spring*. Hike on the left side of the clearing and enter the open softwood forest. The trail continues on steeper but relatively easy grades, and at 2.4 mi. the trail from the north comes in on the left. Turn right and continue to the summit at 2.5 mi.

Mount Aziscohos, from the Northwest

Distances from ME 16

    to cabin site: 1.7 mi.

    to junction with trail from the north: 2.4 mi.

    to Aziscohos summit: 2.5 mi. (4 km.), 2 hr. 30 min.

From the North

The route from the north begins on ME 16, 1 mi. east of the bridge over the Magalloway River at Aziscohos Dam. At first it leads gradually uphill on an old tote road through open hardwood and mixed forest, then it turns sharply left at 0.5 mi. At 1 mi. the trail enters conifers and crosses a brook at 1.1 mi. After that, it continues more steeply through open conifers and reaches the route coming in from the northwest at 2 mi. To the left, it is 0.1 mi. to the summit.

Mount Aziscohos, from the North

Distances from ME 16

    to brook crossing: 1.1 mi.

    to junction with trail from the northwest: 2 mi.

    to Aziscohos summit: 2.1 mi. (3.4 km.), 2 hr. 10 min.

BALD MOUNTAIN (2443 ft./745 m.)

This small mountain is in a prime location between Mooselookmeguntic and Rangeley lakes. The views, however, are marginal, because despite the mountain's name, the woods have grown up around the bedrock summit. The summit's abandoned tower is in bad repair and may be dangerous to climb. A ski area on the northern slope has been out of business for many years and the ski trails are overgrown. Refer to the USGS Oquossoc quadrangle, 15-minute series and 7.5-minute series.

To reach the hiking trail, go west from Oquossoc on ME 4 to the terminus of that highway at Haines Landing. Turn left (south) before the landing and follow a road paralleling the lake shore for about 1 mi. to the foot of the trail on the left. A short distance from the start of the trail, take the right fork and climb east and southeast to the summit. The trail is well used and easy to see in the hardwood forest at the base of the mountain, but it becomes braided at the higher elevations, where it requires care to stay on the main trail.

Bald Mountain

Distance from road
  to Bald Mountain summit: 1 mi. (1.6 km.), 1 hr.

WEST KENNEBAGO MOUNTAIN (3705 ft./ 1129 m.)

This isolated mountain is north of the Rangeley Lakes and west of Kennebago Lake. There is a firetower on the south peak, which also offers fine views of the area and is the highest of the several summits of the north-south ridge forming the mountain. Refer to the USGS Cupsuptic quadrangle, 15-minute series, and Kennebago quadrangle, 7.5-minute series.

Access to the firewarden's trail is via the Brown Company (now the James River Corp.) system of private roads. Turn north from ME 16 on a company road 4.9 mi. west of the ME 4/16 junction in Oquossoc and 0.3 mi. west of the MFS buildings at Cupsuptic. Drive 3.2 mi. from ME 16 to a junction with a well-maintained, wide gravel road. Turn right (east) and in 5.3 mi. the road reaches the firetower trail, which is marked by an MFS sign.

The trail starts as a road but soon becomes a path and climbs rather steeply. At 0.9 mi. the trail levels out

among conifers and bears left. Then it begins to climb
again, crosses a small stream, and turns sharp right. At
1.4 mi. the trail reaches the warden's camp (3186 ft.), a
picturesque log cabin built in 1911. There is a *spring*
behind the camp 300 ft. to the left. The trail leaves the
camp from the upper right (northwest) corner of the
clearing. At 1.7 mi. it reaches the ridge, where the trail
turns left (south) following the ridge to the firetower.

West Kennebago Mountain

Distances from road

    to warden's camp: 1.4 mi.

    to West Kennebago, southern summit: 2.1 mi. (3.4
    km.), 2 hr.

EAST KENNEBAGO MOUNTAIN (3791 ft./1155 m.)

East of Kennebago Lake, this is a long, wooded ridge
running east-west in T2 R4 T2 R5. (T and R stand for
township and *range;* Maine uses this system to designate its unincorporated towns.)

    This is in part a bushwhack trip. Refer to the USGS
Kennebago Lake quadrangle, 15-minute series, and to
the Kennebago Lake and Quill Hill quadrangles, 7.5-
minute series. East Kennebago also appears on the
Rangeley-Stratton map in this guide.

    On ME 16, 9 miles from ME 16/27 in Stratton, or 9.6
miles from ME 4/16 in Rangeley, turn northwest on a
logging road, cross a bridge over the river, and turn right.
Set altimeter at 1320 ft. Follow the road and take the
right fork at 0.9 mi. (1380 ft.). Cross the stream and take
an immediate left. At 2.2 mi. (1440 ft.) keep left at the
intersection. Continue straight where the road turns left
toward a sandpit (2.5 mi., 1620 ft.). Take a left at a trian-
gle intersection (2.9 mi., 1900 ft.). Pass through a log
yard at 3.5 mi. (2100 ft.). Ignore two left branching roads
at 3.8 mi. (2200 ft.) and 4.2 mi. (2500 ft.). Beyond this

the road is deteriorated, brushy, and has dips for water control. Cross a stream at 2640 ft. and enter another log-yard clearing at 2700 ft. The road then climbs abruptly for a short distance. Go left at a fork and continue on an overgrown path. At a left curling turn, come to a stream crossing, which may be dry (2980 ft.). There are two popular bushwhack routes. One starts just left of the stream, the other about 30 yards beyond the stream. On a 340° heading, the brushy terrain gives way to open forest. Continue the bushwhack into the middle of the col between peaks (3600 ft.). Turn left to 230° and climb through some scrub, then open woods, about 0.5 mi. to the flat summit and register.

Suggestion: Return by reversing your route; the southeast slopes of this peak are steep and ringed with thick spruce. (This trail information was current July 1991.)

East Kennebago Mountain

Distance from gate

to East Kennebago summit: *est.* 5 mi. (8.1 km.), 3 hr. 45 min.

SNOW MOUNTAIN (3960 ft./1207 m.)

Snow Mountain is southwest of Chain of Ponds. There is an abandoned MFS firetower on the summit. The mountain offers extensive views in all directions, including an extended sweep into Canada over Lake Megantic. From the summit, you can see many miles of Benedict Arnold's route to Quebec in 1775, which followed the headwaters of the Dead River past Chain of Ponds and into Quebec Province. Refer to the USGS Chain Lakes quadrangle, 15-minute series, and the Chain of Ponds and Jim Pond quadrangles, 7.5-minute series.

The approach is via a dirt road leading left (west) from ME 27, 0.3 mi. north of the Alder Stream/Jim

Pond town line and 7.5 mi. north of Eustis. Park at a gravel pit 2.8 mi. from ME 27. (The road is passable 0.8 mi. farther.) At 0.3 mi. pass a road on the left to Round Pond. Cross and recross a stream. At 2.1 mi. turn left at a yarding area and cross a stream. At 3.6 mi. turn sharply left and cross a brook. At 4 mi. the road to the left leads to Snow Mountain Pond. The former firewarden's cabin there is now private property. Turn right to the firewarden's trail (sign) and climb steeply north, passing a *spring*. At 5.2 mi. the trail from Big Island Pond comes in on the left. Turn right and climb northeast to the summit.

Descending, don't miss the point where the firewarden's trail turns left and the trail from Big Island Pond goes right.

Snow Mountain

Distances from parking area

    to Snow Mountain Pond: 4 mi., 2 hr.

    to Snow summit: 5.4 mi. (8.7 km.), 3 hr. 10 min.

KIBBY MOUNTAIN (3654 ft./1114 m.)

This remote mountain is in the heart of the wilderness area north of Flagstaff Lake, east of Chain of Ponds, and south of the Canadian Atlantic RR running through Lac-Megantic, P.Q. (Quebec) and Jackman. The Kibby Mountain Trail was restored in 1989, and is periodically maintained. Refer to the USGS Kibby Mountain quadrangle, 7.5-minute series, and *Maine Atlas and Gazetteer* maps 28, 29, 38, and 39.

    From the junction with ME 16 in Stratton, drive ME 27 northwest 17 mi. (3.1 mi. northwest from Snow Mtn. road entrance.) Turn right onto the wide dirt Beaudry Road running parallel to Gold Brook. Drive 9.2 mi. to an abandoned road on the right. Look for a small cairn or possible marking by the rock ledge to the left of the entrance. Park here. This former jeep trail ascends about 2 mi. at an easy grade via two long switchbacks on grassy terrain—delightful hiking and superb winter skiing. The upper 0.5-mi. section to the summit is a steeper footpath. There is an old MFS firetower stand with outstanding, extensive views of the surrounding wilderness.

Kibby Mountain

Distance from parking

   to Kibby summit: *est.* 2.5 mi. (4.0 km.), 1 hr. 30 min.

EUSTIS RIDGE (1623 ft./495 m.)

Eustis Ridge is a fine outlook over Flagstaff Lake, the Bigelow Range, and other peaks to the south. It is right on the road, and there is a state picnic area. Refer to the USGS Stratton and Kennebago Lake quadrangles, 15-minute series, and Tim Mountain quadrangle, 7.5-minute series, if you want to supplement the map in this guide.

   From Stratton, drive north on ME 27 to Cathedral Pines. About 3.5 mi. from Stratton, turn left on a paved road (signs) and drive west 2 mi. to the picnic area.

SADDLEBACK MOUNTAIN AND THE HORN (summit 4116 ft./1255 m. and The Horn 4023 ft./ 1226 m.)

Saddleback Mountain, southeast of Rangeley, is one of Maine's outstanding mountains. It is a long range extending east and west. Pronounced saddles separate its several peaks. Two of the peaks are over 4000 ft.—Saddleback summit and The Horn. The bare summits of both offer far-flung views in all directions. Saddleback, with its widespread areas above treeline, is also unusually exposed. *Caution:* High winds or restricted visibility can be dangerous. You can refer to the USGS Phillips and Rangeley quadrangles, 15-minute series, and Redington and Saddleback Mountain quadrangles, 7.5-minute series, as well as to the map in this guide or map 6 in the MATC's *Guide to the Appalachian Trail in Maine*.

There are several points of interest on the southwestern side of the mountain. Piazza Rock is an enormous overhanging flat boulder with a growth of mature trees, and nearby, the Caves offer ample opportunities for exploration. Both are on the Appalachian Trail, 1.4 mi. north of ME 4. Eddy Pond, one of several small ponds on Saddleback, is particularly attractive.

The Saddleback Mountain Ski Area is on the northwestern slope of the mountain.

Appalachian Trail

To approach Saddleback from the west, follow ME 4 for 32 mi. north from the ME 4/US 2 junction in Farmington or for 9.9 mi. south from the ME 4/16 junction in Rangeley. The Appalachian Trail crosses ME 4 in a steep, winding section of the road. Park on the wide gravel shoulder on the eastern side of the highway.

From ME 4, the Appalachian Trail descends and crosses the Sandy River at 0.1 mi. The trail climbs out of the valley, crossing a gravel logging road at 1.1 mi. At 1.4 mi. the trail passes the Piazza Rock Lean-to (built in 1935 by the Civilian Conservation Corps; reconditioned by the MATC; accommodates six; MFS Campsite). A side trail leads left 500 ft. to the top of Piazza Rock. Not far beyond, on the Appalachian Trail, a side path leads left 100 yd. to the Caves, a series of boulder caves with narrow passages. The Appalachian Trail then climbs steeply, passes along Ethel Pond's western shore, and turns sharp left away from the end of the pond. The trail then continues to rise, passes Mud Pond, and descends slightly to Eddy Pond *(last sure water)*. Watch for a point near the eastern shore of Eddy Pond about 3.2 mi. from ME 4 where the trail, after turning left on a road for a few feet, turns sharply right from the road onto a trail. It rises steeply through conifers, emerging in 0.8 mi. on a scrub-covered slope.

This open crest is particularly interesting, but the cairns are small, the path is not well worn, and the trail is fully exposed. It should not be traveled in bad weather. After nearly 0.8 mi. over rocky slopes and heath, the trail descends slightly into a sag, where a blue-blazed side path (may be hard to see) leads right (south) about 0.1 mi. through scrub to a *spring* (not dependable). The main trail climbs 0.1 mi. farther to the summit.

The Appalachian Trail continues over open slopes, descends steeply into the col between Saddleback and The Horn, and reaches the summit of The Horn 1.6 mi. from the main summit.

For the continuation of the Appalachian Trail beyond The Horn, see the 1992 edition of the MATC *Guide to the Appalachian Trail in Maine.*

Appalachian Trail, Saddleback Mountain
Distances from ME 4

to junction with logging road: 1.1 mi.

to Piazza Rock Lean-to: 1.4 mi.

to Piazza Rock (via side trail): 1.5 mi.

to Saddleback summit: 5.1 mi., 3 hr. 45 min.

to The Horn summit: 6.7 mi. (10.8 km.), 4 hr. 15 min.

MOUNT ABRAHAM (4049 ft./1234 m.)

Mount Abraham (or Abram) lies northwest of Kingfield and south of Sugarloaf and Spaulding mountains. It is an impressive ridge about 4.5 mi. long that runs on a northwest-southeast axis and consists of about eight peaks ranging from 3400 to over 4000 ft. The highest peak, with an abandoned MFS firetower, lies north of the middle of the ridge. The extensive areas above timberline on Abraham give it an unusually alpine appear-

ance for its height. Although the trailless ridge south of
the tower has been traversed, that route is not advisable
since the distances are deceptive and the scrub is very
dense between peaks. *Caution:* The mountain's open-
nessmakes sudden electrical storms unusually dangerous. Watch your weather! Two trails ascend to the abandoned firetower. The Fire Warden's Trail approaches
the mountain from Kingfield. The Mount Abraham Side
Trail, cut in 1987, approaches from the Appalachian
Trail north of Mount Abraham and west of Spaulding
Mountain. Refer to the USGS Kingfield and Phillips
quadrangles, 15-minute series, and Mt. Abraham quadrangle, 7.5-minute series, or map 6 in the MATC *Guide
to the Appalachian Trail in Maine,* if you want to supplement the map in this guide.

Fire Warden's Trail

To reach the trail follow ME 27 north from Kingfield.
Turn left (west) on the paved road (West Kingfield St.) at
Jordan's Lumber Company store, 0.2 mi. north of the
bridge over the Carrabassett River. At 3 mi. from ME 27
the road becomes gravel. Go straight through a crossroad
at 3.5 mi. to 3.7 mi., where the road forks. Go right. From
this point the road is a logging road. At 6 mi. a road turns
left to a new bridge over Rapid Stream. Cross the stream
and follow the road for about 0.5 mi. to the trailhead at a
crossroad. The trail begins straight into the woods.

   The trail follows the south bank of Norton Brook,
crosses the brook, and continues along the north bank,
gradually climbing. In another 0.3 mi. it turns northwest
and then crosses another logging road. To reach this
point by car, turn right at the trailhead and bear left. The
next 2 mi. of the trail, to the abandoned warden's cabin,
skirt the northeast flank of the mountain, crossing four
major brooks. Grades are easy. There is a good *spring* to
the right of the cabin.

From the old cabin (2127 ft.), the trail turns left straight up the slope and climbs steeply through the woods for a mile, then comes out on an old slide with good views. At about 0.1 mi. above the cabin, a side trail leads left to a brook (last sure *water*). The remainder of the trail is completely exposed, except for a few short stretches of scrub. In this section an abandoned telephone line and the few cairns should be followed carefully in bad weather. The trail rises steadily across a boulder field to the firetower.

Fire Warden's Trail

Distances from Rapid Stream
    to crossroad near Norton Brook: 0.5 mi.
    to firewarden's cabin: 3 mi.
    to Abraham summit: 4.5 mi. (7.2 km.), 3 hr. 45 min.

Mount Abraham Side Trail

For the approach to this trail see the description of the Appalachian Trail route to Spaulding Mountain in this guide.

From the junction of the Appalachian Trail and the blue-blazed side trail to the Spaulding Mountain summit, continue south on the Appalachian Trail, descending the cone of Spaulding Mountain to the site of the Spaulding Mountain lean-to with two tentsites, a *spring,* and a privy. A temporary side trail marked by orange tape leads 0.6 mi. north to the old Spaulding Mountain lean-to, which is still functional.

Continue south on the Appalachian Trail to the junction of the Mount Abraham Side Trail. The Appalachian Trail continues southwest, climbing Lone Mountain. Refer to map 6 in the 1992 edition of the MATC *Guide to the Appalachian Trail in Maine*. The Mount Abraham Side Trail leads 1.7 mi. southeast following a very old tote road, climbing gradually then steeply up the south ridge of Mount Abraham, which is characterized by a very dense forest. The trail emerges from the trees and ascends a rock field to the tower.

Mount Abraham Side Trail

Distances from Caribou Valley Rd.

> *to* junction of Appalachian Trail and Spaulding summit trail: 3.9 mi.
>
> *to* site of new Spaulding Mountain campsite: *est.* 4.5 mi.
>
> *to* junction of Appalachian Trail and Mount Abraham Side Trail: *est.* 4.9 mi.
>
> *to* Mount Abraham summit: 6.6 mi. (10.6 km.), 5 hr. 25 min.

CROCKER MOUNTAIN (north peak 4168 ft./ 1270 m. and south peak 4000 ft./1219 m.)

The northern extension of the Crocker–Redington Pond Range, these mountains are 3.5 mi. west of Sugarloaf and separated from it by the Caribou Valley (south branch of the Carrabassett). The summit of Crocker, despite its height, has few views and is heavily wooded to the top. South Crocker Mountain, 1 mi. to the south, has a definite summit with fine views and rises 380 ft. above the col between it and Crocker Mountain. Hikers can approach the mountain via the Appalachian Trail from ME 27 or the Caribou Valley Rd.

Approach via ME 27

For the approach from the north and ME 27, follow the highway 2.6 mi. northwest from the Sugarloaf access road. Park off the highway at this point (sign reading Appalachian Trail crossing). Leaving the south side of the highway, the Appalachian Trail climbs steadily through woods for nearly 1.5 mi. before reaching the northernmost knoll of Crocker. A spruce section begins at about 1 mi. and continues to about 2 mi., where the trail slabs the western side of the ridge through birches.

It continues up the western side of the ridge, reenters conifers at about 3.5 mi., and passes a small stream (usually reliable—last *water*). After that, the trail rises more steeply to the crest and reaches the summit of Crocker at 5.2 mi. The descent into the col begins immediately. The trail leads to the low point of the col and soon begins to climb toward the rocky summit of South Crocker. To reach the summit, take the 150-ft., blue-blazed path (sign) to the right (west), where the Appalachian Trail makes a sharp left turn for the descent to the Caribou Valley.

Crocker and South Crocker via the Appalachian Trail
Distances from ME 27

   to Crocker, north ridge: 1.5 mi.

   to stream in conifers: *est.* 3.5 mi.

   to Crocker summit: 5.2 mi., 4 hr.

   to South Crocker summit (via blue-blazed summit
     trail): 6.2 mi., 4 hr. 30 min.

   to Caribou Valley Rd.: 8.3 mi. (13.4 km.), 5 hr. 30 min.

Approach via Caribou Valley Road

This road leads south from ME 27 1 mi. northwest of the entrance to Sugarloaf. The Appalachian Trail crosses the road 4.5 mi. south of ME 27; 50 yd. beyond this crossing, an old metal gate is usually open.

   The Appalachian Trail leaves the road to the right (west) and climbs steadily but not too steeply through birch woods. Nearly a mile from the road, a blue-blazed trail leads right 0.2 mi. to the Crocker Cirque Campsite (built by the MATC in 1975; it has a two-tent platform, fireplace, and latrine). On the side trail to this campsite is the last sure *water*. Beyond the turn-off to the campsite the Appalachian Trail begins the steep climb to the shoulder of South Crocker. The trail leads up the shoulder through woods for the next mile to the crest of South Crocker. Then it turns sharply right, and at the same

point, the 150-ft. side trail (sign) to the actual summit of
South Crocker leaves to the left. The Appalachian Trail
then descends into the col, from which it climbs steadily
to the summit of North Crocker.

South Crocker and North Crocker via Caribou Valley Rd.
Distances from Caribou Valley Rd.

    to side trail to campsite: 0.9 mi., 35 min.
    to South Crocker summit: 2.1 mi., 2 hr.
    to Crocker summit: 3.1 mi., 2 hr. 45 min.
    to ME 27: 8 mi. (12.9 km.), 5 hr.

SUGARLOAF MOUNTAIN (4237 ft./1291 m.)
SPAULDING MOUNTAIN (3988 ft./1216 m.)

Sugarloaf Mountain

Sugarloaf Mountain is the second-highest mountain in
Maine. Many other peaks are more popular with hikers.
Sugarloaf is known and frequented chiefly for skiing.
The ski area is on the northern slope, and since it is in
one of the heaviest snow belts in the northeastern United
States, spring skiing is frequently good after other areas
farther to the south have closed for the season. For the
hiker the view from the symmetrical, bare cone is well
worth the climb of almost 2500 ft. The number of peaks
visible is perhaps unequaled in the state except from
Katahdin. Spaulding Mountain (3988 ft.) is about 2.5
mi. to the south of Sugarloaf and is connected with it by
a high ridge.

    A rough road (not good enough for cars but easy to
follow on foot in bad weather) has been built to the summit. It starts behind the maintenance-vehicle storage
building at the base, near the ski-area parking lot, and
climbs at first west, then south, and finally east to the
summit. This road, or the network of ski trails on the
mountain, provides an approach from the north. The road
is about 4 mi. long; the ski trails are shorter but steeper.

You can also approach Sugarloaf from the south. The Appalachian Trail leaves the Caribou Valley Road 4.5 mi. south of ME 27. After leaving the road to the east, the trail soon crosses the South Branch of the Carrabassett (dangerous in high water), follows up the stream for a time, and then begins to climb, at first gently and then more steeply. After that, it crosses ledges and skirts the top of a cirque on the western side of Sugarloaf. The last *water* is a stream 1.8 mi. from the road. At 1.9 mi. the Appalachian Trail turns right toward Spaulding Mountain, while the blue-blazed Sugarloaf Side Trail leaves to the left and reaches the summit in 0.6 mi. *Note:* Recent logging has obscured part of the Sugarloaf Trail. Check with the trails chairman of the Maine Chapter for conditions.

Sugarloaf Side Trail

Distances from Caribou Valley Rd.

> *to* junction Sugarloaf Side Trail (via Appalachian Trail): 1.9 mi., 1 hr. 45 min.
> *to* Sugarloaf summit: 2.5 mi. (4 km.), 2 hr. 15 min.

Spaulding Mountain

From its junction with the Sugarloaf Side Trail, the Appalachian Trail (south) traverses the crest of the ridge between Sugarloaf and Spaulding, with views and steep cliffs on the left. At 1.5 mi. the trail begins the ascent of Spaulding, first steeply, then gradually. Near the top, a blue-blazed trail leads left 500 ft. to the summit.

For a description of the Appalachian Trail south of Spaulding, see the Mount Abraham Side Trail description in this guide or the 1992 edition of the MATC *Guide to the Appalachian Trail in Maine.*

Spaulding Mountain

Distance from Caribou Valley Rd.

> *to* Spaulding summit (via Appalachian Trail): 4 mi. (6.4 km.), 3 hr. 25 min.

THE BIGELOW RANGE

LITTLE BIGELOW (3040 ft./927 m.)
AVERY PEAK (4088 ft./1246 m.)
WEST PEAK (4150 ft./1265 m.)
SOUTH HORN (3831 ft./1168 m.)
NORTH HORN (3810 ft./1161 m.)
CRANBERRY PEAK (3213 ft./979 m.)

The Bigelow Range runs east-west for some 12 mi. It is second only to the Katahdin region in interest and opportunities for superb ridge walking. The central features are the twin "cones," Avery Peak and West Peak, which project above the ridge. The equally symmetrical twin "horns," farther west and only slightly lower, are North Horn and South Horn. Still farther west is Cranberry Peak, with its bare ledges. To the east of Avery Peak, but separated from it by a deep notch, lies Little Bigelow Mountain.

The Bigelow Mountain Preserve, established by the people of Maine in a June 1976 referendum, includes the Bigelow Range and the land surrounding it. The 33,000-acre preserve is administered by the Maine Department of Conservation and the Maine Department of Inland Fisheries and Wildlife.

Prior to the New England hurricane of 1938, the western portion of the range was an almost unbroken, uncut softwood forest. That and subsequent storms greatly damaged the forest, and only small uncut sections remain. Water is scarce in some areas of this range.

From Avery Peak, there is a magnificent outlook over the rugged wilderness of peaks, ponds, streams, and extensive Flagstaff Lake—perhaps the best view in the state except for the one from Katahdin.

Flagstaff Lake, a man-made reservoir (Maine's fourth-largest body of water) lies just north of the

Bigelow Range. Like the range, the lake stretches east to west.

West of the Horns lies the Horns Pond, a beautiful mountain tarn. Cranberry Pond, Arnolds Well, and other landmarks are farther west.

In addition to the map in this guide refer to the USGS Stratton and Little Bigelow quadrangles, 15-minute series, Little Bigelow Mountain and the Horns quadrangles, 7.5-minute series, or map 5 in the MATC *Guide to the Appalachian Trail in Maine.*

The Fire Warden's Trail is the shortest approach to the main peaks of the Bigelow Range; but the Horns Pond Trail is longer, less steep, and more interesting. It leads to the Horns Pond, where it joins the Appalachian Trail to follow the ridge between the Horns, over South Horn and West Peak, and on to Avery Peak. As a third approach to the west of the first two trails, the Appalachian Trail runs from ME 27 to the ridge west of the Horns Pond. These trails approach from the south (ME 16/27). A fourth and longer approach, the Bigelow Range Trail from Stratton east to the Appalachian Trail, east of Cranberry Pond, involves more ridge travel up and down the many peaks of the range. It extends the range's full length, from the western end to Avery Peak. A road runs along the southern shore of Flagstaff Lake from the Long Falls Dam Rd. toward Stratton. It offers a fifth approach to the highest peaks via the Safford Brook Trail.

Fire Warden's Trail

A rough dirt road, Stratton Brook Rd. (usually passable) runs east from ME 27 about 3.2 mi. northwest of the Sugarloaf Ski Area access road and 4.5 mi. southeast of Stratton. Drive in, cross the Appalachian Trail at 1 mi., and continue straight ahead, turning left at 1.6 mi. in a logging yarding area. The road beyond the yarding area is very rough. The bridge over the Stratton Brook is washed out.

There is very limited parking here. From this point cross
Stratton Brook and continue on the road. At 0.2 mi. reach
a fork (site of former parking area); go left. (The right
fork descends to a partially destroyed bridge.) From this
point the trail leads north for 0.2 mi., then runs east on the
level for about 0.5 mi. After that, it climbs steeply over
ledges to a shelf. The grade is easy for the next 1.5 mi.,
during which the trail crosses several brooks. At 1.6 mi.
from the parking area, the Horns Pond Trail leaves left
(northwest). At 3 mi. from the Stratton Brook, the trail
runs under the West Peak of Bigelow and the grade
becomes increasingly steep. The trail gains nearly 1700
ft. in the next 1.5 mi. as it climbs north-northeast to the
Bigelow col, where it meets the Appalachian Trail at 3.5
mi. The Avery Memorial Lean-to (accommodates six;
MFS campsite) is located here. The caretaker uses the old
firewarden's cabin, which is kept locked.

From the col, go right (east) via the Appalachian
Trail 0.4 mi. to reach Avery Peak and its abandoned
firetower. To reach West Peak from the col, go left
(west) on the Appalachian Trail about 0.4 mi.

Descending, the trail diverges from the Appalachian
Trail in Bigelow Col at the Avery Lean-to and goes
down to the southwest.

Fire Warden's Trail

Distances from Stratton Brook

    to Horns Pond Trail junction: 1.6 mi.

    to Bigelow Col and Appalachian Trail junction: 3.5
       mi., 3 hr. 40 min.

    to Avery Peak: 3.9 mi., 4 hr.

    to West Peak: 3.9 mi. (6.3 km.), 4 hr.

Horns Pond Trail

This trail starts at the same point as the Fire Warden's
Trail (see above). The Horns Pond Trail diverges left
(northwest) from the Fire Warden's Trail 1.6 mi. from

the Stratton Brook. The Horns Pond Trail heads north-west, climbing gradually. At 3 mi., the trail skirts the southern edge of a former bog area with an excellent view of the South Horn. The trail continues to rise grad-ually, then it gets steeper. At 4.1 mi. the Horns Pond Trail intersects the white-blazed Appalachian Trail. Bear right on the Appalachian Trail for 0.2 mi. to the two Horns Pond lean-tos (caretaker; accommodate six each; MFS campsite). A 50-yd., blue-blazed trail behind the east lean-to leads to the Horns Pond.

Horns Pond Trail

Distances from Stratton Brook

    to start (via Fire Warden's Trail): 1.6 mi.

    to Appalachian Trail: 4.1 mi.

    to Horns Pond lean-tos: 4.3 mi. (6.9 km.), 3 hr.

Appalachian Trail (from the south)

This trail (partly maintained by the Maine Chapter of the AMC) leaves ME 27 2.6 mi. northwest of the Sugarloaf Mountain access road. In the first mile, the trail descends slowly and crosses Stratton Brook Rd. at 0.9 mi. (This road, and the so-called Jones Pond Rd. soon after it, form alternate starting points for the hike.) After the Jones Pond Rd., the trail descends immediately to cross Strat-ton Brook on a footbridge. In the next mile, the trail passes through spruce woods and then joins an old tote road. Turn left on the tote road, which soon crosses a stream. At 1.9 mi. turn right off the road and cross a tote road 2.5 mi. from ME 27. The trail passes an abandoned beaver pond and then climbs gradually but steadily as it approaches the basin of Cranberry Pond, where it passes a *spring* (last sure *water* before the Horns Pond).

At 3.4 mi. the Appalachian Trail turns sharply right (north). The Bigelow Range Trail (sign) continues straight ahead (west). The Appalachian Trail climbs steeply through a boulder field. At 4 mi. it reaches the crest of the ridge. There it turns right (east) and follows the ridge, crossing a minor summit. At 5 mi., where the trail takes a sharp left, there is a lookout 50 ft. to the right over the Horns Pond to the Horns. The trail descends steeply. At 5.1 mi. the Horns Pond Trail comes in on the right. The Appalachian Trail continues along the south shore of the Horns Pond, passing the two Horns Pond lean-tos at 5.3 mi.

From the Horns Pond, the Appalachian Trail continues east, climbing South Horn. At 5.8 mi. the blue-blazed North Horn Trail leads 0.2 mi. left to the North Horn. A little farther on, the Appalachian Trail crosses the South Horn. Then it continues along the crest of the Bigelow Range, reaching West Peak at 8 mi. The trail then descends to the Avery Memorial Lean-to at 8.4 mi., where the Fire Warden's Trail comes in on the right directly in front of the lean-to. The Appalachian Trail continues east, climbing to the summit of Avery Peak at 8.8 mi.

From Avery Peak, the Appalachian Trail descends east to its junction with the Safford Brook Trail. For a description of the Appalachian Trail east of the Safford Brook Trail, see the 1992 edition (map 5) of the MATC *Guide to the Appalachian Trail in Maine*.

The Appalachian Trail (from the south)
Distances from ME 27

   to Stratton Brook Road: 0.9 mi.
   to Stratton Brook: 1 mi.
   to Bigelow Range Trail junction: 3.4 mi.
   to Horns Pond Trail junction: 5.1 mi.
   to Horns Pond lean-tos: 5.3 mi. (8.5 km.), 3 hr. 40 min.
   to South Horn summit: 5.9 mi.
   to West Peak summit: 8 mi.
   to Avery Lean-to and Fire Warden's Trail junction: 8.4 mi., 5 hr. 55 min.
   to Avery Peak: 8.8 mi. (14.2 km.), 6 hr. 15 min.

Bigelow Range Trail

This blue-blazed trail starts at the western end of the range, on ME 27/16 0.5 mi. southeast of Stratton and about 100 yd. northwest of the Eustis-Coplin town line. From the highway, follow a dirt road east. At 0.5 mi. from ME 27/16 the road ends at a clearing. The trail passes through woods for 0.3 mi. Then the trail climbs gradually about 0.2 mi. on a wide logging road. The trail reaches the first barren ledges at 1.9 mi. and bears right. Arnolds Well (a deep cleft in the rocks; *no drinking water*) is 20 ft. to the right. The trail turns up the ledges. There is a good view from the top of the first ledges. The trail leads through scrub and logged areas along the northern edge of the ridge with fine views. After reaching open ledges, it makes a short, steep ascent to Cranberry Peak at 3.2 mi.

After a short, steep descent the trail descends more gradually. Then it follows the north shore of Cranberry Pond, to end at a junction with the Appalachian Trail at 4.9 mi.

Bigelow Range Trail

Distances from ME 27

   to clearing: 0.5 mi.
   to first ledges: 1.9 mi.
   to Cranberry Peak: 3.2 mi., 2 hr. 40 min.
   to Appalachian Trail junction: 4.9 mi. (7.9 km.), 3 hr. 50 min.

Bigelow Range from the North
(Safford Brook Trail and the Appalachian Trail)

This trail begins at Round Barn Field on the shore of Flagstaff Lake, crosses East Flagstaff Rd., and climbs to the Appalachian Trail at Safford Notch.

The trail can be approached by water or by road. Round Barn Field is located on the east side of a cove on the south shore of Flagstaff Lake, which can be identified from the lake by a large sawdust pile on the lake shore. To reach the trail by road, turn north off ME 16 on the blacktop Long Falls Dam Rd. in North New Portland. At 16.7 mi. turn left (northwest) on Bog Brook Rd. (gravel). At about 0.8 mi. the East Flagstaff Rd. leads left (north and west); it crosses Safford Brook at 4 mi. and the trail at 4.5 mi.

From Round Barn Field the trail passes through the woods and crosses East Flagstaff Rd. at 0.3 mi. The trail follows a graded tote road, then climbs steeply, crosses Safford Brook, and enters Safford Notch. At 2.6 mi. reach a junction with the Appalachian Trail.

Fifty yd. east (left) on the Appalachian Trail is a blue-blazed trail south (right) 0.2 mi. to Safford Notch Campsite with two tent platforms and a privy. (The Appalachian Trail east reaches the highest peak of Little Bigelow at 3.7 mi.) The Appalachian Trail west rises steeply toward Avery Peak for a mile, with several excellent vistas. At 3.4 mi. it reaches the crest of the ridge. There, a side trail leads left 500 ft. to the top of Old Man's Head (a cliff on the side of the mountain). The trail continues to climb steeply, reaching the timberline and, shortly thereafter, the abandoned tower on Avery Peak.

Safford Brook Trail and the Appalachian Trail

Distances from Round Barn Field

  to East Flagstaff Rd.: 0.3 mi.
  to Appalachian Trail junction (via Safford Brook Trail): 2.6 mi.
  to Little Bigelow summit (via Appalachian Trail east): 6.3 mi., 4 hr.
  to Avery Peak (via Appalachian Trail west): 4.5 mi. (7.2 km.), 3 hr. 45 min.

LITTLE BIGELOW MOUNTAIN (3040 ft./927 m.)

Little Bigelow lies to the east of the main Bigelow Range, separated from it by a deep notch, known as Safford Notch. It is a long, narrow ridge, with steep cliffs along the southern side. The northern slope descends steadily for some 2 mi. to Flagstaff Lake. The natural structure of the mountain makes extremely rough terrain. The trail is part of the Appalachian Trail and therefore marked with white paint blazes. Refer to the USGS Little Bigelow Mountain quadrangle, 15-minute series and 7.5-minute series, or map 5 in the MATC *Guide to the Appalachian Trail in Maine,* if you want to supplement the map in this guide.

The approach is via the Appalachian Trail. See the Safford Brook description for Avery Peak for the approach from the west. To approach from the east, follow Long Falls Dam Rd. north from North New Portland. At 16.7 mi. the former route of ME 16, Bog Brook Rd. (flowed out by Flagstaff Lake), diverges left. Follow this well-graded road for 0.8 mi. Turn left on East Flagstaff Rd., which crosses the Appalachian Trail in 0.1 mi. The Appalachian Trail leads through hardwoods and follows a brook. At 1.2 mi. a blue-blazed side trail leads right 0.1 mi. across the brook to the Little Bigelow Lean-to. The trail continues through the woods, leaving the brook, and climbs on a series of open ledges which comprise the northeast buttress of the mountain. At 3 mi. it reaches the summit.

Little Bigelow Mountain

Distances from East Flagstaff Rd. (via the Appalachian Trail)

   to Little Bigelow Lean-to: 1.3 mi.
   to Little Bigelow summit: 2.8 mi., 2 hr. 30 min.
   to Avery Peak: 7.5 mi. (12.1 km.), 6 hr.

SECTION 11
Kennebec Valley

This section includes several mountains on the lower and middle sections of the Kennebec River, and other mountains accessible from US 201 and roads running off this highway. There are MFS firetowers on several of these summits. US 201 generally follows the Kennebec River as far as The Forks. It then runs through mountainous country past Parlin Pond to Jackman and on to the Quebec border. ME 15 diverges east from US 201 at Jackman and follows down the Moose River Valley to reach Moosehead Lake at Rockwood.

The highest mountain in this section is Coburn Mountain (3718 ft.). Boundary Bald Mountain is 3640 ft., but the majority of the rest are much lower. Most of the mountains described in this section are in Somerset County; two are in Kennebec County.

MOUNT PISGAH (809 ft./246 m.)

On the summit of Mount Pisgah in Winthrop are a MFS firetower and a relay tower, both with microwave dishes, and a log cabin equipment building. Refer to the USGS Wayne quadrangle, 7.5-minute series.

From the intersection of US 202 and ME 41 in Winthrop, go 3 mi. west on US 202. Turn right (northwest) at Knights of Columbus (formerly St. Stanislas Catholic Church) on the road to North Monmouth. Continue past the Tex Tech Industries factory on the left. At 0.7 mi. the road reaches the crossroads in North Monmouth. (A dam and a bridge over a stream are on the left.) Turn right on New Road and go 0.2 mi. to where it becomes Pisgah Rd. Continue for 2 mi. to the warden's cabin on the right (barn red in 1992). The trail (fire road P-6) follows the line of the driveway, crosses the yard to the rear of the cabin, and immediately crosses a brook (dry in dry weather). After a 0.3-mi. climb following telephone wires, the trail bears left, levels out at a stone wall, and joins a snowmobile road coming in from the right (sign). From the junction, the trail gently rises over a distance of about 0.7 mi., at times following the telephone wires or a jeep road, which also runs from the warden's cabin to the tower. The trail's last 100 ft. traverse open ledges to the summit, where views open up to the west. From the firetower platforms, views in all directions take in the entire sweep of western Maine's mountains, from Pleasant Mountain to Sugarloaf, as well as the Presidentials in New Hampshire. Views of surrounding lakes add sparkle to the scene.

Mount Pisgah

Distance from warden's cabin
to Mount Pisgah summit: 1 mi. (1.6 km.), 45 min.

MONUMENT HILL (660 ft./201 m.)

Monument Hill in Leeds is just west of the Androscoggin Lake and offers good views to the south and southwest from its summit, though in other directions views are largely obscured by trees. On the summit is a granite monument to Leeds soldiers and sailors of the Civil War. Refer to the USGS Turner Center quadrangle, 7.5-minute series.

To reach the trail from US 202 between Lewiston and Augusta, take ME 106 north for 6.2 mi. to Leeds. Take Church Hill Rd. left for 1.0 mi. to North Rd. on the right. The trailhead is at 0.9 mi. (sign) and the well-worn trail is marked by faded and sporadic blue blazes. It leads east and southeast through varied forest and berry patches to the rocky summit.

Monument Hill

Distance from North Rd.
    to summit: 1 mi. (1.6 km.), 40 min.

COOK HILL (472 ft./143 m.)

Cook Hill, in Vassalboro, is topped by a 60-ft. MFS fire-tower with a 360° view, and microwave facilities. Refer to the USGS Vassalboro quadrangle, 15-minute and 7.5-minute series.

From US 201/ME 100 in Vassalboro, take the road northeast at Coburn–Oak Grove School and drive 2 mi. to an unsurfaced service road on the left (northwest) with a double overhead wire. From ME 32 in North Vassalboro, take the same road southwest at the brick factory building and drive 1.2 mi. to the same side road on the right (northwest). For a pleasant walk, or in wet weather, leave the car on the main road. Walk 1 mi., avoiding left turns, to the summit where, besides the towers, is a picnic grove with a table and fireplace.

Cook Hill

Distance from main road
    to Cook summit: 1 mi. (1.6 km.), 30 min.

CHASE HILL (774 ft./235 m.)

This summit in Canaan offers a 360° view from the fire-tower on its summit. Refer to the USGS Skowhegan quadrangle, 15-minute series, or Canaan quadrangle, 7.5-minute series.

From the junction of US 2 and ME 23 east of Canaan Village drive 4 mi. northeast on ME 23 to a town road on the left (west). From the junction of ME 151 and ME 23 in Hartland drive 6 mi. southwest on ME 23 to the same road on the right. After turning onto the town road drive 0.3 mi. to a fork in the gravel road.

Follow the right fork (a small cemetery is just past the junction) for 0.9 mi. to a house on the right, with a jeep road on the left. Park by the jeep road and walk past the warden's cabin and an excellent picnic area with a fireplace and a table (*spring* nearby). It is 0.2 mi. to the tower rising above the trees on the wooded summit. This tower is one of the few in Maine still manned during the forest-fire season.

Chase Hill
Distance from parking lot
   to Chase summit: 0.2 mi. (0.3 km.), 10 min.

KELLY MOUNTAIN (1675 ft./511 m.)

This mountain is in Brighton Plantation, east of Bingham. There is an abandoned MFS firetower on its summit. The present approach is from the northeast. Refer to USGS Kingsbury quadrangle, 7.5-minute series.

   Since use of the firetower ceased, the trail has become overgrown, and hikers should check with the MFS firewarden supervisor in Caratunk before driving to the mountain. To reach the trail, take a woods road leading west from ME 151, 2.7 mi. north of Brighton and 1.6 mi. south of the ME 151/16 junction (Mayfield Corner). Park off the highway at the locked gate at the start of the road. Follow the road around the northern end of Smith Pond to the start of the trail. The warden's cabin is 0.1 mi. farther and straight ahead (*water*).

   The trail goes right, following the telephone line. It climbs gradually through open woods for about 1 mi. and then more steeply for 0.5 mi. to the summit.

Kelly Mountain
Distances from ME 151
   to start of trail (via woods road): 2 mi., 1 hr.
   to Kelly summit: *est.* 3.6 mi. (5.8 km.), 2 hr.

MOXIE BALD MOUNTAIN (2630 ft./802 m.)

This mountain, located in Bald Mountain Township northeast of Bingham, is a long ridge running north to south for about 4 mi. Although the summit is not very high, it has many features of above-timberline summits because of the extended ledges and open crest. The trailless North Peak, easy to reach from the Appalachian Trail, is worth exploring. Refer to the USGS The Forks and Bingham quadrangles, 15-minute series; Bald Mountain Pond and Moxie Pond quadrangles, 7.5-minute series; or map 4 in the MATC *Guide to the Appalachian Trail in Maine.*

The views from the summit are excellent. Katahdin is to the northeast, beyond many other peaks in Piscataquis County; Bigelow, Sugarloaf, and Abraham are to the west; and Coburn and Boundary Bald to the north.

The approach is via the Appalachian Trail, which leaves from a point on a paper-company road just south of Joe's Hole, the southernmost point on Moxie Pond. To reach the trailhead from the south, turn off US 201 in Bingham onto ME 16 and follow it for 0.8 mi. Turn north onto a gravel paper-company road. Two roads join the highway at this point; take the right, which follows Austin Stream for much of its length. At the stop sign, 1.7 mi. from the highway, proceed straight; at 9.9 mi. join the power line for a short distance, and at 10.3 mi., where the road forks, take the left fork. At 14.8 mi. the Appalachian Trail sign is seen on the right. There are few places to park here, but there are some places farther up the road. Be careful not to block camp driveways. (The Appalachian Trail approach to Pleasant Pond Mountain from the east begins a little over 100 yd. north, just beyond a power-line crossing and across from a small boat landing.)

To reach the trailhead from the north leave US 201 at The Forks and take the road toward Indian Pond. At

Lake Moxie Station, 5.3 mi. from the highway, turn south on the road that follows the old railroad bed along Moxie Pond. The road is rough and very narrow in places and there are many camps located on this shore of the lake, so drive carefully. At 8.1 mi. from Lake Moxie Station the sign for the Appalachian Trail and Moxie Bald is located on the left.

The Appalachian Trail up Moxie Bald leaves the east side of the road and crosses Baker Brook (in times of high water hikers may choose to use a tricky two-cable footbridge located just downstream near Joe's Hole). At 0.5 mi. a power line is crossed and at 1.2 mi. a side trail leads south to Joe's Hole Brook Lean-to, with space for six. The trail ascends gradually, then more steeply over open ledges before breaking out above the treeline. At 4.2 mi. reach a junction with a 0.5-mi., blue-blazed side trail used to bypass the summit in bad weather. It rejoins the Appalachian Trail north of the summit along the crest of the mountain. At 4.8 mi. reach the open summit of Moxie Bald with the remains of an old MFS firetower.

Moxie Bald Mountain
Distances from paper-company road via the Appalachian Trail

   to lean-to: 1.2 mi.

   to Moxie Bald summit: 4.8 mi. (7.7 km.), 3 hr. 15 min.

PLEASANT POND MOUNTAIN (2480 ft./756 m.)

On the Appalachian Trail between Moxie Pond and the Kennebec River at Caratunk, Pleasant Pond Mountain has open ledges that offer fine views in all directions. Hikers can approach the mountain from either the east or the west, although the western approach is generally favored. Refer to the USGS The Forks quadrangle, 15- or 7.5-minute series.

From the east the approach by road is the same as for Moxie Bald Mountain. The Appalachian Trail, relocated in 1987 to avoid a 2-mile road walk along the Moxie Pond Rd., leads west up the mountain from a spot on the paper-company road near Joe's Hole, the southernmost tip of Moxie Pond. The trail crosses a power line after 0.1 mi. and ascends to a long ridge, which it follows to the summit 4.9 mi. from the gravel road. A small spring is 0.1 mi. east.

The road approach from the west starts by turning off US 201 to the east at the Maine Forest Service Station in Caratunk. At a spot 0.5 mi. from the highway reach a junction and turn left, following the signs to Pleasant Pond. At 3.7 mi. take the left fork, and in another 0.6 mi. the pavement ends. Continue on the noticeably rougher gravel road another 0.8 mi. to a spot where a narrower gravel road leaves right. Take the road to the right and park soon. At 0.5 mi. from the fork, or 5.6 mi. from US 201, the Pleasant Pond Mountain Lean-to is on the left. The Appalachian Trail leaves the gravel road about 100 yd. beyond it. Parking spots are scarce along this road, but there are a few more turnouts farther back toward the last intersection.

The trail leads steeply uphill. At about 1 mi., pass the remains of an old warden's cabin, and shortly thereafter break out onto open ledges, where all that remains of the old firetower are a couple of concrete and rock footings and some broken glass.

Pleasant Pond Mountain from the east

Distances from paper-company road via the Appalachian Trail

> *to* powerline: 0.1 mi.
>
> *to* Pleasant Pond Mountain summit: 4.9 mi. (7.4 km.), 3 hr. 10 min.

Pleasant Pond Mountain from the west

Distances from Pleasant Pond Mountain Lean-to

to old cabin remains: 0.9 mi.

to Pleasant Pond Mountain summit: 1.2 mi. (1.9 km.), 1 hr. 15 min.

COBURN MOUNTAIN (3718 ft./1130 m.)

This mountain, west of US 201 between The Forks and Jackman, is the highest in the region. It offers excellent views from its abandoned MFS firetower. The mountain formerly supported the Enchanted Mountain Ski Area, but it has been shut down for several years and the ski trails are rapidly growing in; all buildings have been removed.

For the easiest and shortest trail (as of 1986), turn west off US 201 on the ski-area access road (no sign) about 11 mi. north of The Forks and about 16 mi. south of the US 201/ME 15 junction in Jackman. The access road is badly eroded, and only the first quarter mile or so is passable by two-wheel-drive autos, although four-wheel-drive vehicles with a high wheelbase can make it another mile to the location of the former ski-area buildings.

At the base of the mountain is a three-way fork in the road. Take the hard right fork and follow a wide gravel road. A sign on the tree on the left side of the road reads Road 9851. About 100 yd. beyond the sign turn left on a jeep road and begin climbing. About 0.7 mi. from the location of the former ski-area buildings reach the top of the old ski slope, where a new solar-powered radio repeating station is located. Immediately behind the station is a narrow but easily followed footpath marked with alternating orange and blue surveyor's tape that leads very steeply uphill about 0.4 mi. It exits the woods onto the summit at a second, new repeating station and just south of the firetower. Past the firetower and the summit buildings is the old firewarden's trail, which leads off the northeast ridge and circles back down past the few remains of the old warden's cabin onto an old logging track that intersects the jeep road about halfway down the mountain. This trail is much more easily found at the top than at the bottom. For those with compass skills and some bushwacking experience it can make a nice loop trip when combined with the former trail.

Coburn Mountain

Distances from US 201

> *to* base of mountain via access road: *est.* 1.2 mi.
>
> *to* top of ski area: *est.* 2 mi.
>
> *to* summit via new trails: *est.* 2.4 mi. (3.9 km.), 2 hr.

SALLY MOUNTAIN (2221 ft./675 m.)

Sally Mountain is southwest of Jackman, between Wood Pond and Attean Pond. It has a long summit ridge running northeast-southwest, with the highest point at the southwestern end. The northeastern and southeastern slopes rise fairly steeply above two ponds, and the climb to the summit ridge is very steep from these directions. The MFS firetower has been demolished, and although the trail is no longer regularly maintained it gets sufficient use to keep the route clear. Refer to the USGS Attean quadrangle, 15-minute series, and Attean Pond quadrangle, 7.5-minute series..

Leave US 201 on a dirt road to the west just south of Jackman Station and nearly opposite ME 15 east. Follow the dirt road for about 3 mi. until it approaches the stream connecting Wood and Attean ponds, where the Canadian Pacific Railroad crosses. Park here and follow the railroad line to the west for about 1.8 mi. The trail crosses the railroad tracks about 200 ft. beyond a west-facing trail signal post with the marking 770. As of July

1987 the start of the trail is marked by a piece of pipe wrapped in surveyor's tape on the south side of the tracks; there is no sign. The trail, marked by red surveyor's tape on trees, runs fairly level for a time before climbing steeply through a pleasant forest of mixed hardwoods to the summit ridge. Among the rocks and scrub growth of the summit ridge the trail becomes fainter, but it generally runs along the east-facing edge of the ridge on a gradual ascent toward the summit, where four pieces of steel bolted to the rocks mark the former site of the firetower. The views from the top are excellent, taking in several large ponds and mountains from Katahdin to Bigelow to the border peaks.

A more pleasant alternative to hiking along the railroad tracks is making the approach to the trail by canoe. Follow the dirt road mentioned previously to its end at the public landing on Attean Pond. By boat follow the north shore of Attean Pond west. The trail begins at the second established campsite in a small cove directly opposite Birch Island. The trail can be easily followed for about 0.1 mi. to a spot where it crosses the Canadian Pacific tracks.

Sally Mountain

Distances from road

   to start of trail (via railroad line): 1.8 mi.

   to Sally summit: 3 mi. (4.8 km.), 2 hr.

BOUNDARY BALD MOUNTAIN (3640 ft./1107 m.)

This rocky summit is north-northeast of Jackman and about 8 mi. southwest of the Canadian border. Its long, open summit ridge offers 360° views of the mountain and lake country of northern Somerset County. Over the past decade the former firewarden's trail has succumbed to logging operations, blowdown, and lack of maintenance, and it no longer exists. However, the mountain and the collapsed firetower at its top can be reached by a 1.2-mi. bushwhack from the former warden's cabin, now rented to a snowmobile club. Refer to the USGS Penobscot Lake and Long Pond quadrangles, 15-minute series, and Boundary Bald Mountain quadrangle, 7.5-minute series.

From the bridge on US 201 in Jackman, drive north 7.7 mi. to The Falls picnic area on the right. Take the second right after the picnic area (the first right leads back, parallel to the highway). This narrow, unmaintained gravel road leads 5.8 mi. to the former warden's cabin. It is generally suitable for pickup trucks and four-wheel-drive vehicles; some front-wheel-drive vehicles with high clearance might be able to make it most of the way. Drivers may want to carry a saw or shovel to deal with washouts and blowdowns.

Pass over a height-of-land, and at 2.5 mi. cross the Heald Stream gorge and immediately take a right at the fork. The road passes north of Mud Pond and crosses another small stream. At 1.8 mi. after the gorge, take a left at the junction. Another 1.3 mi. of steady uphill driving brings you to the former warden's cabin on the left. Park here, taking care not to block the road. The trail formerly began behind the cabin. Scraps of telephone wire now lead into thick scrub and slash. Set a compass course here.

Boundary Bald Mountain

Distance from former warden's cabin
   to summit: 1.2 mi. (1.9 km.)

SECTION 12
Piscataquis Mountains

This section includes the mountains of Piscataquis County west and southwest of the Katahdin area. Moosehead Lake, about 34 mi. long with an area of 117 square mi., is the state's largest lake. The approach to most of the mountains in this section is through Greenville, a convenient climbing center, at the southern end of the lake. Big Squaw Mountain (3196 ft.), west of Greenville, and Mount Kineo (1806 ft.), reached by water through Rockwood, are the most frequently climbed and best-known peaks in the area. The Appalachian Trail crosses White Cap Mountain (3644 ft.), the highest peak in the section. The Appalachian Trail, in its northeast-southwest course, also passes over the Barren-Chairback Range and close to the interesting and striking Borestone Mountain (1947 ft.).

Lily Bay State Park is on the eastern shore of Moosehead Lake, 8 mi. north of Greenville on the Greenville-Ripogenus Rd. This area of 576 acres offers picnicking, camping, boat launching, and swimming. (In 1974, the Scott Paper Company donated the Squaw Mountain Ski Area and considerable land on that mountain to the state for a park. In 1976, the state added the Little Squaw unit by exchanging land with another paper company.)

An expanding network of private roads, open to the public, serves the wilderness country north of Rockwood. (See the section in the introduction to this guide on the North Maine Woods Association.)

BIG SQUAW MOUNTAIN (3196 ft./974 m.)

Big Squaw Mountain dominates the country to the southwest of Moosehead Lake. It is located west of Greenville and is known for its exceptional views of the lake area. An abandoned firetower (reconditioned in 1985, but now run down) marks the site of the first fire lookout in the state, established in 1905. There is a major state-owned ski area on the mountain's eastern slope. This area is north of the hiking trail. Refer to the USGS Greenville quadrangle, 15-minute series.

From ME 15, turn left (west) on the paper-company road just north of the bridge over Middle Squaw Brook and 5.3 mi. north of Greenville (signs for Maine Public Lands and Big and Little Squaw). Drive up this road for about 1 mi. to where the firewarden's trail leaves the right side of the road (sign reading Big Squaw Mountain Trail). Parking space is on the left.

The trail is easy to follow and leads 2.5 mi. to the warden's cabin. There is *water* near the cabin and also a few hundred yards above. From the cabin the trail heads straight up the steep slope with many rocks placed as stepping stones. Reaching the narrow crest of the ridge, it turns right (north) and climbs another 0.5 mi. to the summit, which is cluttered by three small antennas and their buildings.

From the tower, a short trail leads north to a ledge with a view down over Mirror Lake, an isolated pond on the northeastern spur of the mountain.

A trail has also been cut from the top of the ski lifts and trails to the summit.

Big Squaw Mountain Trail

Distances from paper-company road

  to cabin: 2.5 mi.

  to Squaw summit: 3.3 mi. (5.3 km.), 2 hr. 45 min.

LITTLE SQUAW MOUNTAIN (2126 ft./648 m.)

The hiking trail system of Little Squaw Mountain focuses on the Loop Trail around Big and Little Squaw ponds. Hiking it clockwise gives the best view build-up and is easiest on the terrain. The area can be reached from the Mountain Road trailhead or from the Greenwood Motel parking lot.

The latter trail leaves the south corner of the lot, winds up the ridge to a series of summits with occasional outlooks toward Greenville and Moosehead Lake. Between peaks there are gullies under the cliffs. After passing Papoose Pond, the trail reaches the loop at Little Squaw Pond (about 3.5 miles).

To reach the Mountain Road trailhead mentioned above, go past the parking area on Big Squaw access road, taking the left fork at about 1.8 mi. from ME 16 and continuing for a total of 3 miles to the trailhead.

The right fork follows North Road, which in the future will be improved almost to Indian Pond for carry-in boating. From there an old fishermen's trail connects Indian Pond with Little Notch Pond.

From Mountain Road trailhead, go southeast 0.5 mi. over log walks to Big Squaw Pond and another 0.5 mi. to Little Squaw Pond. The Loop Trail (signed) presents varied terrain and several delightful outlooks over ponds and surrounding mountains. At a high point on the loop, a sign points to the Notch Ponds Trail heading westerly. This trail follows the side hill, and shortly after crossing an old road it branches right a quarter of a mile to an overlook, then drops through a notch down to the ponds.

Little Squaw Mountain

Distances from Greenwood Motel

 to Little Squaw Pond: 3.5 mi., 2 hr.

 to Big Squaw Pond: 4 mi., 2 hr., 30 min.

 to Mountain Road Parking: 4.5 mi. (7.2 km.), 3 hr.

MOUNT KINEO (1806 ft./550 m.)

Mount Kineo, with its sheer southeastern face, rises
spectacularly 800 ft. above Moosehead Lake on a peninsula jutting from the eastern shore of the lake to within 1
mi. of the western shore at Rockwood. The view over
the lake from the summit, where there is a vacant MFS
firetower, is quite remarkable. Refer to the USGS
Moosehead Lake quadrangle, 15-minute series, or
Mount Kineo quadrangle, 7.5-minute series.

To reach the mountain, take a boat from Rockwood.
Since the Mount Kineo Hotel is no longer open, hikers
must take the twice-daily shuttle boat, hire a boat locally, or bring their own. There are two trails up the mountain. The Bridle Trail climbs the western slope. It has
the easiest grades but is the longest. The Indian Trail
climbs from the southwest along the top of the cliff. The
Bridle Trail and the Indian Trail run northwest from the
hotel for 0.8 mi. along the shore under spectacular cliffs
of Kineo flint. At the northwestern end of these cliffs the
trails divide (no sign). The Bridle Trail (no views) continues along the shore 0.3 mi. farther before starting to
climb; the Indian Trail diverges sharply right and rises
along the top of the cliffs. The Indian Trail is the most
interesting and affords the best views. There is *no water*
on either trail.

Mount Kineo

Distances from dock at Kineo Cove

  to Bridle Trail/Indian Trail junction: 0.8 mi.

  to Kineo summit (via Indian Trail): 1 mi., 50 min.

  to Kineo summit (via Bridle Trail): 2 mi. (3.2 km.), 1
    hr. 20 min.

GREEN MOUNTAIN (2395 ft./730 m.)

This mountain is northwest of Pittston Farm and north-east of Boundary Bald Mountain. There is a MFS fire-tower on the highest of its several summits. Refer to the USGS Penobscot Lake quadrangle, 15-minute series, or Foley Pond quadrangle, 7.5-minute series.

Take the Great Northern Paper Company gravel road for 20 mi. north from Rockwood to the tollgate ($4.00 per car). From the tollgate, continue left through Pittston Farm. Beyond Pittston Farm, Boundary Rd. to Green Mountain forks left from North Branch Rd. The trail leaves the right (north) side of the road about 7 mi. beyond this fork.

The trail starts as a steep driveway to the warden's cabin, which it passes in 0.3 mi. It then rises gradually, with several short dips, to the summit. The trail is well worn and easy to follow.

Green Mountain

Distances from North Branch Rd.

  to cabin: 0.3 mi.
  to Green Mountain summit: 1.5 mi. (2.4 km.), 1 hr. 15 min.

LITTLE RUSSELL MOUNTAIN (2400 ft./730 m.)

Little Russell Mountain (about 2400 ft.) is close to the Piscataquis County line in T5 R16, Somerset County. (T and R stand for *township* and *range* and identify unin-corporated areas in Maine.) An abandoned MFS fire-tower is on the summit. Refer to the USGS St. John Pond quadrangle, 15-minute series, and Russell Moun-tain quadrangle, 7.5-minute series.

Take the Great Northern Paper Company road for 20 mi. north from Rockwood to the tollgate ($4.00 per Maine car, $8.00 out-of-state). Take the road right to

Seboomook Dam, and then drive north on the road toward Caucomgomoc Lake. The trail (sign) leaves the right (east) side of the road about 19 mi. north of Seboomook Dam and about 1.3 mi. north of Lost Pond, which is in the saddle (about 1975 ft.) between Russell Mountain and Little Russell Mountain. (There is a MFS campsite at Lost Pond, 0.3 mi. from the road.)

The trail ascends gradually. In its upper half it gets steeper, with expanding views to the north. The trail is wide, well worn, and easy to follow.

Little Russell Mountain

Distance from road
   to Little Russell summit: 1.3 mi. (2.1 km.), 55 min.

SOUBUNGE MOUNTAIN (2104 ft./641 m.)

This mountain is north of Ripogenus Dam and northwest of Doubletop Mountain. An abandoned MFS firetower is on the summit. Refer to the USGS Harrington Lake quadrangle, 15-minute series, or Doubletop Mountain quadrangle, 7.5-minute series.

The trail leaves the north side of Telos Rd. about 8 mi. north of Ripogenus Dam. It runs generally northwest across level country for 1 mi. and then climbs north to the tower.

Soubunge Mountain

Distance from road
   to Soubunge summit: *est.* 2 mi. (3.2 km.), 1 hr. 30 min.

BIG SPENCER MOUNTAIN (3240 ft./988 m.)

Rising sharply from the countryside north of the tiny hamlet of Kokadjo, Big and Little Spencer mountains, by First Roach Pond, are prominent landmarks from many points in the Moosehead area. Big Spencer has a MFS firetower on the northeastern end of its 2-mi. sum-

mit ridge (3230 ft.). The summit is about 0.3 mi. southwest of the tower. The unrestricted views in all directions are beautiful. Refer to the USGS Ragged Lake
quadrangle, 15-minute series, or Big Spencer Mountain
quadrangle, 7.5-minute series.

To reach the trail to the firetower, turn northwest
(left) from Greenville-Ripogenus Rd. on a side road
about 8.3 mi. northeast of Kokadjo and 2 mi. southwest
of Grant Farm, and about 3 mi. north of Sias Hill checkpoint ($4.00 fee per Maine car, $8.00 out-of-state).
Drive 6 mi. on this road. The trail leaves on the left
(south) side of the road (sign) and climbs to the right
(north) of the mountain's nose. In its upper part, beyond
the warden's cabin, the trail is quite steep and gains
more than 1000 vertical feet in the last 0.7 mi. to the
summit. The *last water* is at the warden's cabin.

Big Spencer Mountain

Distance from road
    to Big Spencer summit: *est.* 2 mi. (3.2 km.), 2 hr. 15 min.

LITTLE SPENCER MOUNTAIN (3040 ft./927 m.)

Like its partner, Big Spencer, the elongated mass of Little Spencer forms a prominent landmark in the Moosehead area. For years the trail was just a flagged herd
path used mostly by people staying at a local camp near
Spencer Pond. The challenging trail starts out on a
wooded easy grade, but soon climbs steeply, crosses
several sloping rockpiles, and ascends through a narrow
chimney. There are great views of the Moosehead Lake
area from several rock outlooks and the summit. Refer
to the USGS Lobster Mountain quadrangle, 7.5-minute
series, and maps 41 and 49 in the DeLorme *Maine Atlas
and Gazetteer.*

To reach the trail, head north from the Kokadjo
General Store and take the left fork at 1.3 mi. Travel

northwest on the gravel road and turn right at about 8.3 mi. Little Spencer is now a very clear mountain profile ahead. Continue on the road and watch for trail signs on the right at 10.3 mi.

Caution: Use care when climbing through the steep chimney section. Hikers up ahead can dislodge loose rocks to injure climbers below. Send one person through at a time.

Little Spencer Mountain

Distance from road

>   *to* Little Spencer summit: *est.* 2 mi. (3.2 km.), 2 hr. 15 min.

NESUNTABUNT MOUNTAIN (1550 ft./472 m.)

This mountain, part of the Maine Public Reserve Land, is found in T1 R11. Its summit offers some of the best views of the Katahdin range from the south as well as views over Nahmakanta Lake. Wadleigh Stream Lean-to on the Appalachian Trail is about 2 mi. away. Refer to the USGS Rainbow Lake West quadrangle, 7.5-minute series, and map 1 of the MATC *Guide to the Appalachian Trail in Maine.*

From ME 11, take the road northwest at Bear Brook, about 16 mi. northeast of Brownville Junction. Follow for about 25 mi. toward the northwest end of Nahmakanta Lake. There is a checkpoint at Jo-Mary Campground. Where the Appalachian Trail crosses this road, follow it south to the north summit. A 250-ft. side trail leads to splendid views.

Nesuntabunt Mountain

Distance from Appalachian Trail crossing

>   *to* north summit: 1.2 mi. (1.9 km.), 45 min.

NUMBER FOUR MOUNTAIN (2890 ft./881 m.)

This summit, with a vacant MFS firetower, is at the
northern end of the jumbled mountain mass lying
between Kokadjo on the north, Lily Bay on the west,
and Big Lyford and the West Branch Ponds on the east.
Baker Mountain (3520 ft.) and Lily Bay Mountain
(3228 ft.), other major peaks in this mass, are higher but
have no trails. Refer to the USGS First Roach Pond
quadrangle, 15-minute series, or Number Four Mountain quadrangle, 7.5-minute series.

Turn off Greenville-Ripogenus Rd. onto Frenchtown
Rd., which is about 8.5 mi. northeast of Lily Bay and 1
mi. south of Kokadjo. The trail, not maintained but easy
to follow, leaves the south side of Frenchtown Rd. 3.5
mi. from the intersection. The trail runs southwest, with
little change in grade, for over 2 mi., passing through an
out-of-use timber yarding area at 0.5 mi. Then, crossing
Lagoon Brook (*last water*), it runs through the clearing
where the fire warden's cabin used to be. From this
point, surveyor's flags mark the trail, which climbs, first
gradually and finally more steeply, through white birch
and spruce to the summit ridge. The tower is locked.

Number Four Mountain
Distances from Frenchtown Rd.
  to cabin site: 2.3 mi., 1 hr. 20 min.
  to firetower: 3.8 mi. (6.1 km.), 2 hr. 30 min.

WHITE CAP MOUNTAIN (3644 ft./1111 m.)

White Cap Mountain is the highest point on the
Appalachian Trail between Katahdin and Bigelow, and
also the highest mountain in this section. There are outstanding views from its summit. Refer to the USGS
First Roach Pond and Jo-Mary Mountain quadrangles,
15-minute series; the Big Shanty Mountain quadrangle,

7.5-minute series; or map 2 in the MATC *Guide to the Appalachian Trail in Maine.*

White Brook Trail

The Appalachian Trail in the Gulf Hagas–White Cap area has been relocated and now leads from Pleasant River past the Hermitage and then turns northeast to parallel Gulf Hagas Brook to Gulf Hagas Mountain, West Peak, and Hay Mountain. To reach the White Brook Trail—the former route of the Appalachian Trail, and still maintained by the MATC—turn left (northwest) off ME 11 5.5 mi. north of Brownville Junction. The sign (Katahdin Iron Works) at the turnoff marks the start of a 6.8-mi. drive on a gravel road from ME 11 to a gate at the Iron Works, a very interesting State Historical Memorial with a blast furnace and a beehive charcoal burner. Register at the gate and pay a fee to the caretaker. Bear right after driving through the gate and cross the West Branch of Pleasant River. At about 3 mi. fork right. About 5.8 mi. from the Iron Works, the road crosses the high, narrow bridge over White Brook. At the next junction continue straight ahead up the west side of White Brook. (The left fork leads to Hay Brook and Gulf Hagas.) Follow the major gravel road for 3.8 mi., taking the main branch at each fork, and park well off the road where it crosses two brooks. The trail follows an old logging road for 1.0 mi. to a large wood yard. The White Cap–Hay Mountain sag is clearly visible from this yard. Depending on logging operations this road may be impassable.

A blue-blazed trail leaves the left side of the road and climbs the southern slope toward the sag through a heavily logged area.

At 0.4 mi. the trail crosses White Brook near the ruins of the warden's cabin. From there it climbs more steeply and reaches the junction with the Appalachian

Trail at 1 mi. Turn right and climb the last steep stretch to the summit at 2.1 mi. There are panoramic views from the open ledge. They take in Saddlerock (2998 ft.), Little Spruce (3274 ft.), Baker (3520 ft.), Big Squaw (3196 ft.), Hay (3244 ft.), and Big Spencer (3240 ft.), along with the vast lake country to the north, rising to the Katahdin range. The view is one of the finest in the state.

White Brook Trail

Distances from road at wood yard

   to White Brook crossing: 0.5 mi.

   to Appalachian Trail junction: 1 mi.

   to White Cap summit (via the Appalachian Trail): 2.1 mi. (3.4 km.), 1 hr. 30 min.

GULF HAGAS

Just off the Appalachian Trail between the Barren-Chairback Range and White Cap Mountain, Gulf Hagas is a unique scenic area consisting of a deep, narrow, slate canyon about 4 mi. long on the West Branch of the Pleasant River in northern Piscataquis County. The West Branch falls about 400 ft. in the 4 mi., and in many places the canyon's vertical slate walls force the river into very narrow channels that form a series of waterfalls, rapids, chutes, and pools. The falls are particularly spectacular in late spring during peak runoff. During winter, ice builds up on the walls and, because the sun rarely reaches certain faces, often lasts into late June.

The St. Regis and Great Northern paper companies own the property. In 1969 the canyon was designated a Registered Natural Landmark, and the owners agreed to set aside 500 acres, including all of the canyon, for the public's enjoyment. While retaining ownership, the paper companies have agreed not to harvest wood on the reserved land as long as the area is designated a landmark.

Loggers first harvested the area more than a century ago when Pleasant River Rd., the approach from both ends of the canyon, was built. Trails were cut to the rim of the canyon in the last century but fell into disuse. The last extensive logging took place during the 1930s, when new trails were cut. The trails are still well marked and well maintained. The trail system runs near the rim of the canyon, with frequent side trails to viewpoints and falls. By using the old Pleasant River Rd., hikers can make a circuit from the south. Refer to USGS First Roach Pond, Sebec Lake, and Sebec quadrangles, 15-minute series; the Barren Mountain East quadrangle, 7.5-minute series; or map 2 in the MATC *Guide to the Appalachian Trail in Maine.*

See the preceding description of the approach to White Cap Mountain. After crossing the high bridge 5.8 mi. from the Katahdin Iron Works, go left off the major gravel road at the first junction. Follow this logging road for about 1.8 mi. to Hay Brook, which is about 7.5 mi. from the Iron Works. The approach road is rocky and rough but generally passable. A campground with tentsites lies along the West Branch of Pleasant River. Reservations can be made (fee) at the control gate at Katahdin Iron Works.

From the parking area, cross Hay Brook and follow Pleasant River Rd., past Pugwash Pond, for 0.7 mi. There, the Appalachian Trail comes in from the left. Continue straight ahead. The trail shortly reaches the Hermitage, a beautiful stand of tall white pines now owned by the Nature Conservancy (a log cabin and other buildings have been removed). From the Hermitage area follow the white-blazed Appalachian Trail northwest along Pleasant River Rd. for 0.9 mi. to Gulf Hagas Brook, where the relocated Appalachian Trail turns sharply right to follow Gulf Hagas Brook. Continue straight ahead and cross Gulf Hagas Brook (no bridge and dangerous in high water). Immediately after the crossing, the Screw Auger Falls Trail leaves left and descends steeply along the rim of the canyon to Gulf Hagas Brook, where it passes a series of spectacular waterfalls visible from viewpoints to the left of the falls trail.

A new rim trail section continues west, and at 0.7 mi. a side trail leads left to Hammond Street Pitch, a point high above the canyon offering a fine view of the gorge. Return to the rim trail and turn left (at 0.9 mi. a connector road leads 0.2 mi. back to the Pleasant River Road). Continuing along the rim, at 1.2 mi. from Pleasant River Rd. is a series of side paths leading to views of the Jaws, where the river squeezes around a slate spur and narrows in many places. Back on the rim trail, at 1.8 mi. from Pleasant River Rd., a spur trail leads to a viewpoint below Buttermilk Falls. After that, the canyon gradually becomes more shallow and at times the trail approaches the banks of the West Branch. At 1.9 mi. from Pleasant River Rd., the trail passes Stair Falls, and at 2.8 mi. it reaches the ledge above Billings Falls, where the narrowed river drops into a large pool. In another 0.1 mi. the trail bears sharply away from the river. (At this point a short side trail leads left to the edge of the river near a rocky island called Head of the Gulf, where there are some interesting logging artifacts.) The trail rejoins Pleasant River Rd. in another 0.2 mi. Turn right (southeast) to follow Pleasant River Rd. along the side of the mountain high above Gulf Hagas back to Screw Auger Falls, the Hermitage, and Hay Brook. Although it is often very marshy and wet, the road offers a quicker return than the rim trail.

Gulf Hagas Circuit

Distances from campground

    to Appalachian Trail junction: 0.7 mi.

    to Screw Auger Falls Trail junction: 1.7 mi.

    to rim trail junction: 2.1 mi.

to spur trail to Hammond Street Pitch (via rim trail):
    est. 2.3 mi.
to side paths to the Jaws outlook: 3 mi.
to side trail to Buttermilk Falls: 3.4 mi.
to Stair Falls: 3.8 mi.
to ledge above Billings Falls: 4.4 mi.
to side trail to Head of the Gulf: 4.5 mi.
to Pleasant River Rd.: 4.7 mi.
to rim trail junction (via Pleasant Valley Rd.): 6.7 mi.
to Gulf Hagas Brook: 7.1 mi.
to campground: 8.8 mi. (14.2 km.), 7 hr. 30 min.

CHAIRBACK MOUNTAIN (2219 ft./676 m.)

This interesting, open peak is at the eastern end of the
Barren-Chairback Range. It is a day hike from a logging
road south of the West Branch of the Pleasant River.
Refer to the USGS Sebec and Sebec Lake quadrangles,
15-minute series; Silver Lake and Barren Mountain East
quadrangles, 7.5-minute series; or map 3 in the MATC
Guide to the Appalachian Trail in Maine.

From Katahdin Iron Works follow the gravel St.
Regis Paper Company road. At about 3 mi. take the left
fork at the LLPC (Little Lyford Pond Camps) sign. The
right fork leads to Gulf Hagas.

Park at 6.7 mi. from the Iron Works, short of where
the Appalachian Trail crosses the road. Then descend
0.2 mi. to the Appalachian Trail. Follow it south as it
climbs a short way on a hauling road, then turns sharply
left. At 1.2 mi. the Appalachian Trail reaches the top of
a ridge, and a side trail leads right 0.2 mi. to East Chairback Pond. Continue over a series of ridges. The last
half mile of the climb rises over very steep talus slope to
reach the summit, with its outstanding views.

Chairback Mountain

Distances from parking (via the Appalachian Trail)

to side trail to East Chairback Pond: 1.9 mi., 1 hr. 15 min.

to Chairback summit (via the Appalachian Trail): 4.1
mi. (6.6 km.), 2 hr. 35 min.

BARREN MOUNTAIN (2660 ft./811 m.)

Barren Mountain, at its western end, is the highest and
most accessible mountain of the Barren-Chairback
Range. It is in Elliotsville Plantation (USGS Sebec Lake
quadrangle, 15-minute series, and Barren Mountain West
and Barren Mountain East quadrangles, 7.5-minute
series). There are interesting outlooks from Barren Slide
and Barren Ledges over Bodfish Intervale, Lake Onawa,
and Borestone Mountain. The panorama from the abandoned firetower on the summit is excellent.

To climb Barren Mountain via the Appalachian
Trail, drive from Monson on Elliotsville Rd. 11.8 mi. to
Bodfish Farm and park. Follow the Long Pond tote road
1.6 mi. to the junction with the Appalachian Trail. Then
drive 1.6 mi. on the tote road and park. The Appalachian
Trail follows the road 150 ft. and leaves southeast.

Leave the road right (north) on the Appalachian Trail
and descend 0.1 mi. Cross Long Pond Stream at the normally knee-deep ford. The trail turns east, passing Slu-
gundy Gorge. At 0.9 mi. it reaches a blue-blazed side
trail leading 150 yds. to Long Pond Stream Lean-to.

After the junction, the main trail climbs the northwestern slope of Barren Mountain. At 1.8 mi. another
blue-blazed side trail leads south to the head of Barren
Slide, an interesting mass of boulders with a view west.
A little farther, the main trail crosses the head of Barren
Ledges, from which there is a striking view. The route
then bears left and winds along the northern slope of the
range over rough terrain to the base of the cone. From

there, it climbs steeply through boulders for a short distance to the summit firetower.

(The Appalachian Trail continues northeast over the remaining peaks of the range to the valley of the West Branch of the Pleasant River. This hike is a camping trip of several days over rough terrain. See the 1992 edition of the MATC *Guide to the Appalachian Trail in Maine* if you plan to take the trip across the range.)

Barren Mountain

Distances from Long Pond tote road (via the Appalachian Trail)

> *to* side trail to Long Pond Stream Lean-to: 0.9 mi.
> *to* side trail to Barren Slide: 1.8 mi., 1 hr. 30 min.
> *to* Barren Mountain summit: 3.9 mi. (6.3 km.), 3 hr.

LITTLE WILSON FALLS

A worthwhile side trip in this area is to Little Wilson Falls, a striking 57-ft. waterfall in the canyon gouged through slate by Little Wilson Stream. Driving from Monson on Elliotsville Rd., park just before crossing Big Wilson Bridge. Go left on a faint dirt road (formerly the Appalachian Trail). At 0.8 mi. pass MFS Little Wilson Campsite and cross Little Wilson Stream. At 2 mi. turn left on the relocated Appalachian Trail, and at 2.1 mi. cross Little Wilson Stream. At 2.4 mi. reach the rim of ledge to an outstanding view of the 57-ft. falls and a deep slate canyon.

Little Wilson Falls

Distances from Big Wilson Bridge

> *to* MFS campsite: 0.8 mi.
> *to* Little Wilson Falls: 2.4 mi. (3.7 km.), 1 hr. 25 min.

BORESTONE MOUNTAIN (1947 ft./593 m.)

Spelled Boarstone on USGS and other maps, this small but rugged mountain complete with its two peaks and three small ponds well up on the southwestern slope, rises above Lake Onawa. The views from the bare summits are excellent. The National Audubon Society sanctuary established there welcomes hikers year-round on the Moore's Ponds Route. They are open dawn to dusk. From June 1 to October 31, nature programs, a self-guided tour, and a staffed interpretive center halfway up are available. Fees are $1.50 for adults, $1.00 for students, and group rates with prearrangement. No dogs or guns are allowed in the sanctuary. Refer to the USGS Sebec Lake quadrangle, 15-minute series.

Moore's Ponds Route

From Monson follow Elliotsville Rd. After crossing the Big Wilson Bridge at 9 mi., bear left and cross the Canadian Pacific Railroad tracks in another 0.7 mi. The route to Borestone leads right 0.1 mi. beyond the railroad, following a private road through a gate. The road climbs steadily through switchbacks and then runs along a shelf to Sunrise Pond, the lowest of the three Moore's ponds, where it ends. The other two ponds are known as Midday and Sunset. Follow the trail, blazed with green triangles, around the southeastern end of Sunrise Pond and cross the outlet. After that, the trail, turning north and then east, climbs steeply up the main cone to the open western peak. It descends slightly into the saddle and then rises to the higher eastern peak.

Moore's Ponds Route

Distances from Elliotsville Rd.

    to Sunrise: 1 mi., 40 min.

    to Borestone, western peak: 1.8 mi., 1 hr. 20 min.

    to Borestone, eastern peak: 2 mi. (3.2 km.), 1 hr. 30 min.

HIGH CUT HILL (955 ft./291 m.)

High Cut Hill is in Garland, just south of the Penobscot-Piscataquis county line. There is a magnificent 360° view. Refer to the USGS Dover-Foxcroft quadrangle, 15-minute series, or 7.5-minute series.

Approach by turning west off ME 15 onto ME 94 at West Charleston four corners. Drive 3.2 mi. to a dirt road on the right. (From Garland go north 1.0 mi. and east 1.6 mi.) The trail ascends north through open pasture to the summit. The first 0.5 mi. are drivable, but parking is limited.

High Cut Hill

Distances from paved road
   to High Cut summit: 1.3 mi. (2.1 km.), 55 min.

APPENDIX
The New England Trail Conference and the Appalachian Trail

NEW ENGLAND TRAIL CONFERENCE

The New England Trail Conference was organized in 1917 to develop the hiking possibilities of New England and to coordinate the work of local organizations. The conference serves as a clearinghouse for information about trail maintenance and trail use both for organized groups and for individuals.

The annual meeting of this organization is held in the spring. Representatives of mountaineering and outing clubs from all over New England come together for a full day and evening program of reports, talks, and illustrated lectures on mountain climbing, hiking, and trails and shelters. All sessions are open to the public.

The work of the conference is directed by the chairman, who is elected by the executive committee. For information, contact the chairman, Forrest House, 33 Knollwood Drive, E. Longmeadow MA 01028 (203-342-1425 or 413-732-3719).

THE APPALACHIAN TRAIL (AT)

The Appalachian National Scenic Trail (AT) is a continuous marked footpath extending through the mountainous regions of the east for two thousand miles, from Katahdin in Maine to Springer Mountain in Georgia. Its maintenance is a volunteer project carried on by organizations and individuals, coordinated by the Appalachian

Trail Conference (ATC). The trail west of Old Speck through the White Mountains in New Hampshire uses numerous AMC trails for its route, and AMC chapters maintain parts of the Appalachian Trail in Maine, Massachusetts, Connecticut, and New York. The AMC has been a member of the conference from its inception.

In Maine, the Appalachian National Scenic Trail is maintained by the Maine Appalachian Trail Club, Inc. (MATC), also a member of the Appalachian Trail Conference. This club is comprised of individual members and organizations including such diverse groups as the AMC's Maine chapter, college outing clubs, fish and game clubs, and children's camps.

The Appalachian Trail starts in Maine at the summit of Katahdin; goes by Rainbow, Nahmakanta and Jo-Mary lakes and Crawford Pond; traverses White Cap, the Barren-Chairback Range, and Moxie Bald; crosses the Great Bend of the Dead River, in part following the Arnold Trail; goes over the Bigelow Range, the Crockers, Spaulding, Saddleback, Baldpate, Old Speck, and the Mahoosucs; and reaches the New Hampshire line at Carlo Col.

Due to the remote locations and changes brought on by storms, lumbering, beaver activity, etc., it is not advisable to attempt travel on the Appalachian Trail (other than by the routes described in this book) without explicit directions and maps. Both are incorporated in the *Guide to the Appalachian Trail in Maine* (twelfth edition, 1992) published by the Maine Appalachian Trail Club. It is available at many bookstores; from the Secretary, Maine Appalachian Trail Club, PO Box 283, Augusta ME 04330 (also for memberships and trail information); or from the Appalachian Trail Conference, Box 236, Harpers Ferry WV 25425. More detailed information on the sections of the Appalachian Trail described as approaches to some of the mountains discussed in this book will also be found in the MATC guide.

Glossary

blaze a trail marking on a tree or rock, painted and/or cut

blazed marked with paint (blazes) on trees or rocks

bluff a high bank or hill with a cliff face overlooking a valley

boggy muddy, swampy

boulder large, detached, somewhat rounded rock

box canyon rock formation with vertical walls and flat bottom

bushwhack to hike through woods or brush without a trail

buttress a rock mass projecting outward from a mountain or hill

cairn pile of rocks to mark trail

cataract waterfall

cirque upper end of valley with half-bowl shape (scoured by glacier)

cliff high, steep rock face

col low point on a ridge between two mountains; saddle

crag rugged, often overhanging rock eminence

flume a ravine or gorge with a stream running through it

grade steepness of trail or road; ratio of vertical to horizontal distance

graded trail well-constructed trail with smoothed footway

gulf a cirque

gully small, steep-sided valley

headwall steep slope at the head of a valley, especially a cirque

height-of-land highest point reached by a trail or road

knob a rounded minor summit

lean-to shelter

ledge a large body of rock; or, but not usually in this book, a horizontal shelf across a cliff

ledgy having exposed ledges, usually giving views

outcrops large rocks projecting out of the soil

plateau high, flat area

potable drinkable

ravine steep-sided valley

ridge highest spine joining two or more mountains, or leading up to a mountain

runoff brook a brook usually dry (intermittent), except shortly after rain or snow melt

saddle lowest, flattish part of ridge connecting two mountains; col

scrub low trees near treeline

shelter building, usually of wood, with roof and three or four sides, for camping

shoulder point where rising ridge levels off or descends slightly before rising higher to a summit

slab (n.) a smooth, somewhat steeply sloping ledge

slab (v.) to travel in a direction parallel to the contour of a slope

slide steep slope where a landslide has carried away soil and vegetation

spur a minor summit projecting from a larger one

spur trail a side path to a point off a main trail

strata layers of rock

summit highest point on a mountain; or, a point higher than any other point in its neighborhood

switchback zigzag traverse of a steep slope

tarn a small pond, often at high elevation or with no outlet

timberline elevation that marks the upper limit of commercial timber

treeline elevation above which trees do not grow

INDEX

Notes: **Boldface** denotes trail name
ALL CAPS denotes section name

About the
Appalachian Mountain Club

The Appalachian Mountain Club pursues a vigorous conservation agenda while encouraging responsible recreation, based on the philosophy that succcessful, long-term conservation depends upon firsthand experience of the natural environment. Fifty-four thousand members have joined the AMC to pursue their interests in hiking, canoeing, skiing, walking, rock climbing, bicycling, camping, kayaking, and backpacking, and—at the same time—to help safeguard the environment in which these activities are possible.

Since it was founded in 1876, the Club has been at the forefront of the environmental protection movement. By cofounding several of New England's leading environmental organizations, and working in coalition with these and many more groups, the AMC has positively influenced legislation and public opinion.

Volunteers in each chapter lead hundreds of outdoor activities and excursions and offer introductory instruction in backcountry sports. The AMC education department offers members and the public a wide range of workshops, from introductory camping to the intensive Mountain Leadership School taught on the trails of the White Mountains.

The most recent efforts in the AMC conservation program include river protection, Northern Forest Lands policy, Sterling Forest (NY) preservation, and support for the Clean Air Act.

The AMC's research department focuses on the forces affecting the ecosystem, including ozone levels, acid rain and fog, climate change, rare flora and habitat protection, and air quality and visibility.

AMC Trails

The AMC trails program maintains over 1,400 miles of trail (including 350 miles of the Appalachian Trail) and more than 50 shelters in the Northeast. Through a coordinated effort of volunteers, seasonal crews, and program staff, the AMC contributes more than 10,000 hours of public service work each summer in the area from Washington, D.C. to Maine.

In addition to supporting our work by becoming an AMC member, hikers can donate time as volunteers. The club offers four unique weekly volunteer base camps in New Hampshire, Maine, Massachusetts, and New York. We also sponsor ten-day service projects throughout the United States, Adopt-a-Trail programs, trails day events, trail skills workshops, and chapter and camp volunteer projects.

The AMC has a longstanding connection to Acadia National Park. Working in cooperation with the National Park Service and Friends of Acadia, the AMC Trails Program provides many opportunities to preserve the park's resources. These include half-day volunteer projects for guests at AMC's Echo Lake Camp, ten-day service projects, weeklong volunteer crews in the fall, and trails day events. For more information on these public service volunteer opportunities, contact the AMC Trails Program, Pinkham Notch Visitor Center, P.O. Box 298, Gorham NH 03581; 603-466-2721.

The club operates eight alpine huts in the White Mountains that provide shelter, bunks and blankets, and hearty meals for hikers. Pinkham Notch Visitor Center, at the foot of Mt. Washington, is base camp to the adventurous and the ideal location for individuals and families new to outdoor recreation. Comfortable bunkrooms, mountain hospitality, and home-cooked, family-style meals make Pinkham Notch Visitor Center a fun and affordable choice for lodging. For reservations, call 603-466-2727.

At the AMC headquarters in Boston and at Pinkham Notch Visitor Center in New Hampshire, the bookstore and information center stock the entire line of AMC publications, as well as other trail and river guides, maps, reference materials, and the latest articles on conservation issues. Guidebooks and other AMC gifts are available by mail order (AMC, P.O. Box 298, Gorham NH 03581), or call toll-free 800-262-4455. Also available from the bookstore or by subscription is *Appalachia,* the country's oldest mountaineering and conservation journal.

Begin a New Adventure—Join the AMC

We invite you to join the Appalachian Mountain Club and share the benefits of membership. Every member receives *AMC Outdoors*, the membership magazine that, ten times a year, brings you not only news about environmental issues and AMC projects, but also listings of outdoor activities, workshops, excursions, and volunteer opportunities. Members also enjoy discounts on AMC books, maps, educational workshops, and guided hikes, as well as reduced fees at all AMC huts and lodges in Massachusetts and New Hampshire.

To join, send a check for $40 for an adult membership, or $65 for a family membership to AMC, Dept. S7, 5 Joy Street, Boston MA 02108; or call 617-523-0636 for payment by Visa or MasterCard.

S7